BEWITCHED

SECRETS FROM COMEDY GENIUS SOL SAKS

CAROLYN HAYNES

Kelledge Hall Press

Acclaim

"A first-class account woven into a captivating story of one of our nation's top writers, Mr. Sol Saks. Comments from Saks and several brilliant Bewitched-actors, will forever elevate your perspective."
—Carolyn Jeffers, LA Times

"Carolyn has written a lovely book about my Dad. In it, she has re-told many stories of his: a lot of which I remember—some I had forgotten, and some I had never heard. Throughout the book, I can hear echoes of my Dad's voice. Dad always told stories.
Carolyn took notes. Thank you, Carolyn."
—Mary Saks

BEWITCHED

Copyright © 2021 Carolyn Haynes

ISBN-9798698294535

LCCN: TXu002274373

Bewitched/Secrets from Comedy Genius Sol Saks

Los Angeles, California

Printed in the United States of America

All rights reserved under International Copyright Law. Contents and/or cover may not be reproduced in whole or in part without the expressed written consent of the Publisher.

Photographs courtesy of the Saks family.

Note: Distribution of 12% of all royalties advances to local and worldwide charities.

SOL SAKS

Dedication

It's an everyday privilege, Linda, Jennipher, Jill, Jessica, my first-fourth Cathy, my adorable grandchildren, and my amazing sister, Gloria, to call you my family.

I lovingly dedicate this book to you, my inspiration and priceless blessing. You indeed are more than I could have possibly imagined.

Acknowledgment

As with any significant project, it takes a great team to combine all the elements in a book. So, I want to extend my personal and most profound gratitude to:

Linda, Jennipher, Jill, Jessica, my first fourth **Cathy**, my incredible daughters, and **Gloria,** my fantastic sister—thank you for your invaluable input. From reading my early drafts to advising on the cover to always being honest, supportive, and the most caring and generous of people! I love you all very much.

Social Media Friends, you are the best on the planet. You've patiently helped me navigate the ever-changing technology and cheered me with your lovely, supportive—sometimes hysterical comments. You've shared, tweeted, retweeted, reblogged my posts, prayed for me, and read and reviewed my books! You are amazing!

Shehanne Moore, Brilliant, prolific author and, blessed to say, meh bonnie friend, thanks for generously sharing your expertise as an author. Your cheery hello on Friday mornings from Dundee, Scotland, always brought a touch of paradise. Your fun stories about watching Bewitched as a young girl added the elusive touch that every book needs.

Daphne O'Neal, Actress, Design writer, and Public Speaker—thank you for writing down your thoughts on the Bewitched characters who made a difference in your life. It's a testament to the actor's heart beneath the surface of the character they portrayed.

Mary Saks, Sol's daughter, writer, and the best storyteller, for your invaluable assistance, patiently sorting through pictures and old memories and adding stories, and a blurb, as only you could do. What fun you are.

Carolyn Jeffers, from the LA Times, thank you for reading my manuscript, making notes, and for the invaluable review.

I am incredibly blessed to have you all in my life!

Preface

It was a blessed and challenging job working with Sol Saks, the creator of Bewitched. I never dreamed it would continue all these years later. I took notes on stories Sol told before we began a day of writing. Years later, many incredible people shared their experiences through social media, some as they rushed home, as children from school to watch Bewitched, met with friends to have nose-twitching contests or saw kindness in Samantha that they found inspiring. Regardless of the controversy surrounding one of TV's most popular shows, there's hidden wisdom from someone who traveled a path and left a gift for a reader to discover. He said for those who have ears to hear and eyes to see. So, as you continue to read, my wish is that you'll unearth the hidden treasure lying beneath or wrapped in each word, for they came from a God who loves, a man who tried, and a young woman good at taking notes.

Introduction

Bewitched is an unveiled glimpse into a writer's heart who moved through the wonders of the entertainment industry within rarified air. He brought laughter to ease the pain, left signposts to success, stepping stones to help, unanswered questions for you to ponder, and a lifetime of gratitude expressed. More blessings than magic.

SOL SAKS

TABLE OF CONTENT

ACCLAIM	2
DEDICATION	4
ACKNOWLEDGMENT	5
PREFACE	6
INTRODUCTION	7
1	**11**
WHO IS SOL SAKS, AND WHY IS HE *BEWITCHED*?	11
YOUR PERSONAL INVITATION	13
DEARLY BELOVED	35
2	**38**
THE RADIO DAYS	38
RED SKELTON	41
ED GARDNER BING CROSBY BETTY HUTTON	42
DINAH SHORE	48
FANNY BRICE	50
HATTIE MCDANIEL	54
DANNY KAYE	60
OZZIE, HARRIET, DAVID, AND RICKY NELSON	64
3	**66**
TELEVISION	66
JOAN DAVIS AND JIM BACKUS	66
LUCY & RICHARD LUCY & DESI	68
JOAN CAUFIELD & BARRY NELSON	71
HOWARD DUFF & IDA LUPINO	72
4	**80**
A PROMISE OF PARADISE	80
MEETING SOL SAKS	81
A GIFT FROM A GRACIOUS HOST	93
5	**96**
SO WAS BORN THE LEGEND	96
A STRONG SUPPORTING CAST	104
PAUL LYNDE/UNCLE ARTHUR	104
MARION LORNE/AUNT CLARA	105

ALICE PEARCE/GLADYS KRAVITZ	106
CALLING DR. BOMBAY/BERNARD FOX	107
BEWITCHING SECRETARY'S	107
LEFT—DIANA & ERIN MURPHY	108
TABITHA—THE SPINOFF—LISA HARTMAN	108
THEME SONG	109
THE MAGICAL LOCATION	109
SAMANTHA-SERENA SIMILARITIES	111
THE TOURNAMENT OF ROSE PARADE COMMERCIAL	111
THE FAMOUS CHRISTMAS EPISODE	112
THE BEWITCHED ROSE	114
THE BEWITCHED BARBIE DOLL	119

6	121

ALISON, SOL, AND HOLLYWOOD	121
DENNIS WEAVER	127
LOS GATOS, JOHN STEINBECK, AND MARY	134

7	139

WHY DIDN'T YOU WRITE MORE EPISODES FOR BEWITCHED?	139
AGNES ROBERTSON MOOREHEAD	140
ELIZABETH AND FAMILY	142
ELIZABETH'S LEGACY LIVES ON	148
DICK YORK	150
DICK SARGENT	155
DAVID WHITE	157

8	160

WITHIN THE SECRET GARDEN	160
WARNING…LUNCHING WITH COMEDY WRITERS	166
MOMENTS WITH MARVIN KAPLAN	172
SITTING WITH THE CREATOR OF *M*A*S*H*, LARRY GELBART	173

9	175

APPLAUSE, DISAPPOINTMENTS, AND HIS LAST WRITING CLASS	175
HOLLYWOOD AGEISM	185

10	190

"WHAT BETTER TEACHER THAN SOL SAKS?" –NORMAN LEER	190

SOL SAKS

11	**201**
"Cary Grant Did A Lot for Me" –Sol Saks	201
12	**208**
The Fair-Haired Boy At CBS	208
13	**214**
Inspirations Last Journey to the Silver Screen	214
Bewitched the Movie	216
An Honored Visit	221
I Would Enjoy Hearing from You!	224
About the Author	225

1

Who is Sol Saks, and Why is He *Bewitched*?

*"Humor is used for feelings
that are too deep for tears."
—Sol Saks*

"Now in my late nineties, I can still see the tears in my mother's eyes as she told of the days Germany, Russia, and Austria criminally divided her nation of Poland. As a child, to hear that the country and people were in constant conflict and turmoil was frightening. I heard explicit stories of how these invaders brutally took their possessions, their virtue, and ultimately the lives of loved ones. The vividly revealed atrocities played in my young mind; the painful cries of war became real, resting like a weight upon my chest."—Sol Saks

Once there lived a man amid the spaces of time, a genius of comedy, a shy man wanting to entertain people with words. He endeavored to evoke emotions and share ideas by clever arrangements of phrases born in his imagination. They flowed from a rarified place where only a few privileged souls may enter. But, did he recognize the privilege? What road was traveled, where did this comedy come from, and what was the price paid for success? These were but a few questions asked of the quiet-natured Sol Saks.

As I drove down the metropolitan store-lined stretch of Ventura Boulevard in Sherman Oaks, memories of those days and provocative inquiries came flooding back. I was seconds away from the familiar street I would turn onto to meet Sol for work many years ago. This narrow winding street led to a creative world of word-wrapped ideas that became entertainment for countless thousands. Here it was; I saw the sign reading Cedros Avenue, and with it came a strange sense of the passage of time.

A moment of breathlessness captured my attention as I made a right on Cedros and followed the sun-dappled road as it merged into Sutton Street. I pulled up in front of his former home and was shocked to see a high chain-link fence covered in dark green heavy plastic sheeting, somewhat obscuring my view. The dwelling where Sol, his wife, their children lived, and his cleverly built office (The Treehouse) were no longer there. Still sitting in my car, I could only see the new construction of a second story rising between the old familiar pine trees. Sadness surrounded me as I gazed at the weeds and debris.

SOL SAKS

The brevity of life hung heavily in the air as I remembered his dreams, his hard-fought battles, and his well-deserved victories. Looking at where the treetop office once was, a vivid memory drifted from the now vacant space.

Suddenly blazing through my mind, the question I asked my eventual friend transported me back in time. "Why don't you write an autobiography, Sol?"

His surprisingly pained expression pinned me to my chair. He turned away and stared through the picture windows overlooking Sutton Street, the very spot I'm in today. A deep sadness appeared on his face as he confessed with a hint of a tear in his weary eyes,

> To write a successful book about yourself takes a brave person, you must let the reader in, and that brave I'm not! Maybe it will be written by someone else one day.

Painful memories, haunting words, and several disturbing sights seen as a child encompassed this now weathered soul. Yet, how did he rise above them, or did he? What lay behind his troubled eyes? Those telling phrases so often conveyed with a joke, poignant questions, and distant looks that brought back memories he haltingly shared. His very thoughts formed his writing style, bringing laughter to countless people. Humor, Sol said, was used to take the edge off the truth.

Whether this provider of laughter stood before an audience or wrote behind a desk, wealth was stored and shrouded in jailed pain. Yet this dear man had the inner strength and motivation to use his pain to build something productive, to move forward in a favored society. Like a stream of light illuminating the darkness, I saw the priceless gift Sol left to me; a glimpse into the mind of not just a comic but humanity.

Overwhelmed with gratitude, I drove away without another glance at the hasty discards. I finally understood that for Sol to write about or revisit those days was a door he could not open; he would not consider that journey. However, maybe I could make the journey. Perhaps I could follow his wishes and write the experiences he shared; to deliver his hope that, in some small way, would help someone rise higher.

Your Personal Invitation

*"We travel, some of us forever,
to seek other places, other lives,
other souls."*
--Anais Nin

    Well, here we are, dear treasured reader. I walked through the door left open for me to respectfully visit portions of one hundred years of a beautiful life, then condensed them just for you between the pages of this book you now hold in your hands. My invitation lies within, to a journey back in time, with the priceless ticket paid for by a man of considerable substance, Mr. Sol Saks.

    You may want to grab a cup of tea before we begin, then settle in for a captivating view, a snapshot of the world when the eventual man of words made his humble entry into the world. So please join me as we view destiny in the making, after which we will return to a cozy glimpse of the family's hidden garden. Our first destination begins with a remembrance by Sol in the distant 1800s in war-torn Poland.

    My father would interrupt the grim stories of Poland with a disturbing yet uplifting tale told to him by his father. When Poland was under siege, the British were bombing Fort McHenry, an important port city in Baltimore, Maryland, in a young America. The common roots of these wars were hateful greed. Yet, with unimaginable chaos in America, screams from the dying, blood-spattered walls, blaring guns, and bodies strewn about the encampment, a man stood that would bring hope. The weary, heartbroken Francis Scott Key lingered unharmed but in terror as gunfire subsided amid smoke-filled air. In shell-shocked disbelief, Francis gasped at the indescribable carnage with the unique heart of a poet. He battled in the courts as a lawyer but never shot a gun until this day. Finally, he turned his head from the nightmare and observed that the American flag was still standing. Through his tears, inspiration enveloped his soul. The words given to this poet seem to be engraved forever in his mind as he wrote the national anthem for America. One particular stanza, the land of the free and home of the brave, found its way around the world. It resided most profoundly within my grandmother's heart, bringing light to the painful darkness of the time.

SOL SAKS

Sol concludes,
> My mother said; that his words were like hopeful arrows striking her heart and the hearts of her family, friends, and neighbors, who were considered the unfortunate disenfranchised. These stories were my first insight into the power of words.

Medicine came in the form of words held together by musical notes easing the pain of grief. Francis confided that he believed the words he wrote were a gift to share; he would later see a progressively steady flow of Jewish families making their way to America, many settling in New York. Sol remembered that Francis learned the impact of his written words and humbly replied, "I now know for certain I was but a humble scribe writing as each word dropped into my soul. No one could make such an impact accept God."

Trailing years later, on the departure's fringe, two young people were destined to meet and usher into the world our star of this book, an adorable bundle of hidden residing talent. Destinies' path blazed a way through those dark days, finding a young Sarah Finkelstein and a dynamic Jacob Saks, distant relatives. An unseen protecting love brought them safely together, and soon the veil of fear shrouding their minds moved aside for a time, exposing a captivating view of only a heart of love and possibilities. Amid their dream, the ignited words of Francis Scott Key still blazed and filled the hearts of Sarah and Jacob.

They eventually married, talking all the while about possibilities and the music of Mr. Key that flamed dreams of New York City and the freedom it would offer. Over dinner one evening with family, a rough-looking uncle asked if anyone had heard of an organization on the Lower East Side of Manhattan in New York run by compassionate American Jews. Sarah and Jacob sat motionless while waiting for an answer. Finally, the uncle smiled between mouthfuls of food, and said it was called The Hebrew Immigrant Aid Society or HIAS, considered an iconic sanctuary. Enthralled with the prospects of this organization, Jacob asked the uncle in a whisper about the possibilities of escape. Could he find work, make a living, raise a healthy family, rest, and sleep at night without fear? A million questions surfaced until the disheveled uncle put down his fork. Everyone stared in his direction in complete silence. He quietly described the organization as providing much-needed comfort and aid to thousands of Jews fleeing pogroms (exterminations) in Russia and Eastern Europe. HIAS sounded like heaven, but fear was a presence so palpable in Poland that Sarah and Jacob knew that if they looked too long in any direction, they would see this murderous ghostly form. How could they possibly escape?

They needed to find the courage to hope for such a glorious dream. They kept busy, helping where they could while attempting to dream during unimaginable horrors of the slaughter of friends and neighbors, homes looted, and the constant threat of anti-Semitic hell on earth. Each day seemed like an eternity to Sarah and Jacob as they waited for information.

Then came a single loud knock at the door, signaling that successful news had finally arrived. A war-battled and clever uncle had covertly contacted HIAS for them. He relayed that each family member sold a treasured item to raise the money to make the purchase. No Passports or visas—no papers were required at all, just the purchase of a ticket in those days. Then came an uncomfortable pause as he explained that, sadly, they could only secure passage for one, and there was no guarantee for boarding the vessel leading to freedom.

Pregnant with their first child, Sarah thought it best for her to wait. They thanked him, kissed him goodbye, and he left for home. The thought of separation became numbingly painful for the couple. Jacob, with tears streaming, held Sarah's face between his hands, promising he would work hard to bring her and their child to America quickly. Through the painful weight of separation, the young couple attempted cautious optimism at the prospects of freedom.

The following day, through their seared, scared, haunted minds, tear-stained faces, and weary bodies, Sarah and Jacob met briefly with the entire family in the uncle's basement to express their gratitude and for Jacob to say a quiet goodbye. Then, in a whisper of departing words, each family member assured Jacob that "no matter what, we will keep in contact, take care of Sarah and the baby, and God willing, we'll try to follow one day." Finally, Sarah and Jacob hugged each relative, slipped out unobserved by anyone on the lane, walked home, and fell asleep in each other's arms.

Through the next few days, fear threatened to take hold, but they determined not to let one word of discouragement pass their lips. Finally, the long-awaited day was but a sunrise away. For Jacob, the reality of leaving his remaining family and friends was a mixture of painful guilt and a heartbreaking farewell. Surrounded by the thoughts of love and support of their family, Sarah and Jacob summoned the courage to begin planning for the morning of departure. They followed the advice of staying calm and not bringing attention to themselves. To pack only one bag as if spending a short day picnicking in the woods: attach his small suitcase to his bike, then, at the designated point—detour to the ship.

With the sunrise, Sarah made breakfast, as usual, then they left the house for what looked like a simple adventure through the woods. An experience, indeed; a three-hour bike ride, an arduous journey of perseverance. Sarah had to stop several times to rest, but Jacob's loving encouragement helped her continue. The closer they drew to the ship, the more painful the thoughts of separation became.

Ahead lay a dense brush area; they slowly walked their bikes through the tangle, briefly revealing a sight in the distance, reviving their tired spirits. The massive transportation ship to freedom loomed ever-larger in their minds as they continued further over the tree-covered dirt path. Could Jacob board the vessel? Was anyone watching? Their hearts were pounding, and their legs were weak from the journey. It was just a couple more feet of dirt path before they would enter the dock area, casually park their bikes, then slowly make their way to the ship.

Reaching the end of the path without incident, Jacob stopped suddenly. He turned to look at Sarah, held her hands in his, and asked her not to accompany him to the dock area, to please say goodbye to him in this seclusion. As tears filled Sarah's eyes and rushed down her lovely face, she hesitantly agreed. Camouflaged by fragrant rustling bushes, they clung tightly to each other as they kissed goodbye.

Jacob wiped the tears from both their faces and, with one longing look at Sarah, quietly hid his bike within a bush, untied his suitcase, then slowly made his way out into the open dock area. Sarah clung to the branches as she watched from behind the bushes breathlessly as Jacob walked out into the open, then began climbing up the long-rising gangplank without cover. With each step, she held her breath in fear.

The threat of being shot still echoed in the ears of this beloved couple. Jacob reached the middle, turned, and the two took one soul-piercing look at each other, and with the memory of sacrifices made—he continued to put one foot in front of the other until he reached the top of the gangplank; exhausted. Not wanting to bring any more attention to themselves, Sarah, trembling, reluctantly turned and walked to her bike for the long ride home.

Arriving aboard the ship and immediately into a division of wealth and class, grief-stricken Jacob successfully surrendered his ticket. He had made it just in time to hear the blast from the ship's horn above him announcing the transport departure. The massive heralding blare shot through the air, tearing through Sarah's heart. She stopped beneath the trees crying uncontrollably before finding the strength to continue her journey home. With the heart of a scholar and poet, Jacob lingered at the ship's railing until he could no longer see any vestige of the area Sarah was traveling. Then, with his suitcase in hand, he descended the many stairs to the lower part of the vessel, called steerage.

The bright sunlight diminished with every few steps, dimming the way before him. As he reached the last stair, musty air pervaded the long narrow corridor. Lingering fatigue became pronounced; he paused, then entered the daunting dark passageway stretching in the distance. Overwhelmed at what lay ahead, Jacob's legs faltered as he leaned against the wall until he gained composure. He wondered if he had made the right choice to leave Sarah. Using the sides of the ships-wall to steady him as the vessel moved, Jacob continued to a large, musty smoke-filled room crowded with upset people.

There was no limit set on steerage tickets sold, no restrictions on smoking, drinking, or anything that would facilitate privacy or good manners; Jacob found it almost impossible to remain positive. He struggled through the crush of people to the far corner of the claustrophobic room, finding just enough space for his suitcase, which Jacob quickly placed on the floor and sat upon to rest. Leaning back on the ship's wall, he struggled to keep hope alive and his bride's face before him.

The journey would take several weeks, and doubt was a constant companion. How could he endure the lack of privacy and unsanitary conditions? Nevertheless, he held the belief in freedom close while convincing himself it was worth the hardship for the chance to bring his family to America. Jacob closed his weary, burning eyes, and thoughts of Sarah returned, helping him ease into a deep sleep; within a moment, Jacob slid off his suitcase onto the floor, jolting him awake with fright. Startled—Jacob forgetting where he was, looked around in embarrassed horror. Then, holding back a slight hint of laughter, he shook his head and returned to sit again upon his suitcase.

As night fell, weary passengers within the room laid down where they were, huddling together for warmth. The gentle, comforting hum from the ship and the gentle rocking lulled each frightened soul to sleep. But sleep for some did not remain peaceful. Shocking sights from the war they left behind still lingered vividly somewhere inside. A nightmare of the horrors would visit one woman this night. Jailed in her memory was the sight of her family and only child slaughtered as she stood helplessly watching. She awakened with an excruciatingly painful scream, waking almost everyone and filling their thoughts with tragedy.

The following morning, anxiety and fear permeated the room. With Sarah's comforting ways on his mind, Jacob wanted to bring hope and decided to meet people. Introducing himself, he tentatively said good morning to those around him. His calming voice began a slow interruption through the heavy cloud of discouragement. It was but moments when the uncomfortable feelings eased, uncovering a commonality.

SOL SAKS

Jacob learned that morning that one person could change the lives around him. Inspired, a retiring Jacob continued to bravely take steps to help comfort and assist those he could. Life views broadened for this poet while nurturing new acquaintances from different religions and cultures. Later, some of these shipmates would contact him in New York and remain life-long friends. What were undesirable conditions were simply a covering of treasures hidden just for Jacob Saks.

The long adventurous journey ended, and the grief Jacob arrived with had eased a bit. Parting with handshakes and best wishes, Jacob grabbed his suitcase in anticipation of seeing New York for the first time. He took one long look at the room that had once terrified him, smiled, and climbed to the top-side steerage. At that moment, he determined Sarah would not come to America in these conditions. With one last glance back, Jacob turned his attention toward the New York harbor that should appear on the horizon at any moment. His head flooded with the wonder of freedom as the massive ship cut through the water. Dolphins glided playfully alongside, hugging the vessel. It was like these beautiful creatures were welcoming the ship to America. The sounds and sights of such beauty were glorious. The fresh, crisp ocean air rushing past his face seemed to whisper that life was improving. He stretched out his arms to the sky and breathed in the fragrant sea air of America.

One by one, steerage passengers filed up the stairs, many of which were his new acquaintances. They band together, their eyes glued to the distant horizon. As the harbor appeared, cheering arose amidst thunderous roars of laughter and tears. Any remaining passengers rushed up the stairs to see freedom ahead, pushing and shoving for just one glimpse of the land of their dreams.

A hush fell over the crowd as one passenger stepped onto an outer railing, almost falling overboard, and pointed to an object in the distance; the Statue of Liberty. Tears rolled down the cheeks of many in a breathless stare. The generous gift of freedom was growing closer. Some bowed their head in prayer; others cried. The home of the free was there before them, and they had arrived to witness the splendor. All stood in excited wonder as the ship docked and the gangplank was secured. Jacob and the multitude positioned themselves to disembark when suddenly uniformed health officers immediately boarded. For the war-torn, this sight was terrifying. Women fainted, children cried, and fear replaced the heartfelt joy of the battered passengers.

When the captain and crew realized their fear, the captain announced, "Please stay calm; this is a simple procedure to confirm that all are healthy." A sigh of relief echoed over the crowd as they listened for instructions.

Immediately processed were first and second-class passengers and, if healthy, allowed to enter the United States without going through Ellis Island. Unfortunately, those in steerage like Jacob and the hundreds remaining did not have that option. Instead, they waited for a small ferry to take them to the Island's immigration station for processing. Weary travelers slowly walked into the awaiting ferry filling every available space. Then, reaching Ellis Island, each one exited carrying all their belongings.

They first passed through the baggage room on the ground floor. The room contained hundreds of large steamer trunks, beautiful suitcases, and people dressed in elegant clothing hurrying to claim their baggage. One fashionably dressed woman gasped in disgust as she put her gloved hand over her nose. She stared with contempt at the steerage crowd as they moved through. Having nothing to pick up but merely passing through was difficult enough for Jacob, but seeing the response of this privileged woman, made him pleased Sarah was not there to feel the heartbreak of ignorant disrespect.

Anger filled Jacob while being pushed, shoved, and sandwiched between the mass of humanity. Suddenly interrupting his thoughts was the hand of a new friend as he reached out to pat Jacob on the back. With resolve, Jacob whispered that someday, God willing, he would travel again, and his baggage would be in this very room waiting for him. Jacob kept close to his friend until they passed the baggage room. They waved goodbye and gave a reassuring smile as the force of the crowd parted the two men. Once through the room, a steep winding staircase lay before Jacob, leading to the registry on the second floor.

Doctors stood vigilantly above, peering over the rail at each person climbing the stairs for any visible sign of a health problem. Jacob stopped briefly to catch his breath and noticed the doctors taking notes on each ascending passenger. Though Jacob was in good health, he closed his eyes in prayer; his poet's heart was pounding in anticipation. Then, taking a deep breath, Jacob climbed the stairs while the doctors watched his every step.

Reaching the top, moving past the doctors scrutinizing gaze, he breathed a sigh of relief, then entered a large room with people waiting for further examination. The stress and sadness of this ordeal were palpable. Jacob watched intently while another doctor in his white coat gave a six-second health examination. Those that passed were free to go to the final room to confirm their identification. Those not passing received an X made with chalk on their lapel and then herded like cattle to the railed area leading to a sequestered room for further examinations.

SOL SAKS

Jacob held fiercely to hope as he overheard the following cryptic statements. Anyone considered a risk by not passing the legal inspection would be marked with a second X and detained for extensive inquiries. With the discomfort of hunger, a million fears raced through his mind.

Waiting for this six-second test seemed like an eternity, but with exacting precision, his turn arrived. The doctor went through his routine, looked past Jacob, and hollered, "Okay, next!" Jacob quietly moved ahead, listening to the directions given to the legal inspection. He found the room and sat, then he was quickly asked 29 identifying questions with the help of an interpreter. His mind was spinning while watching them check each answer he gave against the ship manifest. If his answers did not match the officials' information, the next stop was detainment. The ordeal was fraught with anxiety. Reaching the end, the interpreter smiled and said he could leave. Relieved, Jacob picked up his suitcase and left the room.

While clutching his prized landing card, he effortlessly journeyed down the stairs, breathing a sigh of relief as he walked out to freedom. He paused to feel the sun on his face, silently prayed for those held back, then continued with gratitude. Jacob felt fortunate as he spotted the smiling representative from HIAS; his journey in liberty began.

Jacob later learned that some friends in overnight detainment were held for months until there was time to make further investigations. Then—when the background probes were complete, they received a landing card, some with names misspelled, then finally let into the United States. One couple was returned to their country, free of charge, and told they were part of the unfortunate 2 percent. Through a feeling of conflict at the seeming injustice, Jacob found work and worked diligently for the next two years—sometimes seven days a week until he had enough money to send for Sarah and his son. Sadly, one problem loomed, distressing Sarah significantly; again, there was only enough money for one ticket. Their first child Joe was 18 months old, and only children 12 months of age or younger could travel free. A meticulously honest woman, Sarah would step into the shadows of a lie today. She said Joe was just 12 months old, smiled, then the two boarded for America, relieved and excited.

Jacob kept his promise that Sarah would not have the Ellis Island experience as he did; his bride and son came through Canada on a cleaner ship with a cot for each passenger and Jacob to meet them. The long, almost unbearable wait was finally at an end. Jacob's eyes began to tear as he spotted Sarah in the distance. Overwhelmed to see her, he began running toward her then stopped abruptly overcome at first sight of his child, beautiful Sarah, held in her arms. His breath caught in his throat as he quickly moved to embrace them both.

Sarah and Jacob were gloriously together again in the country of their dreams, parents yet still newlyweds.

At first glance, New York was everything Sarah had imagined; unmeasurable joy filled her to overflowing. But unfortunately, it was a matter of days when she realized that anti-Semitism was quietly present in New York. Immigration was at an all-time high; reported was that 8 million immigrants left their countries, and millions were migrating to America. The news unsettled the longtime New York residents suffering challenges of their own. Prejudice lurked in the dark corners of their new country, and a grey cloud of disappointment hovered over Sarah for a time.

She later told the story that the disappointing reality caused bitterness in Jacob that he found hard to shake. Each morning while sweeping the walkway, he angrily attempted to brush away the glaring looks and the quietly spoken anti-semantic words lingering in his mind. But unfortunately, the trauma the war caused overshadowed the covert prejudice in New York, and to Jacob, it appeared to be Poland again.

One saving grace was that this couple had a unique advantage over most Americans, mainly a misunderstood benefit often hated. They had gained wisdom and determined stamina from the atrocities left behind, giving them an ability to push past insults vigorously and find the bright spot of success. Though hidden mental scars remained, they soon learned about many lovely—generous people in America. Jacob fought to use his anger to succeed, and Sarah held fast to her faith as life slowly gave them wings to fly. They eventually entered the flow of their new country and increased their family. Though the words, the land of the free and home of the brave, did not shine as they once did, they held fast to the possibilities of better days.

The overcrowded treeless streets of New York became an energetic blend of immigrant cultures. Amidst the gray of the buildings and walkways, the bright aroma of delicious ethnic foods filled the air with rare, exciting spices and beautifully appointed crafts handed down through the generations. No country is without its problems—and America was no exception. America was experiencing civil wars, and New York, the effects of internal political and civil corruption. The hardships of these adversities brought growth to some and others to a destructive approach to life. However, America had not known the degree of suppression as did the millions now entering. A great deal of pain filled the overcrowded streets with differences in lifestyles bringing a constant irritant. Each new arrival struggled to survive, becoming an ugly objection to those who had never experienced such violence. Those not broken by the extreme experience they left behind spent their days working with a resolve that brought dark suppressive envy because of their success.

SOL SAKS

Working within the mix of cultures, including Americans, lived a few who did not possess a gallant work ethic. They preferred instead to steal rather than contribute to society. Some spread well-crafted lies, convincing communities that immigrants alone were responsible for the growing poverty that spread like the ravages of cancer. Sadly, prejudice, once covert, began showing in loud hateful speech, slurs written on walls, and rocks thrown through windows. The fallout of its painful growing effects found its way to the Saks family. Sarah was pregnant and expecting any day. This baby would be born into the escalating hatred that reminded Sarah of the horrors of her youth—rendering her heartbroken until his arrival.

From the first moment love brought Sarah and Jacob's newest addition into the world, this tiny bundle wore a look of intense curiosity. As Sarah gazed in wonder upon his face, she considered him a small force of nature, and Jacob agreed to name their son Saul which in Hebrew means to ask or question, and in time the name proved fitting. Saul was regularly called Sol by his family members, and the name stuck but modifying it did not change its meaning. Almost ninety years later, Sol said,

> While still a young boy, I sat enveloped as if in the center of an adventurous book. I leaned back in my chair to hear my mother tell me about December 10, 1910, the day of my birth. She made the day sound magical. She explained that she thought I was a determined spark of light undeterred by the bitter cold while making my premier appearance in the world. Hearing her refer to me as a spark of light has always been a lovely thought.
>
> Impatiently waiting at home to meet me were my two brothers, Joseph and Harry, and sister, Dora helping to prepare for a family celebration in honor of me. My mother's eyes sparkled as she painted a picture with words. These were her words as she described the day I was born. 'New York City, my son, was experiencing record cold days with streets covered in piles of glistening snow; clean white snowflakes provided a noise barrier with every falling crystal soothing my weary, saddened ears. Yet, on those snowy days, the thoughts of the city's inhabitants turned toward Christmas while carefully navigating the icy walkways. Bundled from head to toe, they were almost unrecognizable. The eyes of many were the only exposed part of their bodies.
>
> Amid 11 degrees of bone-chilling cold, people stopped to gaze through the warm, inviting Christmas windows on this reported coldest day. Moments of calm reached into their hearts as they stood, momentarily huddled together, blissfully blind, for one suspended breath to each other's differences.

BEWITCHED

Sarah's story concludes,

> Christmas lights cast twinkling reflections that bounced off the snow, and encircled carolers gathered on street corners. Though many may not have celebrated Christmas, moments of rest captured the minds and hearts of the community. The news of Enrico Caruso appearing at the Metropolitan Opera House spread across all cultures like warm sunshine. He would sing Giacomo Puccini's La Fanciulla de West, conducted by Arturo Toscanini.
>
> If you were lucky enough to hear the voice of Caruso as he sang, worry and hatred melted from your heart as if each note came from a mighty angel. It brought the holiday celebration to an exceptional level; love took its preeminent place on those bitterly cold days in December. Several family members and friends may have celebrated different holiday traditions. Still, foreign cultures took a deep breath, relaxing for that brief time of joy and peace, and began observing the season with customs they brought from their countries.'

Sarah regained her strength and resolve, and with it, the simple joys of life found their way back to the Saks. They continued contributing to society while doing their best to show kindness to neighbors who occasionally were rude. Sol crawling then walking, seemed fascinated with everything within his sight. Curious about life around him and beyond, a never-ending barrage of questions poured forth from this happy soul. Sol looked back in sadness as he remembered those days as a child.

> Life changed at that point; for the first time, I felt fear, a crushing feeling. I stopped asking questions and retreated into my thoughts. I think I was in school then, but I remember people I liked slowly becoming distant and angry. President William Howard Taft held office then, and the heated conversation in our shop was that he didn't fix the growing prejudice causing harm to countless people. Instead, the focus was on the exciting period of technological and stylistic experimentation for moviemakers.

For the most part, the new technology helped divert the mind and brighten outlooks, but it wasn't the answer to the underlying anger. With a steady increase, cinema matured into an artistic medium, transforming into a popular method of silent storytelling, while crime and misunderstanding of cultures grew steadily worse. Sarah often wove into a story the exciting discovery of movies, helping her family through the confusion. Then, with soft music playing in the background, Sarah would recite captivating accounts of the people endeavoring to make the world a kinder place to live.

SOL SAKS

Though all present enjoyed her thrilling stories, they ignited a fire for storytelling in Sol that remained. An adorable package of humanity with infinite possibilities arrived on earth that cold winter day so many years ago with hidden talents unique to him alone. It was all ahead of him. It would be many years of battling prejudice, alluring crime, his misunderstood longings, and struggling through his discouraging thoughts before turning in the best possible writing. But success came; his writing earned him money, then came recognition.

The Hollywood Reporter, a popular show business news magazine, would interview a candid Sol Saks, quoting,

"I was the skinny kid with the glasses and the big nose who would not get a girl, and I told jokes at parties—somebody else's jokes! I wasn't funny as a kid or as a grown-up. But I knew I wanted to be a writer at about age 13, but I don't remember writing much."

The curious, wide-eyed young interviewer leaned in and asked Sol to tell him more about what the early 1900s were like and what else shaped his thinking. There was a long pause as Sol smiled, then said,

There were many firsts for the country when I was a child. My parents told me about most events, but several impacted me. I'll give you a snapshot of the world when I was a boy. In 1910—Jack Johnson, the first black boxer, beat Tommy Burns for the Heavyweight Boxing Championship. That was one of the stories of courage and controversy my dad told us about when we were older. The Boy Scouts found their way from England to America, an exciting time. Sadly, I found out it was for everyone except the Jews. I ran to the mirror as a little boy, wondering why they excluded Jews and thinking something must be wrong with me. But how could that be? I thought to write to King Edward VII, "Bertie."

He was England's beloved king then and was known as a man who brought people together even in America. I was sure he didn't know about this oversight. My mother told me of his kindness, courage, and love for people but advised me not to write to a man so painfully busy. So, I determined I would try to be like "Bertie;" maybe I could join the Boy Scouts. But, unfortunately, compassion, courage, and love still didn't get me into the Scouts.

Family stories directed my attention to the First Electric Self-Start installed in a Cadillac by General Motors, which became an exciting time in family conversation. I think my love for adventure began when I heard stories of the discovery of Machu Picchu.

Sol continues,

> First, the name and location intrigued me. Next, my mother loved Puccini's opera Madame Butterfly and regaled us with the story.

The Manhattan Sweatshop Fire hit New York, and my mother cried when she told us about the devastation and the injustice; I wanted to help. But, within days came the first Indianapolis 500 race in all its excitement and eclipsed the tragedy; that puzzled me. People appeared to forget, going about their day as if nothing had happened until the Sinking of the Titanic. I was still a child, but hearing my parents talking about these events made life somber. The introduction of Girl Scouts of America was a sharp reminder that girls of immigrant parents were not welcome. I had sisters that I loved, and it was a painful reality. That, of course, has changed, as has the Boy Scouts.

In 1913—came the first Cross Word Puzzle, and it was fun as we got older. Ah, then the 16th Amendment! The collection of taxes on income. No one, except the government, was happy about that!

Mr. Ford introducing the Assembly Line was a bright spot. It was something open to all people. My father talked about Fords and the Federal Trade Commission; these were new and might hold possibilities for everyone. Soon, thunderous news rocked the hearts of all. World War I began in Europe. War, the word alone, was frightening for my family and friends. But fear covered all of America when a German U-boat torpedoed the British-owned steamship Lusitania, killing over a thousand people, including over one hundred Americans. The disaster led to the United States entering the war. All who fled to America feared that the devastation would reach them again. With thousands of men at war, women took new roles discovering they were stronger than they believed, bringing about The Women's Suffrage Movement.

In a serene rented home in Omaha, a Roman Catholic priest, while working for the diocese of Omaha, founded The City of Little Men, later called Boys Town, a revolutionary accomplishment. Though segregation was prominent and hatred thought appropriate, Father Flanagan believed that all boys deserved a second chance regardless of race or religion. As a result, he saw no barriers, which caused many problems for Boys Town. But through the hatred and threats of violence, he continued to give America a glimpse of the type of love England's King Bertie had. Years later, the quote of Margaret Mead, an American cultural anthropologist, remembers this band of brave women and one lone man.

SOL SAKS

Sol continues,

> 'Never doubt that a small group of thoughtful, committed citizens can change the world. Indeed, it's the only thing that ever has.'
>
> An inspiring quote that stuck with me all these years, keeping me focused on moving forward. These examples inspired me to dream beyond my limitations, easing the cloud of doom. I concentrated on Joseph Pulitzer's stand on integrity and the Pulitzer Prize. I found the rewarding thought of inspiring people out of their limitations exciting. Our friends and neighbors from Russia were devastated when they heard of the execution of Mata Hari, Czar Nicholas Romanov II, and his family. I was a child, but I listened intently to the conversations and saw the pain of grief. It's only now that I'm in my nineties that I see these profound life events leading me to write.
>
> The war was ending about the same time as the brutal demise of the Romanov Dynasty. A glimmer of hope appeared amidst waves of grief. The world, though celebrating, was worn and tired. Before civilization could recuperate, hope again was lost at the global outbreak of the Spanish Influenza that continued until 1920. There was much more, but I'll end with two courageous women: Lady Astor, American by birth, was sworn in as the reported first female member of the British Parliament. I believe one woman before her did not take the position because of her Irish nationalist opinions. Then, Emma Goldman, a writer, was arrested and jailed for Advocating Birth Control. She died in 1940, twenty years before the FDA approved the first sale of birth-control pills.

Sol was nearing his one-hundredth birthday when he first spoke of his younger sister Lilly with me. A whisper of sadness surrounded his voice as he recalled life with her and events that shaped their thinking as children. These following childhood events were clear and tangible in his mind, as he said with a smile;

> As our family entered the 1920s, the KKK claimed to have four million members, more than all the Jews in the United States. Amid this turmoil and despite protestations, President Woodrow Wilson nominated Louis D. Brandeis to the Supreme Court in 1916, the first Jew to serve on the Court. Many non-Jewish people were outraged at this news. But, by the time I was old enough to understand, my parents would balance these harsh truths of life with the less reported stories of people making productive contributions to the world. One that made a big impression on me was hearing about the determination of Harry Gordon Selfridge.

Sol concludes,

> Raised in poverty without his father, he rose through calamities and hatred. American-born, he founded a magnificent London-based department store called Selfridges. His story fueled my imagination. I wanted to learn how this man who worked at a store we knew called Marshall Fields in Chicago became one of the most respected and wealthy retail magnates in the United Kingdom. So I read everything I could get my hands on about Selfridge, known as the 'Earl of Oxford Street. Learning to rise above a poverty way of thinking, prejudice, and angry stares helped me better deal with the insidious germ of hatred spreading like a plague.

The infectious thinking slipped through the cracks of humanity, finding its way into minds and homes unguarded. Hatred, it is said, arrives in many forms, but its mission is always to steal, kill and destroy. Unfortunately, Sarah and Jacob knew this only too well. Their modest family life grew more difficult with each passing day. Sarah worried for her children and Jacob as they walked the streets, harassed by angry stares or whispered slurs. But however tricky life became, there was a silent prayer from Sarah, asking for protection for her family and help them to make this world a better place to live. This ignorant hate was what she fled from, but Sarah held fast to hope. She knew people could change, and life could be better, but the choice would start with her. Sarah determined not to respond in kind. She did not accept or return the insult if hatred came to her. Instead, Sarah guarded her heart remaining above the disease of hatred. Though lacking a formal education, Sarah set an example. Children, strangers, and friends learned how to add to life around them, to live above the fray.

As exciting, progressive, and artistic as the city of New York was, Jacob and Sarah Saks grew uncomfortable with their living conditions. Maybe now was the time to experience a long-time dream of moving their family of six children to sunny, warm California. Then, at least in the sun's warmth, they might find comfort as they worked. Dreamy imaginings of blossoming fruit trees, warm days wrapped in fragrant air, and expanded days of business opportunities captured their minds and hearts. While Jacob made the exciting arrangements, Sarah packed as many bags of clothes as she could for each of them. While gathering the needs of her family, she told the children of adventurous experiences ahead. Finally, the long-awaited day arrived, and the excited Saks family boarded the train.

As the train passed through mountainous terrain, over open stretches of uninhabited land, and the occasional grand views of massive deep-blue lakes in the distance, Sarah entertained the children and Jacob with stories. From stories she heard as a child and the sites passing before them, she captivated their imaginations, calmed fears of the unknown, and changed the long-confined ride into a wonderous possibility-filled voyage.

While passing above Fort Wayne, Indiana, a porter interrupted Sarah's well-crafted diversion by bringing disturbing information. Apologizing to the tired family, he informed them of a mistake. The tickets they purchased went only as far as Chicago. Shocked, Jacob questioned another porter-in-charge who confirmed the heartbreaking news. There was nothing Jacob could do. All finances went for these tickets. They would have to leave the train in Chicago. The Hebrew Immigrant Aid Society, HIAS, was advised of the error, and they quickly began working on new arrangements for the Saks family. A wave of fatigue settled upon Sarah. Numbness encompassed her; not one story filled her head. Finally, the dazed and disappointed family gathered their belongings. The train stopped, and the confused family walked to the exit waiting for the door to open.

They could hear the sound of the wind as it drove the snow past the train window, eclipsing the station's view. Jacob stepped out first, then reached for the hands of his frightened children. Stepping from the adventurous train, the familiar despair of icy cold wrapped itself around the family. But now, this cold was accompanied by a strong buffeting wind. Jacob took the lead, instructing everyone to hold hands. Holding tightly to the string of hand-holding children, Sarah, clasping the hand of the last child, struggled to hold back her tears. As each one descended into the piercing cold wind, they held tight as they battled against the wind force. They were in strange surroundings and knew no one in Chicago. Huddled together, Jacob began to worry that HIAS had not received the message. Sarah stood in speechless fear, trying to comfort their children, and force back the memories from the past. Their faces near frozen, Jacob reassured them that everything would be alright. He gathered their suitcases and moved them into the shelter of the station building.

The children peered through the icy window while the train that carried their stories built up steam. Sol remembered that the sound of escaping steam from the train brought an image to his mind of a giant broom sweeping their dreams away. He can still see the conductor stepping onto the train platform, hanging onto the rail as he tilted into space and hollered all-aboard! The haunting sound of a whistle rang out as the engine escalated in power. It shook the platform and rattled the windows of the station building; each child jumped in fright. The sights and sounds became painful.

BEWITCHED

Tears filled the eyes of the Saks family as the train slowly departed in a cloud of smoke, taking with it their dreams.

Still standing at the window, the children turned and ran to Sarah, looking frightened and stranded. All eyes looked to Jacob for direction. Sarah sat quietly in prayer while the younger children took comfort in her smiling face. An hour passed, and the despair was mounting when they heard in the distance a voice calling, "Saks family?" There, to meet them, was the ever-dependable lifeline of HIAS. Each able family member picked up a suitcase and followed the HIAS representative to an old bus. Sol said that boarding the bus was like entering a sanctuary. He and his family were numb from the cold and exhausted. Each one found a seat without uttering a word.

Feeling the warmth and safety of the bus, young Sol fell asleep the moment he sat down. Forty-five minutes passed, which seemed but a moment to Sol when the jolt of the bus stopping awakened him. He opened his eyes to see a large, towering gray office building with a sign he said he would never forget.

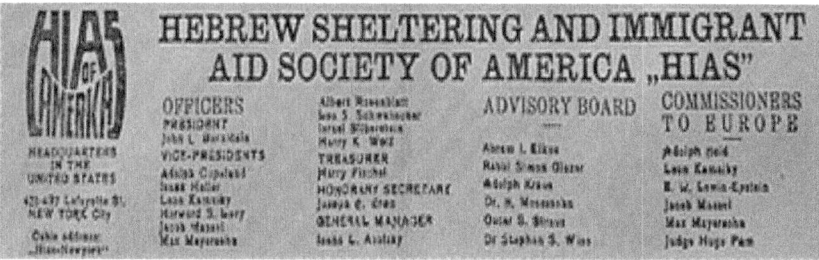

While staring at the imposing sign above, Sol became transfixed in the private universe behind his eyes until his mother's voice broke through his thoughts, saying, "It's time to leave the bus." Jacob instructed the children to quietly and respectfully follow him. The gray building loomed over the bus and sidewalk, casting a large shadow that eclipsed the little bit of sun peeking through the clouds. Standing waiting to follow their father, Sol overheard his older brothers talking about an orphanage asylum, and he became terrified. His legs suddenly felt weak as the family exited the bus and passed through the door of the somber-looking building. A few moments of terror passed before Sol realized this was not an orphanage. Instead, this building housed kind people who immediately addressed his parent's concerns with guidance and emotional support. His initial fear of going to an orphanage was now gratefully quenched.

Though just as cold as New York, Chicago slowly began to sound promising—and maybe the Saks family would continue their dream to California later.

SOL SAKS

That momentary fright of children being without parents, and placed into an orphanage, deepened Sol's awareness of the fragility of life and the importance of family. Eventually, this awareness increased his desire to be successful.

HIAS found living quarters for the Saks family with a shop at the forefront. It was perfect, and Jacob, an industrious man, opened a paint shop. In previous days, Jacob noticed the need for houses to be painted and put himself forward as a painter. Though he knew little about house painting, he learned on the job. A homeowner would see his work and tell him that was not the way to paint a house, then show him and let him go. Another homeowner would explain that he was holding the brush wrong and then show him; he persevered until homeowners were pleased.

While on these jobs, he ordered extra paint and brushes until he had enough to open a store someday. The day arrived, and each child helped in the store after school; and when Sarah was not cooking or baking and heard the shop doorbell, she would run to lend a hand. Sol recalls fondly his mother baking the best bread and the glorious fragrance drifting into the paint store. As customers entered, they were cheered by the tantalizing aroma and told Jacob that he should sell bread with his paint. Sol and his family only had store-bought bread when they ran out; this occasionally happened at the end of the week because Sarah was busy in the store.

Chicago became home. Continuing to California faded from their minds, for everyone but Sol. Prosperity was emerging for the Saks family, yet Sol dreamed of something different for himself. An unsettling feeling of now even being different from his family began an ever-growing, uncomfortable presence within him. Then, Sol met a student at school that said a local radio station was interviewing young boys to play parts for a Storytime drama. A spark ignited in young Sol, and he asked his family for permission to audition. Sarah recognized a dissatisfaction in her son and convinced Jacob to let Sol try. The audition went well; Sol landed the coveted job and immediately began learning from seasoned actors while still helping in the store after school. Finally, the big day arrived when Sol received his first paycheck! He ran home, his feet barely touching the ground. Flying through the paint shop door, young Sol gallantly presented his father with his wages. Although beaming with satisfaction, as days passed, a powerful frustration threatened to overtake Sol; being a child actor was not for him.

The loud daunting criticism, discussions, arguments, and rewritten commentaries, pierced the ears and souls of all those at work. Each show had to be better than the next, putting the producers and staff under extreme pressure. Sol couldn't imagine this type of work as a profession.

BEWITCHED

Those words flying through the air culminated in a chaotic charge through the atmosphere affecting all in the studio. Lines immediately changed before airtime, direction seemed to come from everyone, and confusion escalated. Finally, with no time to rehearse the new dialogue, the assistant director broke the chaos with a bellow, something like the jarring sound of shattering glass. He screamed out five seconds to airtime, and the producers exhaled and sat back. But the unbelievably nervous actors stood weak-kneed alone before microphones trembling, some with glistening beads of sweat on their brows. Sol became disillusioned with this highly prized position, deciding that acting was not for him. There were too many bosses, and he had no control over the words he spoke, so he quit after his performance.

As Sol approached his teen years, he figured a writer had no boss. He would decide on the dialogue. He would choose when to work. Writing a story began to sound intriguing. One he believes he learned from his mother. Well into his teens, Sol's growing love for the theater started to emerge. When the lights went down, the enchantment began. Sol slipped quietly into the world, unfolding before his eyes. He listened to every word and marveled at the prospect of evoking emotions from the right mix of phrases. He dreamed of being part of the theater environment and a world of unconfined luxury. Hooked by a realm where the good guy wins, the man gets the girl of his dreams, and money is abundant, Sol's imagination soared. The stage became his favorite place to escape the pressures of life. The immediacy of each emotion was palpable, adding a dimension to his life he had not known. A seed of promise in his heart began to grow with the exhilarating reality of possibilities. But was he brave enough to follow? Could he focus on being a part of this dynamic creative process? The word, yes, fired through his mind; the decision and focus came quickly; Sol found his place in destiny.

Sol did his part to help in the paint store while attending school. Though it was required and expected, first and foremost, Sol loved his family and wanted to be helpful. However, overflowing with varied teen emotions came the beginning of a disconnect from duty. An unfamiliar dimension of joy took center stage in Sol's life. It was like receiving a precious gift and learning to handle being set apart. Joy was always a missing element in his life; now, it seemed to flood him with distraction. When seated in the theater, this new exhilarating sensation captivated his soul like an addiction. Sol found that it occupied his mind causing him to daydream a great deal of the time. His family and friends became increasingly impatient with his growing lack of enthusiasm for work in the paint store and school. Sol struggled to understand this newfound journey.

SOL SAKS

No one, including his teachers, had answers. No one he knew made money from writing. The jobs available to Sol became an irritating obligation. It appeared inevitable and frightening to Sol that he would break away from the family business one day.

Sol in Harrison High School

Was this what growing up was all about, Sol wondered. From the vantage point of experience at the age of 90, Sol said,

I now realize that an exceptional process was starting; the painful criticism for being stubborn was because people loved me and didn't understand. How could they? I didn't understand. If I had, maybe I could forgive them. But unfortunately, information was not as readily available then, and talking about feelings was not done. So unforgiveness slowly turned to anger, then bitterness. With each passing day, the pressure of prejudice we experienced in school, in our neighborhood, and in the paint store became an increasingly evident visitor; it especially took a toll on my mother. I could see the pain on her face. Where was the freedom she dreamed of for her family? I learned that if I smiled, my mother smiled. So, I pretended to be happy. Though I did have friends in school, for the most part, they were Jewish, like Friedman, Chester, Klein, and Turek. My Non-Jewish friends and I could only visit while in school. In my yearbook, kids wrote that I was a pal to everyone and I was one of the five horsemen—a nerdy group of Jews and non-Jews. I had many interests in school but could only join Biology Club, Fencing, and a couple more. Jewish children had an invisible leash around their necks.

We could go just so far, but no further, not ever! I always wondered about the truth of my existence. What was wrong with being Jewish?

Sol continues,

> I understood that being rude, unkind, lying, and physically unclean were unacceptable, but I thought I was a kind boy, took baths, and wore clean clothes. As I said, discussions or questions about such things were not part of our lives—ignorant imaginings ruled the air.
>
> We were fighting to survive, with no time to figure it out. The result caused a disturbing, lingering anger as I witnessed this strange hypocrisy throughout our community. It was easy for some people to throw a verbal stone, to try to kill the difference, and the culprit seemed upsettingly relieved for the time they were throwing. But soon, almost cancerous thinking began and became contagious, similar to a plague. More people engaged in verbal stone-throwing and the murder of everyday truth; the plague was spreading. I was grateful for those few people that took the time to find a path to understanding, allowing for diversity, and cultivating a kinder heart—these were complex issues to pursue but incredibly rewarding. I read that every life entering this world is deserving of love; oh, how I hoped that was true. I've carried these and other undefined problems into life with me and possibly, unwittingly passed them on. One thing I've learned, but unfortunately toward the end of my life, is that it's better to be honest, no matter how painful. To sit calmly and talk. Carrying such abuse caused infinite physical, mental, and social problems in my life. To forgive ignorance is crucial and a virtue I have not yet mastered.
>
> One of my students asked me how I got started telling jokes. I told him that as a youngster, my two greatest anxieties were not smelling horrible and not being a sissy. So, I told someone else's funny stories to cover my vulnerability. Eventually, I found that most of my friends felt the same way. The anxiety lessened, and I started figuring out original jokes.

While in Harrison High School, that theater seed continued to grow. Confidence steered Sol now, and he took the chance to hone his language skills. Learning became focused as he found a path to his destiny. Attending college at night, Sol entered the North-Western University of Journalism with a glimpse of his dream floating before him. He developed writing skills and secured that coveted job with lasered motivation. He worked during the day as an apprentice reporter for a local newspaper while remaining helpful in the family paint store. Sol remembers,

> In the early days of my career, on August 6, 1945, an American B-29 bomber dropped the first deployed atomic bomb over the Japanese city of Hiroshima.

SOL SAKS

Sol continues,

> This horrific incident gave me three different and separate shocks. The horror of this new death-dealing invention came first. Then, a few weeks later, the second, I heard, with disgust, a joke about the same horrendous weapon. Finally, a few years passed when the third shock arrived; I found myself writing a joke about the atomic bomb; I paused for a considerable time to take in this strange discovery.
>
> Comedy, I have learned, can bring to light things that can hurt and delight—but once brought to light in a respectful comedic form, they never seem to hurt as much. As I grow as a writer, I see people finding peace when they can laugh, even in the face of tragedy.
>
> When I worked in radio as a kid, I wrongly thought many things. For example, I believed a writer would not have any boss except the writer himself. Boy, was I wrong! I later found that writing for television; I had several. But comedy taught me to lighten up, and when I did, I saw a signpost in life that said I could fly solo. I believe we all need to shine at some time or another. If we can't do it any other way, we'll wear a lampshade for a hat, enter a cake at the county fair, try a double gainer off the diving board, offer to fight any man in the bar, or tell jokes. The last is by no means the least dangerous. But, to some of us, it's the only way left.

Sol Saks

Dearly Beloved

In 1938, Sol, as a young man of 28, wrote an insightful article for the **Chicago Daily News** called **Dearly Beloved**. It was only one of many, but his talent was unmistakable, his pain substantial, and his love for humanity fearless. I am presenting his work in the original form without further editing.

Mummy Was Dead, Everybody Was Crying, but He knew She'd Wake Up and Take Him Home Again.

"Dearly beloved, we are gathered here…"

Grownups were so silly sometimes. Don't cry, don't cry, they said, when you bumped your head or cut your finger. You are seven years old and a little man now. Besides, it isn't going to help one bit if you cry. And here they were all whimpering just like 3-year-old Mary Louise when somebody took her wagon.

All because Mummy was dead.

As soon as the minister was finished, Mummy would get out of the box and come and take him home. Mummy wouldn't leave him alone. When it thundered and lightened, you were frightened, but if Mummy were there, she would put her arms around you, and you weren't frightened anymore; because Mummy wouldn't let anybody hurt you.

"…For she bequeathed to those she loved a heritage…a treasure of memories…"

She told you fairy tales, mostly about the beautiful princess and the gray-eyed prince who was good and kind but very jealous. He thought that the princess had done something awful bad. Something worse than fibbing, worse even than stealing. And the princess had become very angry and said when was going away and would never come back until he trusted her.

Then you would tell Mummy the rest of the story because the end was the part that you liked best. The prince sent for the princess and said he was sorry, and the princess forgave him, and they lived happily ever after.

When Mummy was working, you would ask Mrs. O'Flaherty, who took care of you, to tell you when it was time for Mummy to come home. Then you would wait for her on the corner because you could not go across the street on account of the automobiles. Mummy would wave to you from far off, and she would have a present for you, but you would pretend that you didn't see it. Then she would give it to you and shout, "Surprise!"

They had a lot of fun until Mummy lost her job and then she was very sad, and she didn't bring home any more presents. They ate mostly potatoes and crackers and milk and many times Mummy didn't eat with him because she said she had just had a big meal in a restaurant.

"...Doubly blessed are those that live not for themselves, but for others..."

One night he was telling her about Georgie Prender's new red bicycle and how rich Georgie's father was, and he had said, "I'll bet Georgie Prender never goes hungry, does he Mummy?" He didn't mean anything by it really, he didn't. He just said it as he would say, I'll bet that automobile can go 100 miles an hour. But it hurt Mummy. He could see that it hurt her terribly, worse than the time when she burned her hand on the stove.

She took him right downstairs and asked Mrs. O'Flaherty to take care of him. Then she went out, even though it was late at night. He tried his hardest to keep awake, but he fell asleep before she came home. The next day she brought home an armful of groceries and a red bicycle because she had another job, only now she was working nights.

He said to her, "Gee, Mummy, you didn't have to buy me this bicycle. I don't care if I have nothing else to eat in my life but old potatoes. I wouldn't care. Honest, Mummy." And she grabbed him and squeezed him until it hurt, but he didn't cry.

When it rained, they would dress warm and walk in the rain. The rain was so nice and soft on his face that he would get tingly all over. Then they would buy popcorn and feed it to the birds. Mummy said that the birds like the popcorn twice as much in the rain because no one else would feed them then.

Then one day she got that nasty old letter. She started to laugh, but it wasn't a nice laugh like when he told her about Denny O'Flaherty falling into the flour.

It was almost like crying. Then she started laughing and crying at the same time, and Mrs. O'Flaherty came running upstairs and called the doctor, and Mummy was sick in bed and had medicine and everything. He had picked up the letter, and he could read it because it didn't have any hard words. It only said, "I need you, Mary." Then Mummy died.

Now Mummy was over there in the big box, and everybody was crying. Aunt Bertha, who lived very far away, was there, and last night when she thought he was sleeping, she had said to Mrs. O'Flaherty:

"I suppose that now I'll have to take care of the kid."

He didn't want Aunt Bertha to take care of him. She would never walk in the rain and feed popcorn to birds. He wanted to wait for Mummy. Mummy would feel very sad if she came home and he wasn't waiting for her. If Aunt Bertha would make him go, he would run away from home. He would even rather live in an orphan asylum where they beat you and made you scrub floors.

"Hello, Jimmy," said the man who sat down next to him. Jimmy could see that the man had tears in his eyes,

"How would you like to come home with me?" Jimmy saw that through the tears, his eyes were gray. Jimmy said:

"I'd like that fine. But I couldn't live with you always, only until Mummy comes home."

"All right, Jimmy, we'll wait for Mummy together, and may she rest forever in peace. Amen."

2

The Radio Days

"TV gives everyone an image,
But radio gives birth to a million
Images in a million brains".
—*Peggy Noonan*

Well-finished with college courses, Sol was ready to launch into the larger world of words. Though he wanted to be a writer, he didn't want to sit at the dining room table, write nights, or work for a newspaper that didn't pay well. Earning a good living, being independent, and having a home of his own were paramount. As a rookie just out of college in the 1930s, the good-paying writing jobs were in radio, so Sol attended the interviews. He earned money by selling occasional short stories in periodicals such as Atlantic Monthly. When the Chicago Daily News published his short stories, they became helpful in landing writing jobs for Chicago-based radio programs in the 1930s. He was paid $20 for his first radio script. Sol laughingly remembers,

> I started writing on a radio show called *Uncle Walter's Dog House* in Chicago. I got the job by sending dozens of letters to advertising agencies. In those days, ad agencies produced radio shows. Consequently, I only went out with girls that could type.

Radio Soap Operas were big in Chicago then and needed good writers. When the help-wanted announcements went out for writers, the room filled with writers for drama. But Sol noticed that if they mentioned comedy, the room would empty. That was an inner cue for Sol; he remained patiently waiting as each person left. He remembered the furrowed brows and a couple of angry glances from writers as they passed him. Undeterred, Sol sat determined, with a hint of fear knocking at his heart in the now vacant and cold room. Several minutes passed before the door opened, and a solemn-looking man stood quietly at the threshold. He looked over at Sol with a disappointed look, took a deep breath, shook his head, and exhaled in exhausted disgust as he continued gazing. Finally, he asked if Sol could write comedy. Sol, though intimidated, bravely told the man that he would write anything needed. Sol got the job on the spot.

Interestingly, the Chicago-based *William Morris Talent Agency* saw a promising writer in Sol and signed a contract to represent him.

BEWITCHED

Sol was specializing in Westerns and airplane scripts at the time, putting jokes here and there in otherwise serious storylines. Sol did not realize it at the time, but his reputation as a comedy writer was born, and a path to success lay before him. Sol explains,

> I continued getting small jobs writing western stories and airplane stories. I'd never been out West and never up in an airplane. While writing a story about planes, my instructions were to refer to the aileron. So, I wrote, "The aileron isn't working!" I didn't know what an aileron was or if such a thing existed. But, those were my instructions given by the producers, and I followed them, and we didn't get any letters of complaints. I finally learned this aileron object was something at the trailing edge of the craft that controlled the balance. Who knew?

Sol dreamed of transitioning to drama, but comedy writing became his forte and the means to his eventual fortune. About a year later, in the 1940s, radio began its slow decline in Chicago—and became the home of soap operas. The family paint store increased in popularity and revenue, and Jacob gradually opened three more stores. All in the Saks family were living comfortably. The dream Sarah and Jacob had was finally before them. However, with this burgeoning comfort came an increasing restlessness to Sol; it was that time he knew would come, his opportunity to spread his professional wings. He was a married man and wanted to provide a better living for Anne and himself.
Sol said,

> I couldn't get on the soap opera shows, even though I could write drama. It was a frustrating time. All the avenues that were open to me were now closed without explanation. For a time, I wondered if writing was the wrong choice. Maybe I should stay and work full-time with my family as they suggested. The decisions I had to make were not easy for me and somewhat frightening. When I finally decided to take a chance on writing, with what I felt was right for me, the next decision was to move to New York or Los Angeles. My wife Anne and I discussed it with my family, which was difficult as I was the only one that did not stay in the family business. My family was not sorry to see me go. They were always joking and telling me I was not a good businessman. Maybe they were right; I know my mind was always in the writing world. Anne was a brave soul and said she would back any decision I made. One day, I overheard my father talking to a customer while handing him his paint cans.

Sol continues,

> He said that a man of substance; can make a living anywhere. Though not directed at me, his words significantly strengthened my life. I took a deep breath and then talked to Anne. We considered that New York had Theater, and California had Movies and celebrities. It was one coast or the other. I looked at Anne as she sat confidently waiting for my decision, and I jokingly said,
>
> "Let's go to Los Angeles; it's a better ride!"
>
> Anne laughed and said,
>
> I agree; I'll pack!"

My family smiled at my reasonings but shook their heads in disbelief as they wished us good luck. I think my mother was worried. She hung on to my father's arm as we left that day. Anne and I had borrowed a car and motored west on Route 66. Before we left, my agent told me Hollywood was dying for comedy writers. So, when Anne and I arrived in Los Angeles, my first call was to the agency to let them know I was available immediately. Then I made many phone calls inquiring about possible work. I found Hollywood was not dying for comedy writers! Still, I wasn't worried. My agent at *The William Morris Agency* in Chicago had referred me to their Los Angeles office. Supposedly, you could not get work without an agent in Hollywood, so I felt confident. We then rented a small apartment, which Anne quickly made into a comfortable home while I continued looking and calling for work.

I made more calls to the agency but couldn't get an appointment. So, I put on my best suit and went to the office, but I still couldn't get in or make an appointment. Now I was worried! I immediately went to an advertising company that produced television shows and quickly earned a reputation for being a maverick. I don't consider myself that way; I just wanted to work. The advertising company put me on *The Red Skelton Show,* featuring comedy skits, gags, and vignettes. I got paid directly; the agency didn't get their ten percent which got their attention. Now they called and asked me to come in at my convenience—no less.

BEWITCHED

Red Skelton

Richard Red Skelton premiered his radio show on October 7, 1941, called The Raleigh Cigarette Program. He began developing his comedic and pantomime skills from the age of 10. Red became part of a traveling medicine show developing his unique routines. His radio show involved several recurring characters, all played by him. Red was much-loved and admired by his audience. He maintained a brilliant program of comedy for all listeners. The audience could relax in a healthy diversion from cares in this armchair escape for the moments it aired. Letters of thanks poured in, saying they felt refreshed and relaxed at the show's end.

It was into this rarified atmosphere Sol entered as a rookie. He remembers his frightening steps into writing for the show as a desperate, random groping for something funny. A feeling similar to the nightmare actors have of being on stage and forgetting their lines. Yet, though his heart pounded with uncertainty, he held on to courage and gave his best.

Sol continues,

> It was an exciting time, my first job in California, writing for Red Skelton, and I got $200.00 a week! As you can imagine, being the rookie and on my first big job, I was nervous and preoccupied with a mental barrage of 'what-ifs.' Then, I got a message that the *William Morris Agency* had called several times. I couldn't leave to return their calls and was moving toward overwhelmed. So, I took a deep breath and planned to go to the office on my day off. But, before the day came, an agent arrived at the show to see me. I stood motionless, in disbelief, and I was speechless. They were now pursuing me. Some years later, a new writer asked me how he could get an agent. My response was to become a success first.

SOL SAKS

Sol continues,

> A strange twist, I know that some publishers or large sections of studios, and producers, will not even consider your work unless submitted through an agent. They say it is to avoid lawsuits and save time reading through the myriad of submissions; this is the practice.
>
> But on the positive side, if you can find an agent interested in your work and feels he can make money from it, you are in a good spot. Otherwise, it is something close to getting a bank loan; prove to them you don't need one. Anyway, working with Red Skelton was inspiring. He was very talented, and I learned a lot from him. He was also kind and generous to everyone connected with his show. Though I admired him, I always looked for a way to advance myself. So, I asked my agent to call me with any shows looking for writers, and he did. I was writing with Red Skelton for two weeks when I got a call that Duffy's Tavern, one of the elite shows of its time, needed a fill-in writer. The stars were the treasured Ed Gardner, Bing Crosby, and Betty Hutton. Of course, I went for the interview immediately and expected to make more money. But instead, the producer sternly told me that the head writer only made $250.00 a week, and what was I thinking? A shot of panic hit me, and I was disappointed. But, I reasoned that this was a great opportunity, so I left The Red Skelton Show and wrote the required spot anyway.

Duffy's Tavern

Ed Gardner   Bing Crosby   Betty Hutton

Stressed but determined, Sol submitted his work to the producer, who told him it was good but didn't get the flavor of *Duffy's Tavern*. Sol was now out of work and needed to develop an idea. Walking in the sunshine always helped, so he strolled through a nearby park until a solution arrived, and it did. Sol would make an appointment with Ed Gardner. Sol's idea was outside the considered acceptable avenue to getting a job.

Also, bringing the same script the producer declined was unthinkable. But Sol was convinced he did his best on the script and confidently handed it to Ed.

After the customary introductions, Ed asked Sol to sit as Ed took hold of Sol's neatly bound presentation. Ed remained silent—not making one comment or gesture while reading Sol's creation. Sol said the atmosphere was so tense and uncomfortable that he could hardly breathe. Finally, Ed quietly turned the last page and, with a piercing stare into Sol's eyes, hired him for one day. He would work with Ed and the headmen from CBS for $50.00 that morning. The pressure was enormous.

This day could be a make-or-break moment for the young writer. The blood drained from Sol's head as he breathlessly and, without uttering one word, nodded his head in agreement. Ed stretched out his hand as a welcoming gesture. However, Sol stood frozen for a moment, then quickly shook his hand.

Sol figured they were putting him to the test; to see what kind of a guy he was. Would Sol fall apart under the immense pressure? Could he produce creative ideas while possibly intimidated? Sol held fast to all he learned and wrote everything that was required. It was the end of the most strenuous day Sol had ever experienced, and he was exhausted. Ed came over to Sol and asked if anyone helped him with the original script he showed him. Somewhat dazed, Sol answered, "Well, if they did, they're gonna keep on helping me!"

Sol passed the rigorous test and landed *Duffy's Tavern*. He now would be writing for those three top stars of the day. An enviable accomplishment that brought more pressure than accolades, according to Sol. Sol said in a fretful voice,

> We worked once a week, all day and all through the night. A couple of hours before the broadcast, the producers checked our completed script, then gave them to the actors to rehearse. After all our work, if the writers wanted to see the show, we had to call Ed Gardner's secretary and get tickets. Rain or shine, we would stand in line outside the theater with the rest of the audience! However, the studio's policy was to give any extra tickets to the military if they were in town. The military personnel had a reputation for being loud laughers and beneficial for the show, but this meant the writers were out completely. So, if we could not see the performance, we would meet at the local bar to listen to the production on the radio. Only then would we find out which of our lines passed the editing or who would be working the following week. When I did get in to see the show, I had mixed questions about my choice to be a writer. I watched the actors rehearse once, sat through the editing process, and then enjoyed the performance.

SOL SAKS

Sol continues,

But then, it happened; each actor dropped the script in the trash. Seeing your hard work sitting in the trash like a used tissue was disheartening, a harsh reality. Those sounds of pages filled with hard-crafted words hitting the bin, one after another, stayed with me for a few years. Honestly, I can still recall the sounds if I take a moment. That painful reality regarding our contribution and worth made me wonder if I had made the wrong career choice. I spent many sleepless nights struggling with the loud thoughts vying for an answer. But I had to consider that the dream I worked so hard for was now a reality. Most of my friends who worked hard to be writers never got this far. So how could I complain? I had to put any negative thoughts behind me. The choice to continue as a writer was the correct choice for me.

I read somewhere that we would encounter problems in life even if we made the right choice. Sadly, my friends began to remove their emotional support and close friendship as I became more successful. I never counted on that, and it was painful. Their understandable response was that they would trade places with me any day. I felt suspended in an unfamiliar and most uncomfortable space. Writing became an 80-hour workweek. It was taking a toll on all who wrote for the show. We took uppers to help us stay awake, and for me, a few drinks in the evening to relax so I could sleep.

While at work, I erased all thoughts other than the writing from my mind. Making the deadline took every ounce of dedication, determination, and creativity within me. The last day before shooting, we worked through the night and the next afternoon until the show began, around 2 pm. I'd leave for home on those days, crawl into bed, and immediately fall asleep, only to resume the same grind the following day. At this point, I have to add something. I believe our work schedule also affected each spouse's health. I am in my late nineties now and realize how that must have applied to my wife, Anne. I thought that she was home, safe, protected, and living in somewhat blissful ease, and in most respects, she was. But unfortunately, the sad truth is that what we are unaware of can add to someone else's suffering. Well, maybe I should finish my story. I'll return to this later. On one occasion, we did the show in New York. Our office was a beautiful suite at the Majestic Hotel. We could look across the street at the Algonquin Hotel on Times Square. The view was spectacular and an inspirational dream I used to have as a teenager. A thousand words filled my head as I stood transfixed. I was the rookie then, making $200 a week, which was a better-than-average amount in those days.

Sol continues,

> However, Anne and I lived in California, and I didn't receive any expense money. But on this unique occasion, I wanted Anne to come with me. So, we took money from our savings and rented a small furnished room just off Times Square. It was nothing special, but it did have great views that Anne and I enjoyed. Every night while I was at work, between 7 and 8, Abe Burrows, the head writer, would announce to us that it was time to eat. During the day, Anne would go sightseeing, but at night, she would sit alone listening to the radio, beautifully dressed, and waiting for me to call. When the call came, she left immediately to meet me, and it was fantastic fun having her there with me. We enjoyed a lavish dinner together while having many moments to talk and laugh. In addition, this night, we had the luxury of a couple of memorable dances. There are undefinable moments in time beyond description or explanation, but if you're so blessed, they add a dimension to life that captures and adds to your being forever. That night was the one that lasted the rest of my life.
>
> As we continued our enchanted dance—I noticed it was close to 11 p.m., and I told Anne that this moment reminded me of the Cinderella story. With the music playing, and my eyes on the clock, we stopped dancing, and suddenly all the romance came to a screeching halt. But in this story, Anne and I rushed out the door and down the steps. Nobody lost a shoe, we jumped in the car, and Anne brought me back to work at the Majestic as the clock struck 11 p.m. With tears streaming down her face, she held me close and kissed me goodbye. She knew I'd have to work all night and wondered if life would always have so many lonely stretches. Anne was the one person I could talk to who understood and cared, but I was speechless that night. It was like a picture of a guy going off to jail. Or a man who was cheating on his wife. Then it escalated, and the worst happened; I started to lie.
>
> When she asked me when I got home, I casually said around two. Again, a tear rolled down that lovely face of hers, breaking my heart. If a broken heart was not enough, the look in her eyes as she stared silently straight into mine made my heart sink to the floor. She told me that she was up at three and no husband was in sight. I felt sick and so exhausted that I could not look at her. In a blurry haze, I looked away, telling her I would try to fix my work schedule. Overwhelmed, I secretly wondered if it was possible without quitting. I was at an agonizing crossroads and wondering what to do.

SOL SAKS

Sol continues,

> The strain on all sides was becoming debilitating. Finally, I fixed myself a double scotch and went to bed. The following morning—with pains in my chest and my head pounding, I left before Anne awoke. I headed straight to Abe's office. Walking down the hall, I saw he was writing at his desk. I knocked at his open door, and without looking up, he asked me to come in and sit down. "Abe, excuse me, but I don't work past 9 a.m. I promised my wife I'd be home in the morning. I have a wife, and it's like I have a mistress." Abe finally looked up with a puzzled look and said, "Listen, Sol, this isn't the dress-goods business!" Then he looked back down and continued writing. "Abe, if these are the hours I have to work, I'm going into the dress-goods business!" He looked up at me without a word as I left his office. I worked the remainder of that day with Anne's tears and Abe's frustrating words fixed on my mind. Another long, grinding year passed before I would get a better schedule. Anne, as always, was patient, and I did my best to keep my promise to her. She helped me to have a more balanced life. I would have missed so much if it were not for her. If not for Anne, I never would have relaxed in the garden, learned to listen, daydream, and let my imagination soar among the trees and the fragrance of the flowers. In Anne's atmosphere of tranquility, I finally understood that there was more in life that she wanted, but it was not from me. Until this day, I am not sure if I was home enough or if she accomplished her best dream.

Sol was 99 years old when an interviewer asked,
"How involved were you in shaping the shows back then with your problem-solving skills?"

> I don't know if my problem-solving skills were shaping the shows. In those days, business executives were doing that job, not writers. Most advertising agencies had the clout at that time; they made the decisions. My only responsibility as a writer was to write the script as told, then get lost. We had a concise list to follow. For example, they gave us strict instructions that because of the Holocaust, the word gas should not appear in anything we write. There were many other words, like pregnant. We could refer to the wife as expecting.
>
> Later, the suits, as we called them, ran the shows. The big complaint of the writers was that these men were not writers and had no creativity. The advertising executives got their jobs because they were strictly business, with no creative background.

Sol continues,

> They wanted us to write what they would write if they knew how. In frustrated diatribes, they would instruct us to write as if we were writing for one of our friends! In other words, this is too sophisticated for the general public. I found that the audience was more sophisticated than the suits. Comedy has gotten much better with shows like *Seinfeld* and other good shows. Because writers are more involved, they know their audience is intelligent. Dumbing-down scripts to worried non-creative executives are not happening in those shows. The writers are left to be creative. Like a good composer or painter, a good writer writes for himself. I compare and believe that writing is similar to a tone-deaf musician tuning his violin. I know my work is good when the audience laughs at the joke or line. An accomplished comedian and a good writer know that. You're never sure of what's good, and you're always surprised at what gets a laugh and doesn't.

"Do you have a favorite joke?"

> No one has ever asked me that question, but I remember this joke. The guy says, 'There was this poor widow. She was not always poor. Her husband had a lot of money. But when he died, she had him buried in a rental tuxedo. Babumbum!'
>
> I do have a story about *Duffy's Tavern* you might enjoy. Those long hours that I spoke of were taking a toll on me. Taking those uppers they offered me started affecting my attitude and health, so I tried a new approach. One evening, I refused any pills to stay awake because I was determined to go home early and spend time with my family. I felt good about my decision and knew it was best for me. So I took a deep breath, sat back, pleased with myself, and relaxed until I felt this old familiar calmness. Suddenly, I got this idea for a joke to use in the show. I sat up straight, and all eyes were on me as I delivered my suggestion. They were waiting for something clever, so I said,
>
> 'I would say to Finnigan, a character on *Duffy's Tavern*, how long were you in jail? Finnigan says, 'Well, ah, I went to prison first when I was nineteen.' The other guy says, 'They don't take nineteen-year-old kids in jail.' Finnigan says, 'My mother lied about my age!'
>
> Everyone in the room congratulated me and applauded. Abe Burrows and Bill Manoff, the head writers, loved the funny story. Now, everyone is talking, energized, and rewriting, and they do not want me to go home! So, at 8 p.m., I learned not to say anything intelligent or witty. Why? Because they will make you stay until they capture every word.

SOL SAKS

Sol concludes,

> Not many days passed after that evening that Abe and I finally left the show for good.

Dinah Shore

Though writing for *Duffy's Tavern* was grueling, it was a consistent source of education for Sol, and his reputation for being a hard-working comedy writer was gaining recognition. Sol heard about a vibrant newcomer named Dinah Shore. She had a glorious singing voice, and her confident down-home presence gained her a radio show of her own; *The Dinah Shore Show*. The program employed two veteran writers but needed a third. So, leaving Duffy's, rookie Sol gladly interviewed and received the coveted position.

Born Fannye Rose Shore, Dinah was an instant favorite with her audience. She began her singing career shortly after graduating from Vanderbilt University. Her first exposure to a Radio audience came over New York station WNEW. Dinah entertained her captivated public faithfully every Sunday evening in the comfort of their homes with a series of 15-minute features.

Dinah Shore's meteoric rise throughout the entertainment industry was one of the 20th Century's great success stories, and Sol Saks was there to lend a hand. An instant hit on Radio, Dinah Shore quickly rose to prominence in Television and Film. Sol's first assignment was writing a comedy spot for two announcers selling Camel cigarettes. His work was a successful addition and well-received by Dinah, the suits, and the advertising company. As Sol continued writing for commercial spots, he noticed that Dinah was capable of more.

BEWITCHED

To help her, Sol remarked to the suits that Dinah was another Bing Crosby and could not only sing but talk too. Sol saw an intelligent, thoughtful woman with underused talent and thought maybe he could write something for her to say. His suggestion led to an argument with the head writers. They cited that her job was to sing, not talk. Young Sol had no experience with the politics of the profession and became frustrated. The injustice of short-sighted limitations set upon him to write below his abilities and limits imposed on a brilliant talent became more than Sol could handle, so he quit his job.

However, across the ocean, in undisclosed bunkers, a widespread unimaginable injustice was forming that would be heartbreaking news to Sol.

In September of 1939, the newspapers reported instability in Germany; however, it was not front-page news in America, and the rise of Adolf Hitler was hard to believe. When the devastating words of World War 2 hit the front pages, eligible young men were called to arms, leaving families devastated. Yet, news of the depravity was not fully known or understood by the citizens of the United States. It would be months before the defining word of the Holocaust brought the surreal reality into focus.

Sol desperately wanted to be of service. He filled out his draft card and took the physical. Unfortunately, he failed to meet the medical requirement; it was his eyes. Because wearing his glasses was necessary, the doctor marked Sol as 4F and bluntly dismissed him. It felt like a punch in the stomach. The recruiter sensed the disappointment covering young Sol and called out to him in compassion. He said he could better serve his country by making people laugh through these terrible times. Besides, he was Jewish, and the chances of coming home were slim to none. Though the recruiter meant well, these were hard words to hear. A surge of painful emotions whirled through Sol's mind. The sadness, disappointment, grief, and fear for distant relatives caused many sleepless nights. He struggled through the cloud of mental anxiety and thought, *If I could help people escape their grief and worry for even a moment, maybe that would be a helpful service to my country. Besides, according to my doctor, laughter is a valuable, underused medicine, and comedy is a worthy profession to pursue.*

Sadness eased, and Sol appreciated the words of advice and encouragement. Though the door to serve his country in the manner he chose was closed, he set out to be the best writer possible. The war left many shows without writers and Sol without his new friends. Also, there were those occasional comments from strangers who assumed he did not want to serve. The struggle to remain optimistic was a battle in itself. There were days when Sol found it hard to think of himself as a valuable asset to his country, but he was determined to bring laughter to those at home.

Some jobs were only for a day, weeks, or months but he put everything possible into every word. Sol read the paper daily, staying as current as possible and using the information in his writing. He also wrote to several friends he worked with who were now in the midst of a war. Sadly, within the year, two were killed in action. Sol commented that those times were some of the worst days. He raged at God for leaving him behind. Guilt plagued him at every turn. It was then he learned a valuable lesson. He dreamed one night that a man stood before him. A tall, distinguished man asks him to stop being self-centered and stop thinking of himself.

Shaken when he awoke that morning, Sol had no idea he was selfish in his thoughts. The heaviness lifted as he considered this new information, and a clear viewpoint occurred. He could still be a soldier. A soldier is someone who serves in an organized force on land. He would be a force for those left behind. Sol went to the funerals, helped write the obituaries, and visited bereaved families as often as possible.

Fanny Brice

As the brutal war continued into 1944, a small glimmer of hope seemed to enter between the news lines; the war might be ending. But, many countries were in pain, the sighs of relief mixed with the agonizing tears of grief for the thousands of lost lives. Sol said it was like the world was in a state of mourning.

Amid the pain, a brave young woman in New York stepped out on the edge of humanity and held a torch of brightly shining words. She did her best to entertain and relieve the heartache of millions. A performer shining brighter than most was the exceptional Fanny Brice.

BEWITCHED

Fania Borach changed her name to Fanny Brice or Fannie Brice and became the creator and star of a top-rated radio comedy series. Joy could be found every Sunday evening on CBS starting September 17, 1944, at 6:30 p.m. The show was *Post Toasties Time,* and they needed a writer to help. Sol was thrilled to be of service; he considered it a dream job. You may have been in tears when you turned the radio on at 6:30, but Fannie had you laughing within seconds, and the pain eased for your time spent with her.

Finally, in September of 1945, the war ended. People worldwide were in love with Fannie as she continued to bring laughter that made way for healing, and Sol was in the trenches helping to make it happen. But with all his burgeoning recognition, Sol was still considered a rookie. Even so, on this particular day, the veteran writers invited their recruit to attend a meeting with them at the home of Miss Brice. When the day arrived, they gathered in one car to make the journey. Talking and discussing ideas as they traveled, the driver suddenly interrupted them as he pointed to a palatial estate. "Well, fellas, we're here!" No one spoke as he turned from the road onto the long driveway. They parked the car and, in respectful silence, left the car and knocked on the door. When the door opened, Sol stood speechless. Miss Brice had a butler. He dressed in a proper black suit with tails, a starched shirt, and a bow tie. Greeting them, he led the dazzled group into an opulent living room with an impressive blaze occupying the fireplace. Sol said quietly to himself that the White House should look so good. Dazed, Sol didn't know where to look first.

He had never seen such a beautiful home and was mesmerized. Then like a puff of smoke, the glorious spell vanished when comedic Fanny entered the room. A small white dog walked adoringly next to Fanny, never taking his eyes from her. Her presence filled the room as she greeted all her writers. Sol was captivated by an undefinable something that she possessed.

Sol, in his nineties, remembering that eventful day so many years ago, looked off into the distance with the warmest smile appearing upon his weathered face. The treehouse office and I blurred as Sol again traveled back in time with Fannie. His mouth slightly opened with a gasp at first sight of her. In muffled tones, he whispered,

"That Fanny Brice was quite a lady, and I was so nervous." He leaned his elbows upon his desk, staring into the massive pines while remembering.

I was young, and her bold language made me uncomfortable at first. Women swearing in those days was not done, at least not in this setting. But for some reason, it seemed okay for Fanny. She was kind and very down-to-earth, and we all felt comfortable around her.

SOL SAKS

Sol continues,

> Fanny's intelligent creativity was like a captivating beacon as the meeting progressed, and I relaxed in utter awe of her genius. She was extraordinary! She leaned artistically against her grand piano as we sat on soft, sumptuous velvet couches, entertained like never before. Even now, it makes me laugh as I remember her reaching for a large carved silver bell and then ringing it with a flourish that made us laugh. She was a consummate performer even while holding a meeting. While we were laughing, her maid walked into the room. She was seated dutifully behind a gleaming silver trolley filled with many fancy crustless tea sandwiches, berry-covered custards, coffee, and alcoholic beverages. We pointed to everything we wanted, and her maid served each of us. Fanny, in her silk gown, smoking a cigarette, dramatically waved her flowing silk-clad arm and wished us Bon Appetite! I could hardly eat; I was laughing so much. We ate and drank the best money could buy. I listened intently while never taking my eyes off the extraordinary Miss Brice as the veteran writers explained that this Christmas show would be different. Their script for her would not contain the usual laughter but more emotion. Fanny said, 'Okay, fellas, if you think so, but not too much of that sentimental crap.'

Fanny was the quintessential comedian, and Sol remained forever captivated. Sol described her as an intelligent, thoughtful woman that consistently delivered the best possible performance; she loved her audience. Intouch with the needs of people, Fanny also appreciated the talent and pressures of the writer. She never dismissed their efforts; she applauded them, always holding them in high esteem. She was brilliant and appreciated by all who worked with her.

Fanny died in 1951, leaving an irreplaceable essence in the lives of her audience and all who knew her. On March 26, 1964, radiantly talented Barbara Streisand performed a musical about Fanny's life at the Winter Garden Theatre. The musical played 1,348 performances and received eight Tony Award nominations, including Best Actress, Best Actor, Best Composer and Lyricist, and Best Musical. It was adapted into a motion picture in 1968, starring Streisand in an Academy Award-winning performance. With much bittersweet nostalgia, Sol and Anne attended one of the theatre performances and later the movie.

Sol took a long deep breath as he attempted to explain how they all enjoyed working with an undefinable, charismatic professional woman.

He learned about respecting an audience from her and the trends of each passing season. However, she genuinely liked people, and Sol saw how it came across in her every performance. He leaned back, his hands resting upon his desk as his thoughts, once more, returned to Sutton Street while finishing for the day.

The following morning, after our usual greetings, Sol surprisingly picked up where he had stopped. I quickly grabbed a pencil and yellow writing pad because we were preparing for another fascinating journey. Sol took us back to the time World War 2 was ending. He paced the floor as he relived those days in his mind, explaining:

Fannie Brice's show, *Post Toasties Time,* ended while the demand for television shows grew, along with the need for good writers. Men and women were slowly returning home from the war, many with devastating injuries. The news reported and printed pictures that rendered friends and family speechless and in tears; it was terrible. The advertising companies sent notices saying the need for laughter was vital. But finding humor in the face of these tragedies became almost impossible.

Sol opened the office door and stepped onto the landing in silence for a brief moment breathing in the air. Then stepping inside, he began pacing through the room, becoming more deliberate and animated, then sharply continued:

Between my days of writing for Fannie, I wrote a few episodes for a show called *That's Life* with the much-loved character Beulah. Beulah made guest appearances on another radio series called *Fibber McGee and Molly* now and then, allowing the writers to move with her. But I discovered that Beulah was not a black woman but Marlin Hurt, a white male actor; I was angry over the injustice. I wanted to quit. Though Marlin was brilliant in his performance, many talented black actresses needed work. I reluctantly remained employed as the show grew in controversy. The news reported that Beulah was not what she seemed to be. They went on to describe the guy from Illinois as being Beulah. Finally, this popular Beulah character was passed successfully to deserving actresses. Beulah then became a new series called *The Martin Hurt and Beulah Show.* Almost immediately, the new series became inundated with letters. But strangely, it was a mix of frustration, gratitude, grief over losing loved ones, and unfair treatment. All of us writers received a notice that the faithful listeners needed continuity.

SOL SAKS

Sol continues,
> Pressed for ideas on continuity, we took concerns from many letters and used them for kind, humorous responses with dashes of wisdom within the show. As more letters arrived, they became a bit calmer, more gratitude-filled. Again, the show helped to ease their burdens, and all involved in the show were pleased. With all the refining changes, the wise character of Beulah could now stand on her own, so they renamed the show, *The Beulah Show*.

Hattie McDaniel

A bold, refreshing breeze hit the radio waves and brought Hattie McDaniel to take over the role on November 24, 1947. Hattie earned $1,000 a week for the first season. We writers were pleased and more relaxed to work with a woman with her priceless talent. She doubled the ratings of the original series, and her popularity pleased the NAACP and the networks. Elation spread throughout our writing community as we witnessed a historic first; a black woman as the star of a network radio program. For fourteen years between radio and television, Hattie, through Beulah, added laughter and comfort to her audience. Life was looking up, and writing was exciting.

Returning to those days seemed draining for Sol, and he needed a break. So we walked through the secret garden as he confessed how destiny took him on a sometimes-bumpy road that he struggled with and how strangely correct the recruiter was at the beginning of the war. Though painful, Sol's disappointing rejection into the military was indeed his path of service. But, along with other select writers, he brought help of another kind called laughter.

During the war, Sol graduated from rookie to respected professional at some unobserved point. He could write comedy no matter what was happening around him. He proved he could handle the pressures and deliver consistent quality writing. Sol landed his first job as head writer for one of two writing teams on *The Beulah Show,* starring the brilliant Hattie McDaniel. The other team-head was a man he had worked with before, Sherwood Schwartz. Sol was making his mark, gaining respect, and as a luxury bonus, making life-long friends.

A calming walk amidst the fragrant flowers was just the rest he needed. Finally, we returned to the office for a cup of coffee. Sol walked to his favorite spot, the window overlooking Sutton Street. The steam from his coffee cup fogged a portion of the window before him as he returned to thoughts of Hattie. Standing steadfast looking into the tree-tops, he said,

Hattie had no idea what was funny and what wasn't. But, she had this spontaneous delivery that kept you captivatingly with her every moment. Hattie was a natural talent brimming with that elusive something called charisma. Sometimes, she'd say a line and think it was a joke, which it wasn't, but she'd read it like a joke to a live audience, and they'd still laugh. The audience loved Hattie, and like Fanny, she loved them. Occasionally, a line was not read until the next show because we ran out of time; the laughs were uncontrollably loud and long. Hattie's priceless delivery made even the writers laugh. We did five shows a week, an eighty-hour week for the writers. Boy, we needed a laugh. So, we wrote the character of Hattie to portray the wise housekeeper. In those days, the housekeeper or a kid were the smart ones in the family. But, for Hattie, this is what we called type-casting; she was, in life, a woman of considerable wisdom and added valuable insights to our writing. She brought a dimension to her character you cannot write. But there was always the horrible task of writing the other characters as unintelligent, which was terrible. Making everyone else in the show appear stupid. Most of the characters portrayed those days on tv were slightly dumb. Don't get me wrong, the people who played these characters were bright, talented actors. But, actors needed work, and this was the work the companies were offering; a difficult position.

I remember their frustration and the angry fan letters from their hometown communities. Hattie received hundreds saying she should be ashamed of herself for playing a maid. Hattie was a woman ahead of her time, and these letters were painful.

SOL SAKS

Sol continues,

> She kindly responded that she would rather play a maid in the movies than be one in real life. She was able to help those in need, and that was more important to her. But it seemed futile to explain herself. She told me that anger always blinds people to the truth, and to obtain success, she would learn to deal with another form of rejection. Hattie then showed me a letter from a woman thanking Hattie for her strength of character. The letter was hard to read. Her spelling needed help, but the woman stated that she had learned to think better of herself. She thanked Hattie for showing her that she had choices. Her first choice was to go back to school. She could not buy new clothes but would repair the ones she had and present herself better. Hattie saved that letter; it helped her forget so many negative ones. I'm turning 100 years old at the end of this year. If I could change one thing, it would be that while I worked to achieve my goals, I could have relaxed and laughed more. After all, I did find what I was supposed to do. What remained was to do my best and follow what I knew inside to be correct for me. When I was a boy, my mother taught me something I chose not to take seriously. She told me that the Torah is full of wisdom. That God puts life and death before us, we can choose. Every choice we make from birth to death matters. These choices range from how we treat our loved ones to how we spend money, from whom we bring into our world view, to how we choose our food. In each of these choices, we should always choose life. My mother was a wise woman. Unfortunately, I never realized it when I was young. Now I see that heartbreak, injustice, inequality, greed, jealousy, love, joy, abundance, and health was always before me, and I could choose. I did not know the importance of relaxing. I focused tenaciously and always struggled for balance. Flying in that rarified life-giving atmosphere are the ones who strive amicably to improve life. They work on life-producing answers. Hattie McDaniel was like that, but she and I did not know to use it on ourselves. Hattie always delivered her lines to make people laugh. She may have been crying on the inside, but she chose to give her audience a ray of sunshine. She was a mensch, an honorable, talented woman whose smile often turned to pain when she moved out of the piercing sight of the camera. Despite people's unkindness, there is an art to being grateful and happy. It was an important component that would have made life more enjoyable if we had learned.

Sol slowly rose from his tan leather chair, walked to the door, turned, and said, "This was a good day, Carolyn. See you tomorrow."

There hid a steel inner strength of determination and sense-of-fairness within this quiet, seemingly retiring soul of Sol Saks. He not only believed in equality for every human, but he acted on his belief and fought for their right to obtain what was fair. Knowing that speaking for change could affect his job, Sol stood firm in his convictions. He believed every writer should receive on-screen credit if writing for a show. Unfortunately, the recognition was only to head writers Sol and Sherwin. Determined to correct this injustice, Sol went to the producers armed with a sensitive approach. Impressed with his suggestion and presentation, the producers called the New York office.

Through many conversations and lengthy negotiations, the producers obtained permission. Calling Sol into the office, the producers presented him with victorious news. Sol left the office with triumph in every step; he was thrilled. The credits would now read, 'Sol Saks and Sherwin Schwartz with,' then came the names of each writer. Sol shared the news with the writers, who broke out in roaring cheers. They profusely thanked him for getting them the recognition they thought was an unattainable dream. It was one of those memorable moments that only comes along once in a while.

Sol was extremely grateful that he was able to help. He, Sherwin, and the teams planned a dinner with their wives to meet on the upcoming Friday in honor of the long-awaited elevation. The next few joy-filled workdays comprised some of the best writing for the show. Talk of history-in-the-making filled the atmosphere; creative ideas flowed like never before.

Friday arrived, and so did the families. Everyone assembled for the ending credits and then a celebratory dinner to follow. All dressed in their best attire, holding champagne-filled glasses, and toasting Sol for his brave efforts. The room fell silent as the ending credits rolled, Sol and Sherwood stood in anticipation of hearing their cheers again, but there wasn't much response from either team. Bewildered, Sol and Sherwood asked what was wrong. The team of writers just stood in a long uncomfortable silence as they returned their empty champagne glasses to the table. Finally, a single writer with his eyes cast to the ground replied that dinner was off, then turned and left. Their wives followed in bewilderment while they apologized and hurried away in regret. Devastated and puzzled, Sol canceled dinner reservations, then, in a daze, walked with Anne to their car and returned home.

Sol tried to clear the air on the following workday, but his attempts went unfulfilled. Before long, the Writer's Guild contacted Sol and said his team filed a complaint to the grievance committee.

SOL SAKS

They felt that adding the word (with) and presenting them under the names of head-writers Sol, and Sherwood was diminishing. Sol was perplexed, disappointed, and grieved that his team of writers didn't express their complaint to him that evening or when Sol asked them. When he confronted the writers, they responded in continued resentful silence. Sol never did appear before the committee but spoke with his team, breaking their silence.

Sol reminded them they didn't receive credit for one year, and now they did! They grumbled for a time but most eventually appreciated this breakthrough. The writers' wives, still bearing frustrations, felt it unwise to remain friends with Anne, similar to a punch in the stomach for Anne. Nevertheless, she considered them good friends; they went shopping, had lunch, and met at each other's homes. Now in one short evening, it was gone. Anne told Sol that she felt grief as if something beautiful had died.

Disappointment, grief, and self-doubt lingered long after that momentous evening. Anne and Sol struggled to keep this thoughtful kindness, gone seemingly wrong, come between them. Through these difficult days, Sol, maybe a bit more cautious than before, continued to help where he could. Anne overcame the loss of cherished friends and bravely determined to reach out to those remaining few while opening her heart to possible new friends.

Those writers that remained envious and held a grudge never realized that there is a process to lasting success. Anger and small thinking began clouding their judgment and reflected in their writing; work became scarce. They continually heard the name of Sol Saks circulating gently through the writing community, which fueled their anger. They heard statements: You can count on Sol to deliver, Sol Saks is a hard worker, Saks is a master craftsman, Sol works till the job is done. Gossip seemed a temporary release for these angry, struggling writers. Amidst the accolades, dark rumors emerged announcing that Sol was not what he seemed; he undermined co-workers, and the list grew. According to Sol, it was a problem out of his hands. He tried to explain again, pointing out they were talented, capable writers. But it was as if something was clouding their minds; they did not hear him. Sol would have recommended any of these writers at one time. But, their attitudes and blind anger reduced their skills and reliability; there was nothing more he could do. Sol began to experience sleepless nights resulting in eventual chest pains.

Anne was incredibly concerned and suggested that Sol call Sherwin and relay the situation, saying he would be away at the beach with Anne for the day. Sherwood understood what Sol was experiencing and said he would care for everything. Anne, the voice of reason, afforded Sol the luxury of looking forward to the change of atmosphere and a rest for his weary mind.

Of course, Johnson, their dog, would accompany them; he was part of the family and unusually intelligent. A calming pastime for Sol was teaching Johnson to fetch his slippers. Being the obedient pet, Johnson faithfully accommodated Sol's wish. But this day, he only brought one slipper. So, Sol paused and then asked him to get the other one. Johnson immediately left and brought Sol his other slipper. How could such a dog be left home alone? Besides, he could use a day at the beach too.

Sol's daughter shared a favorite Johnson story that her father loved to tell about when their family pet went missing and a man found him. Seeing information on his dog tag, the man called and said, "Mr. Johnson, I have your dog, Sol." Some moments in life stick with you forever, and this was a good one. So, being such a close threesome, they piled into the car and left for the day.

Ah, this was the life, sitting in the warm sand, silently looking out to the far horizon past the endless sea while a quiet perspective returned with each wave that crashed upon the shore. Finally, the three returned home, relaxed, refreshed, and with good news waiting.

Anne, Sol, & Johnson

SOL SAKS

Sol had a message from his agent. The producers of *The Danny Kaye Show* invited Sol to join their team and write for them; the premier was approaching, and they needed a steady writer they could count on, and they unanimously thought of Sol Saks.

Danny Kaye

Not knowing for sure, Sol suspected that Sherwin had something to do with clearing the fog of rumors which opened new doors. He was especially pleased to work side-by-side with his friend Abe and grateful for the faithful friendship of Sherwin. These two friends and Sol found that producers who were also writers had a broader scope of working dialogue, which helped make a show and the talent successful; it also made for less challenging working conditions. These welcoming producers were confident in Sol's abilities and dedication, and Sol was pleased to work with them in a dream environment.

When the show aired, Danny listened attentively to every word, made notes on every nuance, and checked the timing throughout the show. After all, this show was a first for the beloved comedian. His first radio series was built around him and aired on a prime spot. So, each Saturday, on the CBS radio network at 7 p.m., you could hear Harry James and His Music Makers. Listening within their cozy homes was an enthralled audience and a gloriously happy Danny.

The 1940s was the era of the big bands, and the name Harry James, a master trumpet player, was known worldwide. Harry was married to superstar Betty Grable, a combination loved by producers and audiences. Written into several classic movies of the 1940s were references to one or the other. It was great fun for everyone.

Glowing reviews stated *The Danny Kaye Show* promises to be a sure-fire winner. His show ran from January 6, 1945, to May 31, 1946, with a steady stream of good reviews. The show featured singing—instrumental music—and a variety of comedy sketches. Sol had his work cut out for him with superstars of the day like Eddie Cantor, Eve Arden, and many top-name regulars. Much to Sol's delight, one of the producers was Goodman Ace, said to be one of radio's premier comedy writers.

Also, Sylvia Fine, an intelligent, kind woman and Danny's wife, was a producer, composer, and lyricist. Sylvia worked with Goodman and Abe Burrows; now, Sol is part of the dynamic team. However, the dream Sol so enjoyed soon ended as nervous investors made unreasonable demands. To meet those demands meant working longer hours. Frenzied producers looked to the writers for brilliant dialogue for the actors to ease the pressure. Work for the writers escalated to challenging proportions our young Sol had not experienced, but, if needed, he went without sleep to get the job done. Writers were in a constant state of exhaustion. The actors, producers, and crew ended their day when the show aired—but work for the writer began immediately.

Unknown to Sol was the toll those long grueling hours had on Anne. She kept it a secret, not wanting to add to her husband's already burdened soul. The view of her pressures remained somewhat clouded for Sol. These two thoughtful, sensitive souls were now weary, and life slowly became unbalanced. Nevertheless, Sol remained steadfastly grateful to his loving Anne, and she determined to remain supportive. Anne maintained a beautiful home and a careful eye over their finances while trying to find an interest of her own.

At last, the one long exhausting year of pressured writing finally ended, which might be a reprieve for Anne. Although grateful for the work and experience, Sol left the studio pleased to enjoy the absence of pressure. He went home and slept for two days while Anne cared for everything. When Sol awoke, the heavenly smell of bacon and coffee encouraged him to get out of bed. Yawning and stretching, he made his way to the shower and dressed—then he and Anne sat down to a feast.

The sun streamed through the dining room window, lighting up the room. Sol took a deep breath and relaxed for the first time in a year. While the sun warmed his weary body, Anne told him of a surprise. While he was sleeping, she arranged a beach vacation and began packing. He was thrilled with the news and looked forward to driving along the coast. Sol loved the sea and dreamed of a home someday perched on the warm beach sand. Simply thinking of it helped ease the tightness in his chest.

SOL SAKS

Excited about the prospect of this day, Sol leaned back, felt the sun on his face, then leaned over to kiss Anne. Shortly, they left, hand-in-hand, and began a restful drive together at last. Sol took his time through the winding Malibu Canyon as he and Anne talked non-stop. Finally, they arrived at an elegant hotel with every amenity imaginable, including a maid to unpack for them. Anne was thrilled that the hotel was carrying out her requests. However, on their first night, Anne happened upon a private secluded spot on the sand, and she became excited at the fun possibilities. Like an undercover agent, unobserved, she brought blankets and pillows down from the room, and they fell asleep under the stars. Drifting to sleep together to the meditative sounds of the gently moving waves held within the calming ocean air was a heavenly medicine that removed any pressures left.

Before the sun rose and the community was still asleep—Anne woke Sol, and they hurried to their room, laughing and enjoying the spontaneity of their rather bohemian experience. They emerged from their hotel room in time for lunch served on the terrace. They enjoyed every morsel of a brilliantly prepared lunch, and their eyes and hearts filled with simply each other for the first time in a while. They finished their coffee, then strolled on the sand holding hands, stopping momentarily as the sparkling ocean waves rushed over their feet and reflected on their faces.

Fun-loving Anne suggested they go for a swim; Sol hesitatingly agreed, and they returned to their room to put on swimsuits. They dove beneath the waves crashing over them, laughing and enjoying each other's company. Anne had accomplished her mission. Sol was ready to go back to work and hoped to keep this balance he had found through Anne. What would Sol do without her?

The young couple returned home refreshed and more relaxed than they had been in a long while. It had only been a few days, but the mailbox overflowed with mail. Amongst the letters was a note from Sol's agent that read, 'There is an up-and-coming comedian that needs some help. Would you consider helping him?' The comedian was Danny Thomas, who Sol and Anne had seen in several nightclubs in Chicago.

BEWITCHED

Danny Thomas

Danny, now in Hollywood, got a few radio spots, but the station never mentioned his name; no one knew who this funny guy was. But Sol recognized his voice and was happy to help. Danny's comedy timing always impressed Sol, and there would be no pressure. So, Sol happily wrote a few of the first skits for Danny would perform, and he did them brilliantly. Sol commented that he was the first Lebanese he knew that delivered a joke in a Jewish dialect. Writing and sharing tips with Danny was a joy, but Sol advised Danny that he would have to leave when a call came for a big show.

That awaited call did come, but not until Sol supplied Danny with enough skits to finally get this young comedian's name mentioned on the radio. Sol and Danny said their goodbyes, and Sol was off to the pressures again. Danny and Sol remained lifelong friends.

After writing for nearly eighty years—Sol believed in the importance of learning from history. To build upon the progress of our predecessors is not only wise; it is to value and accept their gifts to us. In this segment, Sol shares a brief, compelling story. It is a gift bestowed and wrapped in words to you, dear reader, hoping it will help somehow.

This true story is about the prevalent regard for writers in the early days of radio and television. The following writing job was for the radio version of *The Adventures of Ozzie & Harriet*. It was a popular variety show and loved by the audience. Ozzie Nelson requested Sol join their writer's team, and Sol gladly accepted. Sol explains,

> Several radio shows were in charge of the scripts and chose the lines they knew would work for them. Sol knew and understood that condition. However, several new changes went undisclosed. First, Ozzie changed his program listing to a story show, meaning the writer would not receive credit. It wasn't until Sol wrote several segments for Ozzie that Sol realized his name did not appear anywhere.

SOL SAKS

Ozzie, Harriet, David, and Ricky Nelson

Sol continues,

>Ozzie explained that his reason for withholding writers-credits was that he did not want to spoil the illusion. He wanted his audience to believe in a different reality. That the stories were happening right as they were listening. To believe each actor made up the lines as the story progressed. Ozzie felt this would bring more enjoyment to the listener. *The Radio Adventures of Ozzie and Harriet* had four writers, and each would write a complete script. Ozzie would take all the radio scripts using the same storyline, then pick out the lines he liked and put them together to make his script. It was a bit like constructing a puzzle. Ozzie became a good editor of his radio scripts. He was not a writer, he never wrote a single line in his life, but Ozzie knew what worked when he saw it. Ozzie was a bandleader in those days and stayed up late. When he'd go to a party, he'd announce he had to go home and write. People were surprised and asked, 'You write the show yourself?' Ozzie replied, 'Oh, well, there's a couple of guys there, but I write the script!' Writers were as disrespected on radio and TV as they once were in the movies. As soon as the writer completed the script, producers didn't want the writer around.

An interviewer asked Sol if he had any regrets. Sol paused for a moment to think. He suddenly remembered a time that made his brow furrow, then spoke out, saying,

>Yes, yes, I never should have taken *The Ozzie and Harriet Show*. It did more harm to my career than good. At least, I thought so at the time.

Sol continues,

> People in my field thought something was wrong because there was no mention of my work. It took me a long time before good jobs came my way again. I struggled with the injustice and was angry. The only jobs I could get were small ones. Finally, Anne reminded me that I gave my best and something good would happen for me. I did Ozzie a lot of good, added to his show, and eventually, I got over the anger, and good jobs came again. Injustices remain in our industry, and I find myself still getting angry. For instance, legal terminology printed in small letters on the back pages of the contract is lethal to the writer. My attorney filed a lawsuit on my behalf some twenty years ago over a considered criminal loophole he found in a big corporation that must remain unnamed. I'm nearly 100 years old, and there is no resolution. The company made millions without compensating me for hours of writing. I haven't found a sure-fire way to deal with the anger that sometimes rises. But I know that it keeps creative ideas from surfacing when it does arise.
>
> My darling wife Anne has been gone for over thirty years, but I still hear her whispers reminding me. 'You gave your best Sol; something good will happen for you, my dear.' Things still are not great for writers, but they are certainly better.

3

Television

*"Movies can and do have tremendous
Influence in shaping young lives in
The realm of entertainment towards
The ideals and objectives of normal adulthood."*
—*Walt Disney*

Joan Davis and Jim Backus

In the early 1950s, radio programs became shows for television. Sol again moved with the tide and went where the jobs were—television. Our story begins within the treetop office, Sol leaning back in his comfortable tan leather chair, his hands clasped behind his head as he told this story to me.

I was offered a writing job as a staff writer for *I Married Joan* starring Joan Davis, and a friend of mine asked me to work with him on the show. It was a popular television show, but something about her bothered me. Also, her sense of comedy was not what I liked to write; I said no. That was the independence I had then. As I mentioned before, I wanted to write drama. I loved working with dramatic actors and was searching for a position. Unfortunately, none of the movie stars wanted to work on TV in those days. If you saw a big-name movie actor on television, you'd know he needed a job and not a good move for an actor. The I Love Lucy Show began to change that stigma.

Writing for radio, you write one line at a time. Writers only participated in one sense, hearing. With television, you'd see the actors you saw them in action. As a result, TV is story-driven and much easier to write.

66

BEWITCHED

Sol continues,
> Hal Kanter, a longtime friend, heard of my decision and called me into his office. He never said hello; he just asked me to sit down. Hal paced the floor, looking preoccupied. I asked him if something was wrong. He turned abruptly with his hands on his hips and said,
> 'Sol, you're a bum!'
> I was stunned. I sat there puzzled, staring at Hal in disbelief.
> 'What do you mean I'm a bum?'
> Moving closer, towering defiantly over me, his hands shot up into the air, his eyes squinting meanly at me,
> 'You could get a job, but you're not working, you're a bum!'
> Anger hit me like a gunshot, and I was speechlessly offended. I had never seen Hal like this. Then, shaking my head in disgust, I jumped out of the chair and left the office without another glance or word. I got in my car and headed home to talk it over with Anne.
> It was lunchtime, and my cheerful Anne had made a wonderful meal and brought it outside into the backyard. Pleased with her accomplishment, she busily placed the food on the table. I, on the other hand, was still frustrated. I was spouting out arguments at Anne like I was still talking to Hal, frustrated and angry. I paced through the yard; I told Anne, the trees, and anyone who would listen, that if we needed something or anyone could give me a reason to write this show, maybe reconsideration would be in order. Exasperated, I could not imagine writing that kind of comedy. Anne calmly asked me to please sit, eat, and calm down. I sat but could do nothing else. She placed her fork gently across her plate, then, in one serene gesture, put her hand on my shoulder. She reminded me that I always wanted a swimming pool in a voice as light as a gentle rain. The heavy fog of anger began clearing, and I remembered being fascinated by people sitting by the water under the sunshine since I was a kid. A lifestyle of comfort, or so it seemed to me. Growing up in Chicago, I read articles about life around swimming pools and those sunny white-sand beaches of California. In an instant, light broke through my dark mood like a beacon. I hit the table in amazement and said yes, then kissed Anne. How could I have forgotten? Looking at the yard, imagining a big pool, I picked up my fork, ate everything on my plate, and then called the pool guys to give me an estimate. It would cost $5,000.00.
> I returned immediately to the producer and told him I would work for five weeks, figuring that would pay for the swimming pool. Then I realized I had to pay income tax, so I renegotiated, saying they had to make it seven weeks.

SOL SAKS

Sol concludes,
> There was this long uncomfortable pause while they thought. The producer knew I was not too fond of Joan and looked at me strangely. The head producer gasped in a sudden inhale as if starved for air, then forcefully told me okay and that I had seven weeks! I took the job and was relieved that they never asked me why. Every line I wrote was so I could buy my dream! I worked the seven weeks and still have the pool, but the shows ended. It was the beginning of a new chapter for me.

Sol's new burgeoning chapter began with his glorious dream realized; the pool he imagined. Empowering feelings surrounded him like a sweet fragrance; he decided he wanted more control of his career. Sol suddenly realized he was now a part of those people he had read about when he was a boy; it was something like magic. Filled with this new exciting revelation, he slipped slowly into their new pool, savoring each moment as he took a victorious swim through the crystal-clear water on that hot summer day.

Then, while floating as if on a cloud, an idea came to Sol that he could not wait to explore. He immediately made an appointment with the CBS-TV producers to pitch his story idea to them. It centered around the original *My Favorite Husband* radio series starring Lucille Ball and Richard Denning. Lucy, at the time, was also engaged in her epic show *I Love Lucy* with her husband, Desi Arnaz.

Lucy & Richard   Lucy & Desi

My Favorite Husband   *I Love Lucy*

Sol remembers,

> I arrived at the CBS building a few minutes early, parked, and sat for a moment, looking up at the CBS logo on the building. I was about to give my first pitch. I wanted to experience every exciting second. I imagined all the people who went before me and wondered if they felt like I did. I could hardly catch my breath; I knew the success stories but wondered how many people never saw their dreams come to fruition. I forced out those negative thoughts and concentrated on people like Ed Sullivan, Lucille Ball, Elvis Presley, my friend Danny Thomas and the enormous list of successful talents that walked through those doors. I would only think of them.
>
> At last, I gathered my courage, nervously climbed out of the car, and entered the iconic building with success on my mind. My head was spinning, and my knees were weak as I signed the register. Grateful to see chairs, I sat down while looking at every celebrity photograph on the wall before me and tried to compose myself. Then, finally, I mentally focused on my story idea. While deep in thought, I heard my name called from some far-off place. When I eventually turned to look, there stood before me a startling authoritative woman staring at me, tapping her foot, waiting for a response. I nervously smiled and, without a word, followed her through a wide hallway clad with signed photographs of movie stars. I had seen this corridor in a magazine when I was a boy and now found it hard to grasp that I was there; it felt like a dream. Suddenly feeling busy-butterflies in the pit of my stomach, she abruptly stopped before two imposing oak doors; I almost ran into her as she knocked upon them, signaling she was there. She pushed both doors open, sternly invited me in, then, without a smile, introduced me. The boardroom was as I imagined. Men in dark suits and ties were seated in opulent black leather chairs surrounding a long, highly polished table with gleaming crystal ashtrays, water glasses, and pitchers of water placed carefully before them. The room looked and smelled like money.
>
> All eyes were on me, and the weakness in my knees began to increase. Thankfully, one man smiled sympathetically and invited me to sit down. There were no further introductions or words. I merely confirmed with my opening statement that CBS owned *My Favorite Husband*. Their interest peaked as a few moved closer to the table while all silently nodded in agreement. I shifted nervously to the edge of my chair, leaned in toward them, and when I did, one producer put his elbows on the table and leaned in also. Thinking his leaning was a good sign, my confidence rose as I explained my idea as simply as possible.

SOL SAKS

Sol concludes,

> The radio version of *My Favorite Husband* is to be a made-for-television series. I heard several muffled hmm's as they looked at each other, then I continued. I would use actors instead of comedians. Their eyes narrowed with brows furrowed as they looked at each other and then asked me to give them a moment. I stepped outside the room for the longest five minutes of my life, then they asked me back to the table. They heartily agreed it would be a great idea, then asked if I could begin next week; covertly overjoyed, I casually agreed. Each energy-charged producer walked over to me, shook my hand, and congratulated me on a superb idea. Later that day, they sent me a substantial contract that I took to my lawyer and friend, then went home to celebrate with Anne.
>
> I returned to CBS late the following day with the signed contract and a suggestion for the leading actors. However, CBS preferred Joan Caufield and Barry Nelson to star in the show. It was one of the first domestic comedies without a comedic actress or actor, and I was pleased with the outcome. The most challenging part of this job was getting a response to the scene. These were the days before Hollywood had laugh tracks—and that was murder because you had to get a spontaneous laugh at the end of every scene. Eventually, CBS decided to use a laugh track, but it didn't go right with the show. So, we did the show live, and they had a guy backstage putting in the laughs. The actors couldn't hear the canned laughs and were told to take a count of one, two, three, or four, then go on to the following line. The studio audience would hear the actors say the line, then, bewildered, watch as the actors silently stood counting. That was our first laugh track.

BEWITCHED

Joan Caufield & Barry Nelson

When the producers applauded Sol for *My Favorite Husband,* Sol was a relatively new writer but held a prominent position on the show. His heart soared with the victory and the possibilities that lay before him. He worked overtime to make every spoken word communicate enjoyment while relishing giving delight to the audience. Everyone at the studio appeared thrilled with this new premise, applauding his creativity.

Yet the producers secretly purchased a new script without consulting him, causing a stinging blow to Sol. After a brief recovery, Sol brought his objection to the director, Norman Tokar, and producer Harry Akerman, saying to purchase a script without his knowledge or at least letting him see it was demeaning. No reply came forth. Later, Sol realized it was a way to make room for him to quit, and quit he did. Now in his nineties and looking back to that eventful day, Sol said,

> It took me a while, but it finally dawned on me that they wanted me to quit because the show was successful, they didn't need me anymore, and I gave them trouble. After I left, the show went down the drain. I don't mean to sound egotistical, but that is what happened. Not because I was such a great writer, but because I was a hard worker. When I left, the man that replaced me wouldn't work the hours I did. I worked on that show from 1953 to 1954 for three episodes—and received my first television writing credit.

CBS continued their professed love for Sol and his presentation despite this apparent rift and continued preparing for new television series. A new comedy was submitted and accepted with the provision to stay with Sol's idea; they hired two dramatic actors, then contacted Sol.

To Sol's delight, he moved on to the short-lived but enjoyable *Mr. Adams and Eve*, starring real-life husband and wife Howard Duff and Ida Lupino. Another challenging opportunity arose for a sophisticated comedy hit, furthering Sol's career and increasing his job opportunities; Sol Saks was happily at the helm. He stayed the course from 1957 to almost the close in 1958.

Many years have passed since those days, but when Sol thinks back, he sometimes wonders, *Maybe I shouldn't have quit My Favorite Husband. Maybe I should have stayed and fought the injustice.* But Sol understood that those regrets must not linger. To protect his writing skills, Sol needed to let all remorse go.

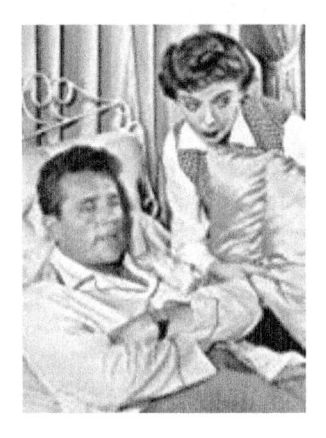

Howard Duff & Ida Lupino

"If you want a place in the sun,
You have to expect a few blisters."
—Loretta Young

Sol's daughter, Mary Saks said,
> Dad was the head writer on *Mr. Adams and Eve* (starring Howard Duff and Ida Lupino) and he hired a new writer—someone whose work he knew and whose skills and comedy sense would fit in with the other writers. Her name was Louella MacFarland. When "the powers that be" in the studio heard about the hire, they called Dad in for a meeting and told him to fire her as she had been blacklisted. He said no and was told to fire her or his job would be in jeopardy. When Ida and Howard heard about that, they went to the "powers" and said that if Sol went, so would they. Dad stayed with the show until the end. So did Louella.

An eager newspaper reporter leaned in and asked Sol, "What was it like to write for this married couple and under such pressure?" Sol smiled, looking off into the distance as many fond memories came to mind, and said,

Writing for Ida's show, *Mr. Adams and Eve,* was interesting, challenging, and rewarding—and I'm proud to have been part of that show. She was doing comedy for the first time because it was difficult for her husband Howard to get work. Her ex-husband had the original idea but wrote a deplorable script, so I took over. His story was about a married couple, both movie stars, and jealous of each other. My thoughts were that it was okay, but it is one episode. How is he going to run three years on that?

I wrote another script based on the original idea, and it did well. The premises were easy to get, I did not have the all-night re-writes, and Ida was incredibly creative. Howard, a nice guy, would give a little trouble now and then because he was disinterested. I would go to their place and have a martini in the early afternoon and chat. I would come home after two martinis with a much-needed premise.

I remember one particular idea came when we all heard their housekeeper call out, 'Broadway-limited in the fifth!' She was giving tips on a horse to Howard from another room. Ida and I started to laugh, so I used that in a script for their show. Both of them loved the idea, and the housekeeper was thrilled.

I eventually left the show because I was going through an era of being tired of writing episodes. I did what I thought best at the time, but I have often regretted leaving. Writing the same characters in the same environment weekly always made me unhappy, no matter what show I was writing. But leaving their show was the first difficult decision for me. I could not deny that the joy and ease of writing left me. But, I had to make a choice. Besides, I could not produce quality writing when those essentials left me. So, I quit and got hired on two shows; *Startime*, an anthology with drama, comedy, and variety directed by Alfred Hitchcock, and *Shirley Temple Theatre*. They kept me busy, and my inspiration returned.

Ida and Howard remained friends with Anna and me for years after the show, through all my different jobs and life's difficulties. As her friend, I must add that the one crucial bit of truth left out from all the writings about Ida is that she was way ahead of her time. She directed a couple of tv movies about a pregnant, unmarried girl. No one would dare write about the subject, which was considered taboo in those days. So there loomed over us all the possibility of being put on that dreaded list they crudely called the blacklist.

SOL SAKS

Sol concludes,

> But no matter the consequence, Ida always followed her instincts, and her instincts came from a good heart, and I believe that is why it worked. She made a success of everything she did for our industry. After Howard died in 1990, everything stopped for Ida. She remembered reading that you must not let grief linger; take a month, then get back to living. So, Ida took a month away from all that was familiar. She told me that it was a matter of deciding—she had to choose. Though pain remained, Ida returned home with a renewed determination to make her days count. Through tears at times, Ida remained grateful for her days with Howard. We remained friends until the day Ida died. She was a great dame!

Sol would start his writing process with a story as each workday began. A tale of something weighing on his mind, a remembrance, or possibly an idea. On this particular day, he had a tattered birthday card written by Ida and Howard clasped in his hand. Ida wrote that she understood why he had to leave the show so many years earlier. However, she wanted to ensure he was not feeling bad about his decision. Ida reminded Sol that CBS had signed the show for a year and that they loved every word Sol placed in front of CBS and her. No one could write for her like Sol, and she appreciated it more than words could express.

Genuinely moved by Ida's sentiments, Sol and I sat silently for a moment. What a beautiful considerate heart lay within each hand-written word. It was no wonder that Sol kept this treasure all these years. Finally, Sol reverently closed the card, placing his hand lovingly upon its cover. Our first hour of the morning became a delightful reminiscence of his friend Ida Lupino. I sat, a bit overwhelmed with invaluable insight and ready to start on his novel. However, he was not finished with this adventure back in time.

A broad, curious smile lit up the face of this dedicated writer sitting across from me. The room was quiet as he began to speak about an evening he and Anne planned a dinner party that included Ida and Howard. I listened intently, poured a cup of hot water, added a squeeze of fresh lemon, then settled in for another adventure. I took notes, just in case he would use them later. Though Sol was present in the room, his thoughts traveled back sixty years, and his very countenance changed as if he was there. Then, taking a long steady breath, Sol closed his eyes, recapturing a moment saying,

> Anne was busy in the kitchen, and I did my best to help her. We were expecting guests in about twenty minutes when the doorbell rang. Not expecting that anyone would be early, Anne looked at me with panic. I tried my best to reassure her as I went to open the door.

BEWITCHED

Sol continues,

> There stood just outside the door, beautiful—exuberant Ida and handsome Howard, both possessing a dynamic presence everyone immediately felt when you were with them. Greeting them with a hug and inviting them in, Howard took Ida by the hand and escorted her into our home. But, Ida abruptly stopped at the threshold, then quickly reached down and took off her shoes. Howard and I stood there watching her in puzzled disbelief. Then, in one dramatic moment, dressed in a stunning Coco Chanel original, she entered with stocking-clad feet and expensive shoes in hand. Anne poked her head out from the kitchen to see what the commotion was and say hello when Ida smiled broadly, said a big hello to Anne, then threw her shoes past me into the house. They slid across the entry hall floor like a bowling ball down the alley. We all gasped as Ida announced, 'Let's get this party started!'
>
> Anne came out of the kitchen laughing and hugged her. Howard and I stood frozen in amazement, then the four of us laughed until it hurt. Ida made a party great even before it began. She added her personal undefinable-priceless quality to everything she did. Her unique friendship added so much to our life, something no amount of money or success can buy.

Sol, enraptured by a delightful memory, shook his head as he stared out the office window, remembering and talking of the days spent with this power-house talent. Suddenly his story stopped. He turned and looked at me with a puzzled smile, then rested the side of his finger across his lips. When I asked if something was wrong, he just looked over at my notes, then pointed to them and said,

"You don't need to keep a record for me today."

"Should I stop?" He stared at the floor, scratching the back of his neck, and with a slightly bewildered tone, said,

"Ah, no. Keep writing; maybe you'll use them someday."

Now I was puzzled. Why would I use these notes? That sounded strange to me. I discounted it as something I would never do. But for a brief moment, there was an uncomfortable pause as we looked at each other. A chilling sadness ran through me and lingered as he quickly turned away, took a deep breath, then continued,

> Ida was a firecracker! Did you know she was born into a show-business family in Camberwell, London, England?

SOL SAKS

Sol continues,

> She shared a story with me with an expression I had not seen on her before, and today is still with me. We were waiting for friends and talking about our childhood and interests when she stopped. I asked if something was wrong, but she remained silent. She looked dazed. I didn't realize she suddenly remembered a day, then a specific time in 1933. Her mother had an audition for a coveted part in a movie called *Her First Affair* and desperately wanted this part, spending days preparing. She studied for hours and even bought clothes befitting the character. She thought Ida would enjoy watching her, so she brought her along. Ida was excited for her mother and sat patiently in the back of the room, looking forward to celebrating with her mom. Then, unexpectantly, the producers spotted Ida and asked her to come forward.
>
> Shocked and frightened, Ida thought she was in trouble. Her mother stood off to the side, bewildered as Ida moved nervously to the front of the room. No one said a word. The producers took a long assessing look at Ida, then handed her the script and asked her to read a couple of lines. She read the line, then the men turned, quietly talked, and hired Ida on the spot.
>
> Her mother, dressed in the character's clothes, tried to hide the tears in her eyes while expressing happiness for Ida, but the bitter disappointment was unmistakable. Ida's mother eventually worked, but they were small parts, and her disappointment became incapacitating. As work for Ida increased, family life decreased in comfort. To help ease the mounting tension, Ida generously contributed most of her pay to her family, but an opportunity that came to Ida sharply separated the ties.
>
> Ida reluctantly moved to Hollywood as a blonde, and there was no stopping her. She was a bundle of natural talent. She could act, sing, direct, produce, and in the 50s, became a prominent filmmaker during the Hollywood studio system. That was unheard of back then! She also formed an independent production company, co-writing and co-producing social-message films. Then, in 1953, remarkable Ida became the first woman to direct a film noir called *The Hitch-Hiker* and several television shows like *Gilligan's Island*. Everyone loved Ida. She had so much talent that it's almost hard to comprehend. Ida and I never talked about her mother again after that day. If the subject did come up, she would suddenly become uneasy. Ida relentlessly set higher goals for herself until, one day, Ida reached an impenetrable barrier. She had to face that she was living with substantial emotional pain.

Sol concludes,

> Keeping busy with movie projects, setting higher goals, then taking that occasional drink to ease the constant discomfort was not the answer. Unable to move forward, Ida knew she had to deal with sleepless nights, painful memories, and self-worth; she took a good look at her life. Success, she found, was a strange position. Like so many of us, Ida had no teaching on handling success. The more she had, the more issues were thrown her way, like jealousy. When jealousy arose, it became bitter cruelty from people who did not understand that talent is a gift and that everyone has an endowment. Ida chose to enhance her talent with study and dedication, which produced success. Though victory in any field unnervingly brings unresolved personal issues to the surface, eventually, being before the public gaze can brutally magnify every flaw to the viewing audience. With all her talent, drive, and conviction, Ida never thought she was pretty. Can you imagine? She believed in the studio press and their opinion of beauty. Those were the days of Hedy Lamar, Rita Hayworth, and Ava Gardner. With studios fixated on box office returns, they groomed their players to bring in top dollar. If Hedy, Rita, Ava, and Ida were standing before you with no makeup, no hair enhancements, and no studio lighting, Ida was just as lovely. However, she did have a depth that separated her that the studio didn't understand. Years of wisdom were evident in my friend's eyes, and I don't think the studios knew how to make money with that particular treasure.

Several years had passed since I sat captivated by that insightful story about Ida Lupino. Her name was not to come up again until on this particular eventful Wednesday when Ida was to make another entrance into his life. The hills of Malibu were on fire, forcing the sea-dweller traffic, usually found on Pacific Coast Highway, to pour into the canyon roads and then the freeway I used to go to work; the always overcrowded San Fernando Valley 101 freeway. As I merged with the freeway traffic for a morning of work with Sol, I found myself trapped. The 101 became a parking lot, and I could not get out.

A gray cloud of smoke moved across the sun, giving an eerie tint of orange to the sky as ash fell on our cars. These were the days before cell phones, so I couldn't tell Sol I would be late. He was very strict about starting at nine-sharp. There was no room for being late. The usual twelve-minute commute took one hour and a half this day. I climbed the circular stairs to the office in a state of nervous exhaustion—expecting to find Sol very unhappy with me.

SOL SAKS

I braced myself—opened the door, and Sol was at his desk with his back to me. His yellow legal pad full of notes lay before him, his pencil in one hand and the phone held tightly pressed against his ear in the other. He turned quickly to look at me and breathed a sigh of relief. Still holding his highly sharpened #2 pencil, Sol covered the end of the phone with his hand as he listened intently to a Malibu policeman he knew. Then, looking up at me with a blank stare and glazed eyes, he whispered that his home in Malibu was in the path of the raging fire, and no one could enter the area. I remained at his desk, attempting to bring calm to the situation.

Since his heart bypass surgery, he was to avoid too much stress. Besides, everything possible to save all homes in the path of the fire was underway, and his policeman friend would keep him updated. Sol committed to waiting as he hung up the phone, realizing there was nothing more to do. As I walked to my desk, I apologized for being late, but Sol shook his head and said,

"Oh, no, it's okay. I realized you must be in traffic when he got the call from the Malibu Police."

He took a deep breath and relaxed back into his chair. His informative and reassuring phone call by the stellar Malibu Police afforded Sol a bit of comfort and me a reprieve. As I moved to my desk, the phone rang, and Sol turned toward me with visible concern; the moment was quite stressful. With every attempt to stay calm, I answered the phone. A woman with a commanding raspy voice said, "Lemee speak ta Sol!"

I asked who was calling, and with a slightly New York street-smart voice, she responded, "Sure honey, tell 'em it's Ida!"

I knew that distinctive voice and immediately had the image of movie star Ida Lupino. My eyes widened, and I may have gasped as I reluctantly put her on hold to relay the message. The timing was perfect; every concern seemed to melt away as they spent the following hour reminiscing and laughing. Ida, bringing their conversation to an end, told Sol she was not feeling well but wanted to get together for lunch when she recovered. Sol happily agreed, ended the call, and began work as usual.

Though the diverting phone call was an immediate stress-reliever—Sol had learned to discipline his thinking, a priceless lesson set before me. Sol thought, *If the worst should happen and my home burns to the ground, I'll accept that outcome.* Sol kept to his writing schedule as the Malibu fires continued to rage for two more harrowing days before finally being extinguished. Another day passed when he received a call that residents could return to their homes.

Early the following morning, his writing completed, Sol drove to Malibu Canyon, leading to his beach house. As he entered the canyon, it looked like a strange science fiction movie punctuated by suffocating smells of burnt timber and chemicals on either side of the road. The surrounding hills stood sadly dotted with massive bare black stretches of earth and pink-covered terrain from a fire retardant called "sky Jello-O."

Once through the canyon, he turned onto his narrow street to see a startling sight. Immediately across the narrow road from his home, the dense brush and trees were burnt to the ground, leaving the homes untouched. With overflowing gratitude, his breath caught in his throat, imagining the courageous firefighters standing on that one-lane strip of asphalt, knocking the blaze down. Exhausted but endlessly grateful, he would relay his heartfelt thanks to the fire department.

The smoke was still clearing when the news found Sol, later that evening, that Ida had died, and would he say a word at her memorial service next week? The news hit him like a sharp punch to his heart, taking, for a moment, his breath away. Struggling to regain his composure, Sol agreed, took the following week off, rested, and prepared for life without Ida. With a heaviness in his heart, Sol held tight to the edges of the podium, holding back the tears, and began with the words,

> Our scaffolding of care is gone. Friends, like Ida, are a rare, once-in-a-lifetime gift; I know she was to Anne and me. I heard a story about unseen scaffolding built around us at certain times in our lives. It's used as necessary assistance in the building or repairing in this life, then removed when the need is gone.
>
> For many of us, Ida was that necessary assistance. I will miss my friend terribly. But I will remain forever grateful for knowing her.

Everyone sat spellbound, some with tissues to dry their eyes. Then, reluctantly, Sol releasing his grip on the podium, stepped away and left with tears threatening to roll down his face. His every moving word, along with a captivating description of the atmosphere in the room, appeared in newspapers reporting Ida's passing. Ida Lupino 1918-1995.

4

A Promise of Paradise

"A good joke is like a pearl, it is beautiful, but it has been created
As protection Against an irritant that got
Inside your shell."

If I'd known the trials of this dream, I might not have pursued it, but listening to that subtle inside direction was the right thing to do; I would have missed many happy moments. When I got to California, I went to every beach up and down Pacific Coast Highway. Malibu was the one people in my industry seemed to value above the rest, so I tried to buy a home in Malibu. I tried for 40 years. The closest I got was an occasional lunch. –Sol Saks

Enjoying a Pacific Ocean view his deck in Malibu-1996

Having acquired his swimming pool, Sol next set a goal to live by the beach, not just any beach. Sol, a man of researched fact-gathering, began seriously looking in Malibu. Sol said he wasn't a good businessman, but I believe he was. Sol surrounded himself with successful people and learned well. He discovered that his contemporaries were basing their opinions on solid facts. Malibu, or Bu as locals call it, is a 21-mile-long narrow strip of coastline. It is primarily home to the extremely wealthy, in a great location with easy access to the studios. On his second visit to this warm and wonderful coast, a simple beachfront house cost $85,000, and he considered that too expensive. Two years later, that house was selling for $125,000. Sol wisely made the purchase and turned the street-level garage into an enviable apartment that was never without an occupant.

His home, perched over the sand, was perfect for renting anytime, but he chose to rent only during August and September. Europeans traditionally vacationed in August and would book the entire month or both. However, September seemed to interest people from the mid-west. After each renter left, Estela was always present to make the house picture-perfect for the next visitor. Money received in August paid the considerable property tax, and in September, the ongoing maintenance. Sol purchased a couple more properties in the San Fernando Valley, which he generously shared with beloved friends and family.

Meeting Sol Saks

An unfamiliar door of opportunity opened wide on this memorable day. I was to meet a writer whose many childhood dreams were now surrounding him. Yet, I was unaware of this humble man's glowing success and the price paid for the goals he set. I would not see the hidden cost until much later. Sol believed jealousy and misunderstanding were part of the toll required and did his best not to complain but move on. At this point, my glimpse into brilliance and the cost begins.

"Hello, I'm Carolyn Haynes. I'm calling about your ad for a part-time assistant." "Yes, Ms. Haynes, I'm Sol Saks, a writer." His voice sounded strained and weak as he asked about my background. Upon continuing with the functions and pay, he asked if I was interested. "Yes, it sounds perfect." Can you send me your resume?" "It will be in the mail today." The worst of grieving the loss of my husband was at an end, and happily, a need to be productive was emerging. As I prepared to start a new page in my life, I was at the end of a maze of my late husband's paperwork, the closing of business interests, and the filing away of unfinished dreams. I quietly closed the door to our filing cabinet while praying for strength to continue.

A few days passed when I got a phone call that would take me on an adventure of a lifetime.

"Hello, Mrs. Haynes, it's Sol Saks calling. I read your resume and wondered if you could stop by for an interview tomorrow?" Still feeling fragile, I didn't think to ask Mr. Saks what he had written. I knew nothing about him, but I cavalierly blurted out, "Absolutely! What time would you like me there?" "Can you be here by 9 in the morning?" "Yes. I need your business address." "Oh, well, I work from home now. My office is upstairs away from the main house. I hope this is not a concern for you?"

SOL SAKS

The thought of a home office was indeed a cause for concern. A fright shot through me, numbing my mind and leaving me breathlessly in the absence of sound. After all, this is my hometown, and I have seen Hollywood up close and personal. The heavy silence continued as I struggled for an answer. My mind was racing, but I haltingly agreed to meet with him.

Within the San Fernando Valley, tucked behind the south side of Ventura Boulevard, are tangles of secluded streets in this peaceful unassuming, yet sophisticated village community of Sherman Oaks. I was searching for Sutton Street—the home of Mr. Sol Saks—and there it was. A ranch-style home enclosed by a brick and black iron wall. Behind the wall stood stately towering pine trees, imposing giant cacti, lovely flowering plants, and delicate pink roses adorning the front garden. I would later learn the gorgeous roses were called the *Bewitched* Rose, named after his television series *Bewitched*.

Brightly colored flowers surrounded a well-tended lawn marked with streams of sunlight and shade—and this day, the gardener was busy working. The blaring sound of his lawnmower droned through the closed windows of my car as I parked at the curb. I sat for a moment, my heart pounding, as I nervously questioned my decision. I walked down the sloping brick driveway and through the black, squeaky iron gate that closed with a bang behind me. I reached the door, rang the doorbell, and waited, but there was no response. Finally, I knocked on the door, and it flew open to the sounds of a vacuum and a rumpled-looking man emerging from a room behind the front door. With a plate of scrambled eggs and toast held precariously in his hands, he said, "Oh, Hello! Ms. Haynes? I'm Sol Saks."

I stood like a deer in the headlights, somewhat frozen, as he gazed at me with a smile. Nodding my head, I managed a breathless yes. "Come in. Excuse all the noise." Quickly turning away and walking into his kitchen, he raised his voice above the racket, "It's a pleasure to meet you. Do you mind if I finish my breakfast?" He turned to look at me, pausing for an answer. I crossed the threshold and raised my voice to the decibels he set, "Of course not. I'm early." Taking one more step into the house, I caught a glimpse of a woman in the sunken living room, feverously vacuuming the carpet. She moved to the far hallway—then disappeared around the corner. Completely out of my comfort zone, I became consumed with Hollywood stories and personal experiences, obliterating my thoughts. Coming from a large Italian family, I also grew up hearing many Mafia stories. His distant voice, inviting me in again, broke through the minutia now camping in my mind, but thoughts encouraging me to leave held me captive in the entry. I felt the urge to turn and run to my car but pushed fear aside and took another step in the hallway.

Mr. Saks looked at me, puzzled, and asked me to follow him to the office. He looked like a nice man, so I encouraged myself to end my over-cautious mind.

We exited the house through the sliding glass doors of his dining room, and the spiral staircase leading up to his office lay a mere few steps in front of us. Reaching the top, he unlocked the door with the care of a banker opening his vault, then stepped across the threshold where the writings of his imagination came to life. As the door opened into this unique 14' by 20' space, it exuded creative energy, history, and poignant memories that seemed to fill every corner. It was a million-dollar treehouse with floor-to-ceiling windows on the north and south sides. An airy, window-clad office atop his one-story home with two lovely calming views; Sutton Street to the south, and his park-like back garden, surrounding an Olympic-size swimming pool to the north. The perfect man cave for Mr. Sol Saks.

The morning sun peeked through the massive pines hedging his front garden and rested gently upon the simple wooden desk that brilliantly matched the tree trunks below. While working at the studios in the early days, Mr. Saks explained he used a Dictaphone that his secretary later transcribed. Now it sat silently at the head of his desk with a wooden sign atop reading; Don't complain and Don't explain.

Another desk at the back of the room was to be mine. Complete with the latest amenities, a state-of-the-art typewriter, and a phone. An orange uncomfortable Danish modern secretarial chair would be mine four hours a day, three days a week. However, surrounding me was old glamorous Hollywood history. A massive pedestaled dictionary stood proudly opened behind my chair. It was the sentinel of all words amongst shelves of reference books. On the right of my desk hung a large, impressive framed movie poster of the movie *Walk Don't Run* starring Cary Grant. It was just like the ones I saw in the theaters when I was a little girl. Behind closed doors on the left was a wealth of scripts, novels, short stories, idea notes, organized office supplies, an electric pot for boiling water, tea bags, instant coffee, and snacks. He shyly apologized, with a hint of laughter at the lack of a powder room, and told me that when his wife Anne was alive, she put her foot down at the inclusion of such a room. She politely articulated that he should come downstairs and use their bathroom. Anne arranged everything her beloved Sol needed within their downstairs en suite. A guest bathroom at the other end of their home was for guests and employees. I believe Anne made a wise decision.

Working in a home office was a first for me and a bit uncomfortable. Mr. Saks, however, seemed a very kind, genuine man with a serious determination to write. Eventually, a sense of safety began to settle upon me. As we continued the interview, he did not talk about his past professional life. Instead, his focus was on his current goals for writing. When I asked about the poster on the wall, he humbly stated that he was involved with the script. I thought *he could be a very accomplished writer, well, maybe.* Though still too shattered to return to acting, this 9 am to 1 pm, three days a week position seemed comfortable and perfectly suited for me. We agreed on my salary, then paused as he read over my resume again, glancing periodically out the window to his backyard. "Well, I think you'd be perfect, Mrs. Haynes. When can you start?" It was the weekend, and we agreed on Monday.

Grief can sometimes impose a tricky state of mind for a season. It seemed this was my time, and I prayed it would not last too long. I wasn't as fearless as before, even though I could not have been in a safer position. It was like diving off a high board into the pool below. I experienced that momentary rush from the pit of my stomach as if diving headlong into a new life. Once in, it's a slow eye-opening revelation. My thoughts reminded me that this is how life continues. Perhaps a deeper pool of life than before with a hint of grandeur and loss. I walked out to my car, a bit more elevated, the minutia clearing, and headed home for a rest. I would prepare for my first day of work; I would reenter the workforce single again, but with a new strange title of widow.

Monday arrived for my first day of work, along with butterflies in my stomach. I entered the crowded, exhaust-filled freeway feeling lost in time. My heart was pounding as I exited a few minutes later. The reality of my husband's death was overwhelming. I slowed the car as I entered Sutton Street, struggling to compose myself. Through my stress, I remembered the streets south of Ventura Boulevard have an intriguing history of old and new Hollywood, a mix of elegant and standard homes and restful gardens; my imagination soared, and my grief eased. I wondered about the history behind each door. These unassuming streets provided a convenient sanctuary for powerful politicians, notable directors, actors, writers, producers, athletes, and the occasional infamous.

The easy access to the beach, studios, and production companies without living in the city is always an attractive plus for most Hollywood entertainers. Sherman Oaks certainly provides all of the above. My new thoughts inspired me; I arrived at my destination a few minutes before nine and was almost euphoric. I parked my car at the curb under the giant pines, walked down the brick drive, through the squeaky black iron gates, and rang the doorbell.

BEWITCHED

The doorknob turned then stopped, and my anxious heart skipped a beat. Finally, it turned again, and the door slowly opened. Much to my surprise, as the door opened, a pleasant woman with a friendly smile and holding a broom greeted me in Spanish. I spoke enough Spanish to know she said hello and asked me to come in. I felt instantly welcomed and relaxed. She pointed in the direction of the office, and I assumed Mr. Saks was already upstairs from her gestures. She walked with me to the sliding glass door leading to the patio, then graciously opened it for me. I turned to say thank you and introduced myself. She smiled and told me her name was Estela. We have remained friends ever since that day.

    I climbed the winding exterior staircase, full of the anticipation of sharing this magical treehouse. I gently opened the door to a very focused writer leaning back in his chair, deep in thought; a character-study, as an actor, I dreamed of seeing. I whispered good morning as I stood at the threshold, then entered. Still somewhat unaware of his impressive background, his all-to-apparent professionalism was perceptible.

    Looking up from his desk, he uttered a quick hello, appearing happy and eager to begin. Before him lay a carefully planned synopsis of his schedules, hopes, and expectations. He expanded on each point on his list in a matter-of-fact conversation, but I found them impossible to remember. His exact caliber was a first for me, and I scrambled for my desk's legal pad and pencil. My breath caught in my throat as I contemplated my abilities and thought, *can I possibly do this?* Pages of notes and a hand-cramp later, Sol finished his preliminary instructions. They included over six weeks of unattended bookkeeping, numerous oversights in rents, rental maintenance, accounts payable and receivable, numerous unsent submissions to literary agents, and so much more. A sudden rush of the reality of this job hit me. I needed to take careful notes as I mentally reached for those dormant skills. I was also setting new goals to fulfill the requirements of this highly disciplined and determined writer. Then he apprised me of his schedule, and I copied it as follows: Writing from 9 to 1 sharp three mornings a week. Afternoons are for meetings, phone calls, answering letters—lunch with friends, and anything non-creative.

    Thursdays, see plays, evenings out, shopping, and Sol never wrote on Sundays, holidays, weekends, or evenings unless irresistibly inspired. He believed that productive time differs from person to person. He was adamant that a writer could achieve his most efficient work within four hours daily.

SOL SAKS

In his book Funny Business, Sol writes,

> Except when driven, keeping up concentration for eight hours a day is a difficult task. I think you will find that if the four hours are pure, uncluttered work time, you will outproduce the nine-to-five writer. Find what time of day or night works best for you. Make a schedule you can stick to as closely as possible and make that time sacred. Also, make everyone around you hold it equally sacred. You will be surprised at how quickly you and they will accept its sanctity. During those hours of writing, you do not make or take phone calls or do anything else except write your determined project. At the end of the time allotted, you quit. Even if you have not written a line, this is very important. It is as essential that you stop on schedule as that you start on time. When the words don't come—don't press, don't quit, don't panic. Don't blame yourself for stupidity; frustration and agony lie in that. Be kind to yourself—be patient, and keep going.

The writing habits of this most prolific writer are, and I believe, will always be current, a pearl of eternal wisdom heeded by many through the ages. After Sol discussed his writing schedule, he moved on to his notes for a new play. He angled his swivel chair of plush tan leather to face the grand expanse of windows and stared out through the treetops to Sutton Street, then turned to look at me, saying,

> Before you arrived this morning, Carolyn, I reviewed my play and would like to make changes. First, I want to get a sense of timing and rhythm. Can you put feeling into each character? Can you do that?

With my acting background, he was anxious for me to read all his written character dialogue aloud. Facing me and moving to the edge of his chair with the command of a seasoned director, he waited expectantly for my answer. It wasn't as demanding as a cold reading for an audition, but reading all the characters and moving through many emotions on my first day was truly overwhelming. I took a deep breath and said I would give it my best. Sol handed me several pages of his play, sat back, then crossed his arms. Struggling to concentrate on what I was doing, I began. I could see him taking notes, which was a lesson in concentration for me. An hour passed, and I was exhausted but hopeful I had done well. He did not respond to my reading but was absorbed in his new notes instead.

Days later, relaxing into the routine, Sol asked me to read aloud the script once more. I read this time as a relaxed actress. I let the dialogue guide me into each character. I suddenly caught a glimpse of his thought-provoking use of words and timing.

Every entertainer dreams of a writer that follows a well-thought-out train of thought. The choice and order of his words evoked the appropriate emotions. I did not have to dig for tears; they flowed with his written words. Sadly, he never wanted to be a comedy writer, and nearing the end of his life, he still said he wanted to write drama. It is the opinion of seasoned professional writers that Sol wrote drama magnificently, and in my humble opinion, I agree.

The weeks passed in an exhausting whirlwind, but I managed to get somewhat close to his pace of excellence in taking dictation and making submissions to studios, agents, and universities. In retrospect, I was fortunate that it was just a part-time job! This dynamo of a writer, who was many years my senior, was an unstoppable, energetic perfectionist when he was working. Sol's spelling, editing, phrasing, and recall were impeccably accurate. Through association, I was becoming good, but he was great. I eventually realized what a marvelous opportunity was before me and hung on by my fingernails. First, I studied the dictionary and shorthand and then called my sister, Gloria, a stellar accountant who gave me more understanding of keeping accurate, professional bank records.

Sol was right out of old Hollywood. His address book was a captivating list of private phone numbers, addresses, and comments from James Dean, Carey Grant, Ida Lupino, Ester Williams, Fernando Lamas, Buddy Ebsen, Tony Curtis, and dozens more. I enjoyed the beginning of each workday story that rivaled any movie, some taking place downstairs in his home. Sol loved entertaining his friends. Throwing a party was part of who he was.

While translating his ideas into words on paper, his countenance was tense, even tired. However, when he leaned back, took a deep breath, and regaled me with fascinating stories, his face took on a more youthful glow. They may have consisted of his days at CBS, family and friends around the pool, or luncheons with top entertainment businesspeople. But his face lit up while in suspended, palpable energy when he spoke of Anne. He looked into a secret place where he could still see her and said,

Always kind was Anne. A supportive woman who put me first. Anne was a terrific cook, Sol sighed. She enjoyed our family, friends, and parties, but beneath it all, she wanted to make more of her life. She was growing into a modern woman. I grew in my field but needed the old-fashioned Anne. The one who helped me to stretch my thinking and to become less selfish. I guess I was still selfish.

Whatever story-of-the-day Sol narrated, it was sure to be a formidable, thought-provoking adventure.

SOL SAKS

While listening, I glimpsed a wonderful sense of humor well-hidden behind his dark-rimmed glasses; I marveled at the fascinating moments of relaxation, teaching me the importance of pacing through the creative process.

The barrage of inspiration paused. Sol rose from his chair and began a brisk walk through the office. Suddenly a delightful look on his face appeared. I witnessed that miraculous moment of a sudden enduement of inspiration. Sol talked a bit then this gifted writer dove into work again like someone instantly hitting a light switch on the wall. With a quick transition back into an immediately focused writer, we were off again to an imaginary place in his ever-so-creative mind. I captured every word on paper as they expanded his already written notes. They filled any blank or slow moments with new revelations, enthusiastically enriching each character. Creative ideas that breathed exciting life into words on the paper. What a gift he possessed! I learned that many character actors who appeared in the plays Sol wrote felt the same way. A favorite of mine was Connie Sawyer.

Connie in 1940s and Connie in 2010 at 98 years!

She had over 140 film and television credits and a career of 85 years. Connie said Sol wrote dialogue so well that it became effortless to step into character and make the part believable. Though she was a brilliant comedian, tears flowed easily while reading a drama written by Sol. Of course, she told Sol, it was because it was so bad it made her weep. They both laughed; Connie could always make Sol laugh. Connie lived to be 105, the oldest member of the Screen Actors Guild and worked with Sol into her late nineties. Sol loved her energy, sense of timing, and her generosity of spirit.

If the end of a workday was with Sol and Connie, I spent a few brief frazzled moments at my desk, leaning back in my chair to catch my breath, then organize for the next whirlwind day. Happily, I built up stamina over time as I moved through my challenges and duties.

First as a secretary, bookkeeper, and property manager, then assisting with writing plays, books, university classes, and occasionally, my favorite moments, working with other actors. Eventually, Sol would ask me to oversee a script on stage and check the timing. But always, my chief job was to listen as he poured out those nagging thoughts, aggravations, and missed opportunities. They seemed to purge the untraveled path to hidden treasures and rivers of inspiration, leading him out of his wilderness.

On this particular day, Sol seemed unusually eager to work but quite irritable. He stated he hadn't slept well, so he used the midnight hours to make more notes for his newest play. Sol clutched his companion-yellow-lined legal pad filled with thoughts and dialogue for me to type. But before handing them to me, he asked if I would fix him a cup of coffee.

While waiting for the water to boil, I began filing the stack of papers on my desk and was surprised that several were medical. Sol must have seen the concern on my face because he started an explanation. After Anne's death, he needed double bypass heart surgery, and at another point in his life, he developed diabetes. I brought him his coffee, sat, and listened to the rest of his struggles. He received news from his doctor earlier that week that another bypass surgery was necessary. Without expressing any concerns, he solemnly said that many moments go into making a life; joy, heartbreak, gain, loss, and for many moments, the attempt to make sense of it all. Then, stopping abruptly, he turned his gaze through the expansive windows beyond his desk to the treetops beyond the windows. Sol told of this unique peaceful view as one that reminded him of his childhood dreams of California and the stories his mother told him of her escape from Poland. Today he attempted to gain a clearer perspective on the bumpy road he traveled leading to this point in his life. Battling through sleep deprivation and medication, Sol deliberated until the mental fog lifted and creativity slowly emerged once again. Before he began to write, his summation was that there were moments in life when you felt like a stranded ship at sea, unable to find a way back to land. Now with his land insight, he reluctantly handed me his pages of sacred notes, then said he would go downstairs to rest, then slowly made his way down the staircase, and I entered every hard-won word into his new play-in-progress. Just two days later, Sol had his second successful bypass surgery.

I waited a couple of days, then went to visit him. I quietly entered the room to an unexpected sight. Sol was sitting in bed telling funny stories to his doctor and two nurses. Everyone was laughing, including Sol. He looked healthier and happier than I had ever seen him. While recuperating in the hospital and surrounded by flowers, his nurses frequently snuck into his room to hear another story.

SOL SAKS

Intermittently, his doctor attempted to share the importance of the elusive art of relaxation. His attending physician's wise and kind words were to have a lasting impact on Sol.

His doctor told of his many patients arriving in Hollywood to enter the entertainment industry carrying varying degrees of heartbreak and dysfunction. Then, with the pressures of the entertainment world, they eventually succumb to a diseased state. Attitude, he reminded Sol is a vital medication, sometimes outweighing the medical treatment. The doctor looked into Sol's eyes intently and said, "Learn to make peace with unproductive, negative memories that plagued you. Happiness is a choice, Sol; begin with those decisions!" Sol knew that cancer and heart disease were prevalent in the entertainment industry and promised the doctor and himself to make changes.

After a couple of days at home, Sol resumed working as usual. He confessed his biggest struggle was achieving the doctor's advice, but he resolved to do his best. While cultivating his newfound mindset, he raised the bar of well-crafted accomplishments higher and higher, as most clever perfectionists do. During the first year, there were days when it was almost impossible to meet his pace. However, my skills exponentially improved as I weathered the roller coaster ride. Within that time, when I thought I was at the end of my rope, quite unexpectantly, he surprised me with a gesture thoughtfully tailored to me alone. One surprise revealed itself during an evening while seated amongst the audience of a theater. The lights went down, and the play we had worked on together began. I was absorbed and listening intently to every word spoken, every phrase he dictated, and I recorded. The spotlight rose to capture the lead actress as she entered with a commanding presence. The theater fell silent. Tension in the room grew as she walked to center stage in her judicial black robe. The bailiff announced loudly, "All stand for Judge Carolyn Haynes!" My breath caught in my throat. I was shocked to hear my name hollered from the stage. My eyes widened, and I gasped in a rush of amazement. That was not the name Sol had chosen for the Judge. I looked across the aisle at Sol to find him looking at me. The lights from the stage sparkled on his glasses, and his face beamed with a broad smile. He had made a last-minute change in the character name. Several cast members knew but kept the secret until the show's end. For the remainder of the play, I was speechless. A lovely kind gesture that remains with me to this day.

Throughout the nail-biting and the occasional harried work days, Estela's soft sense of kindness, efficiency, and calmness, keeping life tidy for Sol, filtered through the air like a summer breeze. Shortly after Anne died, Sol needed help managing his home and fortunately found Estela.

She lived in Los Angeles and didn't drive but took public transportation to every one of her jobs. Estela arrived at Sol's Sherman Oaks home once a week from 8 in the morning and left for her next job at noon. She also took care of his home in Malibu. Again, riding the bus from Los Angeles, Estela exited the bus at the top of his street off Pacific Coast Highway. She walked the quiet narrow road for a mile to his home, had a cup of coffee on the balcony, then cleaned Sol's home from top to bottom. Relaxing for a time, hard-working Estela then reversed her journey back home or to her next job. You always knew when Estela had been there; everything sparkled.

One rainy Friday morning, as I arrived at work, I rang the bell as usual, but no answer. So, I knocked and continued to wait. I stepped back, straining to see up through the second-story windows, but the droplets of rain streaming down the windows made it impossible to see if Sol was sitting at his desk. I tried the door, and it was open. The breathtaking pungent odor of stale food held me at the door. I called out for Sol, but there was no answer. I stood nervously at the threshold for a strange and uncomfortable few moments. I could see the kitchen sink stacked high with dirty dishes and no Estela insight. Something like being in a tv mystery.

I never understood why the person in the mystery movie would walk into the house when it was scary. I should close the door and return to my car. I pushed the door open further and spotted several new shirts sitting neatly on the dining room table in stacks of three, and like that character in the mystery, I walked in and made my way to the dining room. I opened the sliding glass door and climbed the spiral stairs to the office until I could see in the windows. It was hard to see Sol from that angle, and with the high-back leather chair, it looked like no one was there; I saw no movement. I slowly turned the doorknob. Sol abruptly turned his chair and looked in my direction. His sudden movement startled me, and I jumped with a brief scream. I took a deep breath to calm my racing heart and then asked him if everything was okay. Sol shook his head in a frustrating no, then explained that Estela wanted a few days off to visit her family. Puzzled, I just said okay and walked to my desk. Sol put his pencil down, and I could see he was upset. I heard him sigh in frustration, so I plugged in the kettle and made coffee.

Placing his favorite brew on his desk, he quickly picked it up, took a sip, then gazed deeply into the cup. I asked him if he was alright, and without looking up, he hesitantly explained that he didn't know how to use the washing machine and needed clean shirts. Enraged, he had to go to his favorite store and purchase enough shirts to last until Estela returned. I stood with my coffee cup to my mouth, trying to hide my impending laughter. He told me, with frustration, that dirty dishes were piling up, and he also did not use a dishwasher. Laughter was about to burst out.

SOL SAKS

I turned and walked to my desk to gain some composure, then casually volunteered to show him how to use them. He looked at me with the most frustrating facial gestures, then threw his hands in the air, declining my offer, stating that he wasn't good with mechanical things. Within a breath, a sheepish smile lit his face as if waiting for me to volunteer to wash the dishes. It was my turn for a facial gesture, I did not speak a word, but he knew I declined. I smiled, still holding back a roar of laughter, and remained silent. Sol was a man that could make you laugh without the slightest intentions and wholly lost without Estela.

He stood up from his chair, still clutching his coffee in frustration, and began walking silently around the room. As Sol filed past me several times, I gathered the mail and bills on my desk. With the rain now pelting the windows and the wind blowing fiercely, he returned to his desk, and we began to work. Sol returned once more to the most competent man of verbiage.

Through the years I worked and knew Sol, there were many constants: his discipline while working, the importance of supporting his family, independence, and abiding unhappiness. Sadness lingered through even the grandest celebrations until the day he died. Sadness, Sol said, was the building block for his comedy. Yet, through the use of his past, he retained a most incredible gift for writing. He enjoyed millionaire status and, by all outward accounts, a man blessed. Sol lived the dream that most people arriving in Hollywood carry in their hearts and never realize. Working successfully through the Golden Era and modern days of Hollywood, Sol gained respect and admiration in the eyes and hearts of top stars, contemporaries, and many new arrivals. But still, those dark shadows that plague the brilliant gamut of Hollywood talents remained with Sol like an impenetrable wall.

Yet, Sol found a way around those daunting shadows and learned to generously share his approach to writing, combining insights from some of the most ardent writers worldwide and his experiences. With internet access, I have compared notes on writing with several award-winning writers from various eras. Most follow a similar pattern as Sol. He learned from history, discovered success, then paid the lovely gift forward.

This once-in-a-lifetime job could be intoxicating at times, but it fiercely demanded that I consistently acquire more patience, knowledge, speed, and accuracy. Which I would like to think I accomplished over time. However, amid this brilliant-writers dedication and strict schedule, I could rely on the working pendulum to swing back to a relaxed routine. As quickly as he could focus, he returned to a slower pace, a dimension of skill I'd seen from a distance but never worked alongside.

Thursday evenings were his time to see plays, new productions, or a special night out with his family. It was not unusual to get a call on Wednesday inviting you to the Hollywood Bowl for a major concert with several other friends, and what a glorious time that was. Then there were the weekends. Sol stepped into his grey Mercedes, his relaxed room-on-wheels, and turned on his favorite classical music while enjoying the fragrance of expensive leather. He told me that he sold his old grey Mercedes because the leather smell was gone. Hmm, I think he was joking. Then, in a sumptuous world of his own, Sol entered the 101-freeway, exiting onto the winding precipitous Malibu Canyon Road. A few miles into this scenic but somewhat dangerous Canyon, the oppressive summer heat gives way to cool ocean breezes.

Air conditioning in the car cannot compare with the refreshing intoxication that fills the Canyon. They leave any driver serenely energized from the sweltering summer heat of the San Fernando Valley. The well-traveled road cuts through the beautiful Santa Monica Mountains, leaving mountainous cliffs hugging the road and a steep cavernous drop on the other side. As you reach the end, the view expands to a panoramic, breathtaking site of the Pacific Ocean.

A Gift from A Gracious Host

As a recipient of his forward-paying gift, I would like to share a story about one very hot Fourth-Of-July. The weather in the San Fernando Valley hit a record-breaking, brutal 116 degrees. My youngest daughter and I were discussing fun ways to enjoy the day when the phone rang. It was Sol with an invitation to join his family and friends in Malibu for the Independence Day celebration.

Sol told of his Malibu neighbors renting a barge each year filled with fireworks for the community. I later learned the neighbors were actors Danny DiVito of the television series *Taxi* and his wife Rhea Pearlman, who appeared on *Cheers*. Sounding too good to miss, my youngest daughter and I jumped in the car and made our way through Malibu Canyon. After about five miles, the temperature dropped almost thirty degrees. We turned off the air conditioning, opened the windows, and breathed in the fragrant ocean-scented air.

Soon the glorious sight of our beautiful Pacific Ocean with its gliding sailboats appeared in a vast expanse as we emerged from the narrow canyon. We turned onto the busy Pacific Coast Highway overlooking the sea and drove in sublime comfort.

SOL SAKS

His directions were to make a left on PCH, then watch for a shopping center containing stores such as Wolfgang Pucks and several notable markets. Immediately behind that center is the Malibu Police Station on old Malibu Road, make a right, and you will find us. The road was narrow, with cars parked on either side. The sun was setting, and I could not find one spot to park. Stopping in front of Sol's home and wondering what to do, I spotted an official-looking man seated on a chair. Sol had kindly supplied the convenience of valet service for his guests.

Grateful and relieved, my young daughter exited the car, and I walked hand-in-hand down the wooden stairs into a courtyard filled with potted flowers, plants, and the entrance to his home. The homes in that stretch of road are built upon pilings, suspending the dwelling high above the sand. We were about to take a step over the threshold into my first perched home, and I confess I was a bit nervous. I rang the bell, and Sol's lovely daughter Mary opened the door and introduced herself. All fears left as she navigated us through the party with introductions to everyone. We found Sol on his suspended balcony hovering high above the water with friends, telling stories and enjoying the view. We received another warm welcome and introductions to more friends. Standing on the balcony, I could feel the gentle vibrations of each wave as it crashed upon the sand, then gently ran beneath his home. It was an odd sensation. The laughter, mixed with music and the ever-present ocean sounds, captured my heart; heaven-sent moments.

The tide was in, and the orange-yellow sun reflected its glorious rays upon the water as it lingered, dancing on the horizon's edge. The railing floodlights came on and lit up the white luminous-looking sand. With each wave, trails of white foam rested on patches of sand as the sea gently receded. It was such a beautiful sight. The refreshing sea air and the constant relaxing rhythm of the waves seemed to energize us and sweep us into the party atmosphere. We were having such a good time. Moments later, a familiar voice rang out from the kitchen, inviting everyone to help themselves to the most delicious catered food from Wolfgang Pucks. The balcony table held the gorgeous buffet and was immediately surrounded by hungry guests, filling their plates, then moving into the kitchen for beverages.

While enjoying wonderful conversation and this incredible meal, we watched the continuing sunset as it cast a fire-yellow glow on the water while slowly disappearing in a shimmer into the watery skyline. Within moments, the romantic, subtle reflection of the moon appeared in the midnight blue sky and scattered diamond-like dancing lights upon the water. It was simply magical.

The air now, mingling with moonbeams, dipped to 75 degrees. Usually, 75 degrees was lovely. However, this night having just left 116 degrees, was uncomfortably cold. Sol invited anyone needing a jacket to help themselves to his closet. We, the Valley novices, gratefully found jackets, wrapped them around us, and prepared to watch the fireworks. Sol, from his balcony, pointed in the direction of Danny's barge of fireworks, and we stood in child-like anticipation of the event. Moments later, soaring far into the dark starlit sky, firework explosions flooded the heavens in red, white, and blue. Mirrored reflections rested on the water and bounced off the waves; it was fireworks amplified! Voices raised in thrilled tones at the exquisite sight. It was an awe-inspiring, unforgettable memory. I will forever remember that beautiful evening and the gift of such a gracious host.

5

So Was Born the Legend

*"Imagining is creating,
and illusions are its
most rewarding product."*

Promotional photograph for Sol's pilot. Left to right: Elizabeth Montgomery as Samantha, Dick York as Darrin, Agnes Moorehead as Endora

When asked what *Bewitched* was about, Sol spun a story on the spot, to everyone's delight.

> Once upon a time, a beautiful witch named Samantha (Elizabeth Montgomery) met and married a mortal named Darrin Stephens (originally Dick York, later Dick Sargent). While lovely Samantha complies with Darrin's wishes to become a regular suburban housewife, her magical family disapproves of the mixed marriage and frequently interferes in the couple's lives, causing much friction. Episodes often begin with Darrin becoming the victim of a spell, the effects of which wreak havoc with mortals such as his boss (David White), clients, parents, and neighbors.

Sol concludes,

> But, by the epilogue, having triumphed over the devious elements that failed to separate them, Darrin and Samantha most often embrace, ah, all is well. The witches and their male counterparts, called warlocks, are long-lived; while Samantha appears to be a young woman, many episodes suggest she is hundreds of years old. To keep their society secret, witches avoid showing their powers in front of mortals other than Darrin. Their spell effects drive the plot of most episodes and Samantha's continual attempts to hide their supernatural origin from mortals. Witches and warlocks usually use physical gestures along with their conjurations. For example, to perform magic, Samantha often twitches her nose to create a spell. Special visual effects accompanied her nose-twitch with music to highlight such a captivating action.

An Original On-Screen Credit

"How did you come to write the *Bewitched* pilot?"

> I was on a much-needed break from writing. To recharge, I accepted a teaching position at California State University. The change of pace was relaxing and rewarding, leaving my mind free to enjoy those simple pleasures. Anne loved going to the movies, and now I wasn't too busy to see a good one. The idea began when we went to see the 1958 movie *Bell, Book, and Candle* starring James Stewart and Kim Novak. Kim Novak portrays a beautiful young witch who lives in New York City. In this movie, she's attracted to her neighbor, Jimmy Stewart but does not like his fiancé. So she uses her magic to put a spell on him to fall in love with her; however, it all backfires when she falls in love with him. Because he is a mortal, there are problems for her.

SOL SAKS

Sol continues,

It reminded me of an earlier film, made in 1942, named *I Married a Witch* with Veronica Lake that Anne and I had seen earlier. It dawned on me that there wasn't anything like that on television—and suddenly, I was inspired. So, I made notes on my thoughts, filed them away for another time, and continued teaching. One of the first things I taught in class was that we are in a craft. Most people do not know that writing is a craft, like carpentry. You learn the art of carpentry to start with, or else you are a carpenter that doesn't know how to use a hammer. Students would hang around after class with more questions, so I formed a group. Our meeting place was at my house. We served donuts, and I charged nothing. I just ran a workshop for writers. While it grew larger every week, a feeling of emptiness was growing inside me. Finally, I told my wife that something was wrong. If one of my students sells a script, I feel gratitude, joy, and pride. However, the struggle was that I should be getting out my creations. I knew I belonged back in the trenches. So, I told her I would take the next job I had a chance to do.

The next call I got was from Harry Akerman. Harry was now an executive of the television arm of Columbia Pictures and having trouble with an idea, and they remembered me. I realized that it was because *My Favorite Husband* failed that they came to me. They wanted me to do a half-hour show. Harry suggested a relaxed atmosphere for a meeting and asked me if I had a preference. I did, and it was one of my favorites. A place that opened in 1919 and is the oldest restaurant in Hollywood. Musso & Frank Grill, noted then, if not now, as one of the premier deal-making places to do lunch.

Harry loved the idea, and we decided to meet there. The day arrived, and in keeping with relaxation, I brought my son with me. It was a good learning experience for him and a wholesome reality for my contemporaries. Ideas intermingled with every bite of food. The atmosphere was electric. The previous script theme I tucked away found its place in the conversation. Harry put down his fork with intense focus and asked me to tell him more. I enthusiastically told of a witch who comes to earth and lives as a mortal. Harry riveted, took out pen and paper, made notes, and never did finish his lunch. We left on a high, and I knew I was back on track. I could still teach, but not at the exclusion of my writing. Business meetings, from then on, were set at the studio offices, and our next step was to fashion the leading characters and the setting.

BEWITCHED

Sol continues,

> There wasn't much choice in this area. In the 1960s, the female star appearing on television had to be a widow, a wife, or a virgin.
>
> A divorced woman was taboo unless she was a supporting character and very funny. So, our star had to have a husband. Again, minimal choice. By tradition, he had to be a WASP (White Anglo-Saxon Protestant) who loved his mother and was slightly retarded in a charming way. His occupation—had to be white-collar, with enough money so that poverty was never hinted at, but not so much money as to lose the story premises. We picked advertising executive, second in popularity only to real estate salesman. These occupations were desirable because they gave our co-star character free time to come home in the middle of the day when needed and the ability to be someplace where he could be reached by phone when his wife had a funny domestic problem.
>
> These decisions are not as superficial as they sound. The setting in a television series—both comedy and dramatic—must be fertile ground for the twenty-six-story premises needed each season. That is why police stations, newspaper offices, and hospitals are among the most frequently used. However, a small house in the suburbs was almost obligatory for the leading character's home in a comedy. Which rarely has an entry hall, so people coming in and going out never disappear from view. Usually, they don't knock. Answering a door takes up too much production and screen time.
>
> The next step was a storyline; this is crucial in a pilot script. It must establish the main characters, the environment, and the primary conflict and still have a story. At this point, it might be informative to recount some seemingly trivial and superficial problems and incidents that occurred on the long road from concept to the airing of this series—things that may seem irrelevant but strongly influence the final product. The exceptional cast of *Bewitched* contributed immensely to the success of the show. I wish I could take at least partial credit for the brilliant casting, but I can't. I had just finished the first draft of the pilot script when I saw Tammy Grimes in an unmemorable movie, but she was my first choice for the part of Samantha. Watching this fine actress, with her elf-like and ethereal quality, I thought she was perfect for a witch who lived as a mortal, and at this point, the role was named Cassandra, not Samantha!
>
> Bill Dozier, head of Screen Gems at the time, agreed enthusiastically.

SOL SAKS

Sol continues,

> Not only that, but Tammy was his friend, and he knew she was vacationing on the west coast at the time. So that morning, Bill and I traveled out to Malibu, script in hand, to interest Tammy in our project. Tammy later auditioned for the role, and we thought she'd be perfect. It would make a better story to relate that she didn't like the concept, but she did. She would happily do the pilot, except she was contracted to do a musical version of Noel Coward's *Blithe Spirit* and wouldn't be available until the following season. I believed strongly enough in my choice to have been willing to wait, but the studio already had the pilot on their itinerary for the coming season.
>
> Days passed, and though we had not settled on an actress to play Samantha, I was pleased to be on my way to Screen Gems to work with Harry. The Santa-Ana winds were blowing fiercely that day, and the walk from the parking structure was a struggle. I held tight to my briefcase and more notes in the other hand. I struggled through the studio doors, trying to hold on to everything and get into the lobby to straighten my belongings, when, suddenly, the doors opened behind me. Two people laughing and buffeted by the wind were pushed by the wind into the room. Gorgeous long blond hair blew in every direction, eclipsing the woman's face. Laughter came from behind the hair mask, and I stood there laughing too. The wind had rushed past me, blowing my notes everywhere. It took me several moments to gather my notes and put them back in order. The woman pushed the hair from her face and told the receptionist she had an appointment with Harry Ackerman. Not really paying attention, I offered to show the couple to his office, but she said she needed to make a quick stop to comb her hair, so I went ahead of them. I didn't get a good look at her until she was seated with Harry and her once disheveled hair back in place. I was surprised to see Elizabeth Montgomery, the daughter of iconic actor Robert Montgomery seated so composed. She was already making a name for herself as a talented actress. Her husband, director Bill Asher was with her and had an idea for a television series. They were puzzled but agreed and took the script home. I was shocked they called back a few hours later.
>
> They left a message saying they were looking for something they could work on together and loved the script. It was perfect, and both would love to do it. I also had been seeking a distinctive, unique gesture with which Samantha would manifest her magic. (Never done is the work of a creator.)

Sol continues,

> Elizabeth and Bill worked together many times, and the outcome was a success. So, we contracted Bill Asher to direct the first year of the series and produce the rest, a winning combination for all. Cast as the lead was Elizabeth, and Cassandra became Samantha. Elizabeth would simultaneously play Samantha's cousin, Serena, on the show!
>
> Like no other, an emotional high is seeing an idea becoming a reality before your eyes. We were all pleased, shook hands, and Bill got up to leave. He was at the door when he suddenly thought of a bit of news we might be able to include. One of the minor accomplishments of his talented wife was that she could twitch her nose. He had stated that her little wriggle was a nervous tick that she had, and it came out when she was scared or when she got frustrated. But not to worry, she could deliver on demand. So was born the legend. What a day we had!
>
> Then came an occurrence that merely proves the adage that anything that can happen will. While on a family visit to Chicago, I received a call with two pieces of news. The ABC network had accepted the series for the new season, and our star was pregnant. So, strangely in those series of coincidences and happenstances, we cast, I believe, the best possible choice for our lead.
>
> I returned to California to a multitude of intense meetings and a note saying, 'Not the first-time grandiloquent ventures were upset by the biological functions of the star. Find a solution!' Well, now what? So, we got together, and the solution held most in favor; was to have the character, Samantha, go through the pregnancy and birth with the actress, Elizabeth, playing her. Lucille Ball had done it on the I Love Lucy show. Lucy was pregnant, and they wrote it in that way. I resisted this. (Although reminded in my prospectus, I had suggested that to energize the following seasons by the birth of a half-witch, half-mortal child.) After a break in the meeting, I remember impulsively saying an incredulous, 'A pregnant witch?!'
>
> Then, I encountered a critical problem. After completing the first draft, I realized that the protagonist could solve any problem with a twitch of her nose, making it difficult, if not impossible, to sustain suspense. In short, I had no conflict. Conflict, the indispensable element, is one of the first lessons in storytelling. It was finally solved by the witch's husband objecting strongly to witchcraft. He extracted a promise from her that she would kick the habit. I attached a note for all future scripts.

SOL SAKS

Sol continues,

>That magic should solve problems only as a last resort, for the same reason. It seems insignificant, but it might have been the difference between a one-season series and a long-running hit. The final issue with the pregnancy of our star was still unresolved. However, I was confident the studio would find an answer and left the solution in their capable hands. It was time to submit my pilot, and though I was confident, I did feel slightly nervous. I took a deep breath and walked my long-worked-on project into the office called *I, Darrin, Take This Witch, Samantha*. I handed it to one of the producers, who smiled and said he loved the title, congratulated me, then left with my script to start production. That was my last day on the job at *Bewitched*.
>
>I went home to visit Anne, had lunch, and let my agent know I was free to work. It was a sad, uncomfortable day that strangely still stands out in my mind. Somehow, I'd become part of a studio family. I had never thought of working conditions in those terms before, and it was something new and puzzling for me. I could not shake the feeling that I had left my child behind.
>
>Still feeling uncomfortable the following day, I returned to my teaching job. I entered a classroom full of bright, eager students. They generously welcomed me back and barraged me with a myriad of questions. They lifted my spirits as I walked through the aisles, answering their questions. I took a moment to catch up on their progress before we began the class. As I approached my desk, I saw a note that said I had an urgent call. That sickening filling of horror shot through me, and I left the room immediately, thinking something had happened to Anne or the children. But instead, it was the studio with the news that there was a dispute regarding *Bewitched*. They asked me to return as soon as possible for a meeting. I finished the class and attended the meeting. The head of the studio thought that they contracted me to write four out of thirteen episodes. Luckily, by then, I was smart enough to have read the contract small-print, and I had an option stating I didn't have to work. Harry continued to make me a terrific offer. His only requirement was to return and write four out of thirteen episodes. Unfortunately, I had to turn him down. I did not want to write the same episodes over and over again. It's a tough, weekly grind of repetition with little if any creativity.
>
>The studio was not happy with my decision. They grumbled, but they did honor my contract.

BEWITCHED

Sol continues,

> The haunting feeling of something left behind faded somewhat but remained an irritation and hard to move past. That is until I got a call with a great job offer from CBS. I was to head the comedy department. Now, that dispelled the rush to return and retrieve my phantom child. In the meantime, the studio resolved the pregnancy issue with Elizabeth Montgomery, and the studio was going into production on the *Bewitched* pilot I wrote. All was well. So, to use two clichés in the same sentence, the star was a trouper, and the show went on.
>
> The final decision was to "shoot around" the pregnancy. The studio went into production immediately and did long shots and behind-the-head of Elizabeth, making fascinating points of view. On-set also was her husband, series director William Asher. At this point, the producers made the necessary adjustments to the conflict. First, they established in this episode a promise from Samantha Stephens that assured her new husband, Darrin, that she would not use magic, and all seemed well. Then, the executives contacted me with an agreement to continue the pattern into each subsequent installment of the series, with the conflict in each episode surrounding Samantha's failed attempts to keep her promise.
>
> My advice to not use too much magic worked well, much to my relief. They continued finding creative ways to camouflage Elizabeth and completed production three weeks after giving birth to her first child; the audience remained unaware of her pregnancy.
>
> The completed first episode of *I, Darrin, Take This Witch, Samantha* was ready by December 6, 1963, then segued into *Bewitched*. Finally, on Thursday, September 17, 1964, the first produced installment aired starring Elizabeth Montgomery.
>
> While shooting, the producers contacted me. They had more magic ideas, but my continued advice, when they asked, was again not to use too much magic. If magic solves all the problems, you have no show. If a woman can twitch her nose and solve any problem, there's no conflict, no sustainable story. They hesitated with objections, then nervously agreed. *Bewitched* became an immediate hit. The trade papers reported the success of the fresh new show, the television news said the 'ratings continue to escalate,' and viewers wrote glowing letters to the studio. Many objected to the premise, but the letters slowly decreased in volume and objections.

SOL SAKS

Sol concludes,
> The first crossover came in the 1965 episode of ABC's *The Flintstones,* titled *Samantha*. It featured Darrin and Samantha Stephens, who had just moved into the neighborhood.
> By the way, the brilliant sound effects to the nose twitching Samantha were by the talented crew.

It was an honored, destiny-making time working with Sol Saks. Though I may not have fully appreciated it at the time, I had no idea it would continue all these years later. As I read my notes from years ago while listening to Sol's stories, I see the wealth of information packed in his expressed memories. The following is a view of the *Bewitched* ensemble from my notes.

A Strong Supporting Cast

Though Bewitched had a fantastic starring cast, its strong supporting cast members were essential to the show. A unanimous favorite among fans was the character of Uncle Arthur, played by actor Paul Lynde. Sol stands behind Elizabeth in this fun picture, watching Paul prepare for his scene!

Paul Lynde/Uncle Arthur

BEWITCHED

Actress Marion Lorne, an adorable favorite, played Aunt Clara and brought more to the show than people knew. To save money, supporting actors on the show, like Marion, had to provide their clothing. The supporting cast would bring in their selections a week before filming the episode, and then the crew working in wardrobe would clean and iron the clothing to be used on filming day. But, of course—this requirement did not extend to the main actors; they were dressed exclusively by the wardrobe department.

Marion Lorne/Aunt Clara

Marion had clothing and accessories perfect for her character Clara, thrilling the wardrobe department and bringing much joy to their corner of the set. Also, the character Aunt Clara was obsessed with doorknobs in the series. A fun fact is that—Marion was obsessed with them in real life too! She had over one thousand antique doorknobs in her collection. This unique hobby of hers was the inspiration for the character she played. The props department enjoyed using many of her pieces on the show.

With her unique and unusual doorknob collection, quirky Aunt Clara won the heart of Darrin and fans everywhere and smoothed relationships within Samantha's feuding family. Indeed, it was a breath of fresh air for Samantha to finally have a family member accepted by her husband, Darrin.

Daphne O'Neal, Los Angeles actress, Design writer, and Public Speaker, wrote this comment,

The Samantha character on *Bewitched* was my childhood role model. Even though she was super gifted, she was always kind and gracious to mortals, like Aunt Clara and even to Gladys Kravitz!! And she only ever used her powers for good, never out of spite or malice. Even as a preschooler, sitting cross-legged in front of the TV, I knew that was the kind of person I wanted to be.

SOL SAKS

Daphne concludes,
> I believed absolutely that Samantha and Darren were in love and that theirs was an example of a good marriage. Even when they disagreed over fundamental issues, you could still feel the love between them. The strength of my conviction is attributable almost entirely to the skills and enormous gifts of Elizabeth Montgomery and Dick York.
> —Daphne O'Neal
> Instagram: @theDaphneoneal

Alice Pearce played the role of Gladys Kravitz in *Bewitched*. The part of Gladys was a nosy neighbor to the Stephens family. She was always suspicious of the things happening at Darrin and Samantha's, which fed on her ever-so-curious nature!

Alice Pearce/Gladys Kravitz

Poor unnerved Gladys; everyone always thought she was a bit crazy because of what she considered was going on at the Stephens household—the problem was that no one ever seemed to see them!

In 1966, Alice completely disappeared from the show. Sadly, this was because she had passed away from ovarian cancer. Four months before being cast as Gladys, her doctor diagnosed her with this deadly disease. She had surgery, but the prognosis was indeed terminal. Simply wanting to work, Alice chose to keep her illness a secret, so it became a complete shock to fans and the cast when she passed away. A dark cloud seemed to hover over the set, but to honor the strength of this beloved actress, they reverently continued. The phrase, "the show must go on," kept every member moving forward with their jobs while holding Alice in their hearts. Two months after she passed, Alice won an Emmy award for Outstanding Supporting Actress for her role as Gladys.

Another fan favorite was the doctor of the Stephens family. They, of course, could not have a regular doctor; they had a witch doctor. His name was Dr. Bombay, played by the talented Welch actor Bernard Fox, a fifth-generation performer, appearing from 1964 to 1972. Dr. Bombay would appear in episodes in crazy costumes. It is not sure if his outlandish costumes were his own or if he was an exception to that clothing rule. He also appeared as Dr. Bombay multiple times on the Tabitha spin-off.

The report is that although he lived until age 89, heart problems began shortly into the series, altering his life substantially until he passed of heart failure at Valley Presbyterian Hospital in Van Nuys.

Calling Dr. Bombay/Bernard Fox

Initially, the role of Darrin's secretary was a woman seen and not a long-standing or speaking part. Then, it became a regular part and was given to Jill Foster, whose character name was Betty, although not always by that character name. She appeared in ten episodes (1965-1969). But following her were several actresses, including actress Marcia Wallace who also played another secretary in the 1970s, The Bob Newhart Show!

Bewitching Secretary's

Jill Foster & Marcia Wallace

SOL SAKS

Next is the adorable Tabitha or Tabitha's. As soon as the twins started in the role, it was apparent that Erin would be the star and play the role of Tabitha the most. So for all the close-up scenes and dialogue, they chose Erin. Next, for the more extended shots, the producers decided on Diana. After *Bewitched*, Erin made an impact in the world, using her Hollywood status to become an advocate for people with Autism. Her son, Parker, has Autism, and she believes and has first-hand information about this cause. She also wore many hats in Hollywood, becoming a casting director, makeup artist, teacher, and more.

They say art parallels real life, especially in this case. Elizabeth gave birth to her biological daughter Rebecca on June 17th. June 17th also happened to be the birthday of Erin and Diane, the twins playing her on-screen daughter, Tabitha; wow, an interesting coincidence!

Left—Diana & Erin Murphy

Tabitha—The Spinoff—Lisa Hartman

While some of the cast members of *Bewitched* were ready for it to end, fans still wanted more. The audience loved the actress who played the role of Tabitha, so the producers created a spinoff named Tabitha. This show followed Samantha and Darrin's daughter Tabitha as an adult. People were excited about the show; however, it disappointed.

Unfortunately, the original Tabitha was not involved with the spinoff, and they cast talented actress Lisa Hartman to play the role of Tabitha. The break in continuity was disturbing to fans even though Lisa did a remarkable job. Reports say it is for that reason, along with many others, that the spinoff did not do well. Lisa moved to Los Angeles at 19 to pursue music and was signed by a record label the same year she landed the role on *Tabitha*. Though this spinoff ended, Lisa had a very successful acting career. She played the role of Cathy on the successful TV show *Knots Landing*.

Theme Song

Did you know that the famous *Bewitched* theme song used for the opening credits has lyrics? Yes—it's true, and they're fantastic! Jack Keller and Howard Greenfield wrote the theme song for Bewitched. The lyrics are interesting; it's as if Darrin was singing it. It is from his perspective. The lyrics suggest what it would be like if he knew that his wife, Samantha, was a witch. Steve Lawrence sang the brilliant version, but the words went unheard until a few years back.

While the studio prepared for the debut of its first episode, the network experienced a significant time crunch. Steve did not get the lyrics to them soon enough, so they went with the version with only instruments and no vocals.

But a clip can be seen on YouTube of Steve Lawrence singing it, lyrics and all!

https://youtu.be/5O9hr5LBeWg

The Magical Location

The *Bewitched* neighborhood of homes was on Blondie Street within the Warner Brother's lot. At the filming of *Bewitched*, that location saw over 50 years of TV shows and movies filmed, often overlapping. For example, during the filming of *Bewitched*, Ms. Kravitz lived in the same home they used to film, *The Partridge Family*. The two shows were filming simultaneously, so both shows shared the same house during two seasons! If the set of Bewitched looks a little familiar to you, you are not alone. It was a reversed copy of the house used in the movie Gidget in 1959. First, they duplicated the living room and patios from the film. Then, on TV shows Dennis the Menace and I Dream of Jeannie, the exterior of the Bewitched home became theirs; everyone shared. A couple of big-name stars began their careers on Bewitched.

SOL SAKS

One of them was Richard Dreyfuss, cast in his first television role in an episode in 1966 entitled "Man's Best Friend." He played the role of a bratty boy named Rodney.

Samantha and Darrin celebrate in this episode because she has not used her powers in a month; this is when they introduce Rodney. We understand that Samantha used to be his babysitter; at this point, he is older and comes back to tell Samantha that he loves her. However, she does not return his love and tells him that she loves her husband, Darrin. Rodney does not take the news well and uses his magic to turn himself into a dog so that he can stay with Samantha in her home. Darrin loves the dog so much, even though the dog is out to get him. Hmm, what a mess. Samantha needs to use her powers, after all.

Then there was the iconic actor Peter Lawford, one of the "Rat Pack," who played Harrison Woolcott, Serena's wealthy, mortal love interest, in the 1972 eighth season's episode, Serena's Richcaft.

Foreground Peter Lawford—Behind Director Bill Asher
On the *Bewitched* set

By the way, on December 2, 1972, ABC Hanna-Barbera Productions produced the second crossover. An animated TV special for *The ABC Saturday Superstar Movie*, featuring a teenage version of Tabitha and brother Adam visiting their aunt and family who travel with a circus. We wondered if fun-loving Peter had anything to do with that storyline.

BEWITCHED

Samantha-Serena Similarities

The two, both played by Elizabeth, while very different, also had many similarities. Just like Samantha, Serena hung out with Mortals. She also dated them; however, she was not married; she was more of a hippie swinger. She approved of Samantha marrying Darrin, who was just a mortal. Typically the two characters were not filmed in the same scene because that kind of technology was not around yet, but they would try to use a split screen to have them appear simultaneously.

The Tournament of Rose Parade Commercial

In 1966 Elizabeth Montgomery was set to host the Tournament of Roses Parade. In a funny commercial aired late in 1965, the off-screen commentator asked if Elizabeth had a recommendation for a co-host; she did! Elizabeth suggests the beloved Vin Scully, the Dodgers baseball team announcer. (Hollywood and the Dodgers have been a long-time team.) The announcer says, sadly, that Vin is unavailable; he's in Florida playing in a golf tournament. So beautiful Elizabeth twitches her nose to magically summon Vin, mid-swing, from a golf course. From there, it's a battle to see who can be more charming, and of course, Vin says he'd love to join her. It's a wonderfully fun commercial that captured America at that time.

https://www.youtube.com/watch?v=F0JTOrX2T2Q

FORE!

SOL SAKS

The Famous Christmas Episode

The famous Christmas episode, Sisters at Heart, was written by a group of African American high school students in Marcella Saunders' class in Central LA at Jefferson High School. This episode aired on Christmas Eve and was meant as an eye-opening moment while telling the tale of a beautiful story. However, this episode would never air today because of its political incorrectness. Several cast members appear in blackface at some point during the show.

"Would you say that the *Bewitched* series works because it's a husband and wife with cultural differences and a mother-in-law that everyone can relate to, and the witchcraft is just incidental? Also, did you write the Christmas episode?"

There's nothing different, except it happened to be a new premise for television. The daughter and mother-in-law these characters were new people for television, a new attitude. That difference was enjoyable writing. It's usually good writing when it's fun writing, even easy. My premise created room for expanding storylines, but I didn't write or suggest The Christmas Story. When I wrote the pilot, there was a scene where Samantha followed Darrin to the bedroom, exhausted after a party they had given. Then, feeling uneasy because she never left dirty dishes and a mess in the kitchen, she returned to the kitchen. However, Darrin insinuates there will be sex, so she snaps her finger, and the kitchen is now spotless. How many women and men have thought or wished they could do that?

Years after our dear Sol Saks passed, I had the good fortune to meet a beautiful soul in Dundee, Scotland, through social media. Her name is Shehanne Moore, a most talented author and, happy to say, friend. Below is a tribute compilation of texts I received from her.

I wanted to tell you how big a cult thing *Bewitched* was when I was wee. We used to play it in the playground; we had nose-twitching competitions. We all wanted to be Samantha. Just wriggle our noses, and things happen. It was epic. Also, in the 60s, when Tabitha came along, we all thought it was epic and that Tabitha was such a brill name for Sam's daughter. Years later, in 1981, when we were first married and left with a sink full of dirty dishes. I remembered an episode from the TV series that was like this night. We asked friends over one night, thinking if only I were Samantha and could wriggle my nose and clear this up. —Shehanne Moore
https://shehannemoore.wordpress.com

BEWITCHED

Are the Stephens' the first two-broom family on the block?

New Season

abc 9:00 In Color

Elizabeth had three real-life pregnancies during her eight seasons of working on *Bewitched*. As previously said, the producers and writers found creative ways to conceal her first pregnancy in 1964. The second and third became part of the storyline and script. Pregnancy and birth progressed well together, and added the characters of Tabitha and Adam to Elizabeth and Darrin's TV family, enhancing the show's plot and keeping everything looking natural and running smooth! Luckily for fans everywhere and crew, Elizabeth did not need to take a hiatus. She continued seamlessly as the consummate professional that she was.

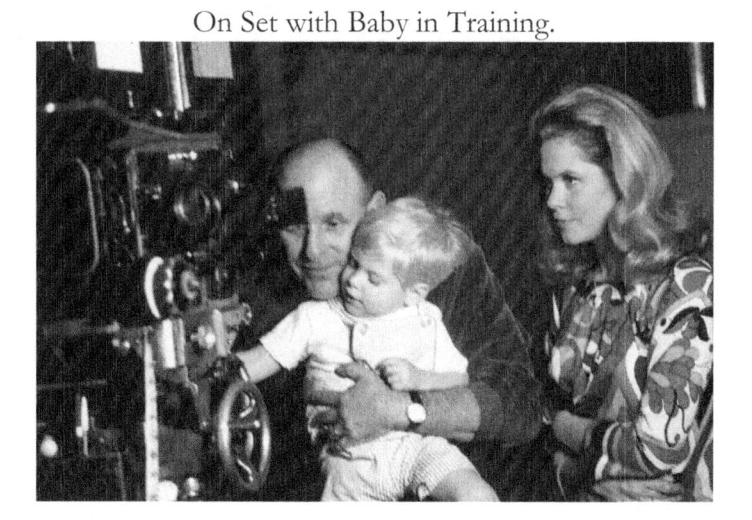

On Set with Baby in Training.

SOL SAKS

"What did you think of the shows with the same premise after *Bewitched*? *I Dream of Jeanie,* for instance."

I got a few calls after *Bewitched* was a success because the studio wanted another pilot. They described the show as the daughter of Elizabeth, a witch also going to New York. I told them they were doing *Bewitched* all over again, another generation of *Bewitched*—I didn't want to do it. They made it anyway, but it didn't last. They did discover, which I accidentally did too, that this out-of-the-world stuff goes way back to the Greeks, where a statue, Pygmalion, comes to life. I later got a call from Screen Gems asking me to do another show, and I thought they meant another hit show. They explained that they wanted another show with a witch—and I said I didn't want to do another one! That other show was *I Dream of Jeanie*! My decision was mentally healthier for me, but not financially. I preferred to write just pilots. Looking back, I don't regret that decision. My name remained in the credits for all 253 episodes. The show finished second in primetime, just behind *Bonanza*, becoming ABC's top series, running eight years, from 1964 to 1972, and inspired a 2005 *Bewitched* feature film.

The Bewitched Rose

"My life is part humor, part roses, part thorns."

—Bret Michaels

The Bewitched Rose

To balance the stress and dark shadows in the entertainment industry, varied beauties of nature subtly whisper to stop and enjoy their presence. Still, Sol passed them in a rush while mentally preparing for his writing day. That is until a letter arrived.

It reads,

> One such remedy for unpleasant moments in life is this lovely rose's fragrance. Your senses are delighted when you stop for a moment to breathe in its sweet perfume. A medium pink Hybrid tea rose was introduced into the United States in 1967. The Germain Seed & Plant Company later chose the marketing name *Bewitched;* in honor of the television series *Bewitched,* which I understand you created. The stock parents are the Hybrid tea rose cultivars, Queen Elizabeth and Tawny Gold. An interesting coincidence between Elizabeth and her golden-haired child. Maybe that is a stretch, but we loved the similarities and hoped you would.
>
> Oh, and by the way, in 1967, your rose won two awards: All-America Rose Selections and Portland Gold Medal.
>
> Congratulations, and we wish you much future success.

Tugging inside his mind were disappointments, tributes Sol longed for but didn't receive. Nonetheless, he battled to think better thoughts; *a rose named after a show I created is a distinct honor, a priceless, unimagined gift. A superbly gorgeous rose named after the work from my imagination dispenses love every day to me, my family, and passersby. I think my parents, especially my mother, would love this rare gesture. I'll keep the letter on my desk to remind me to stop and enjoy the fragrance and form of this time-honored award.*

The battle of depression raged within Sol. The fight to be happy was exhausting. Nevertheless, it would be a habit he must strive to cultivate. Days later, two of these pink *Bewitched* classics arrived, and his gardener planted them proudly in Sol's front garden. These beauties stand five feet tall, bearing large lovely buds and blooms filled with rich intoxicating perfume and held bravely on long dark green stems. Each stately bush clothed with large glossy apple-green foliage resembles holly leaves. Indeed, they would complement any garden.

In the morning, before his stroll along Sutton Street, Sol reminded himself of his doctor's advice. "Make a choice to be happy, Sol." So, he stopped to smell his *Bewitched Roses*. He paused to observe their striking shades of pink and encouraged himself on his good fortune. He began to see that appreciating those seemingly small gifts he overlooked took practice. Soon what he deemed small became cherished and honestly valued.

A new understanding of life as he knew it arrived also. Friends and family who died, leaving lingering, painful grief, seemed to ease as he learned that love never dies.

SOL SAKS

As days, months, and years progressed, Sol mentioned that it was as if they passed through a door into another place, enjoying a better life; it was a knowing he found true. This door, shut to him now, would open one day just for him, and he would see them again. However, for now, he must focus on the life bestowed on him. Sol began to enjoy a richer dimension of everything and everyone around him. He read that the *Bewitched Rose* was now within thousands of gardens worldwide, filling the air with a rich scent. The article brought a lovely feeling of joy that reminded him of the beauty among the thorns, the victory after the struggle. For Sol, the velvet, delicate petals became the beauty of each person that traveled through his life.

All these thoughts rested quietly within Sol as I arrived at Sutton Street for a day of writing. It was the beginning of August, and the morning was warm, sunny, and full of the fragrance of pine and roses. As I walked down the brick driveway, just minutes before nine, I was surprised to find Sol in the front garden admiring the petals of his beautiful roses. The gardener had finished mowing, turning the soil, and cleaning every corner; the garden looked especially appealing. Sol had an early breakfast, had just returned from his morning walk, and motioned me over to take a closer look at the roses. He decided he would like to spend the morning writing outside among the flowers under the stately trees. The gardener had moved a small table and two chairs from the poolside and placed them by the stunning pink roses.

Sol's face beamed while announcing that working within the front landscape might be a refreshing change, and he asked me what I thought; I happily agreed. This movie-set spot looked inspiring, a shaded destination unused until now. I brought what we needed from the office then we began. Streaks of sun beamed like a spotlight through the trees, resting warmly upon the now glowing roses. The warm summer breezes brushed past us, charging the atmosphere with a glorious perfume. I could not help but breathe in its intoxicating fragrance. I was immediately relaxed as if I had finished a glass of champagne. I remarked that we should always work in this very spot. Sol smiled in agreement while becoming inspired by the pulsating nature surrounding him. He leaned forward, looking out in the distance as he began a brief, unusually touching story.

> When I decided to be a writer, there were no thoughts about spin-offs from a show. I only wanted to be good at my chosen profession and maybe even be recognized for my contributions. But first and foremost, I wanted to provide a good living for my family. I find recognitions I've won challenging to describe or put into words.

Pausing for one brief contemplative momentmoment, he reached over to touch a fragrant petal on his roses, then continued,

These, for me, have become honors, enduring awards I treasure. Of course, I admit I would love to receive a Pulitzer. But, I'm finding my most significant rewards are in the battles I've won, like when I was a kid and felt different. No one at that age likes to feel different. I got over it; I'm proud to be Jewish and a child of Polish immigrants.

Sol looked to the corner of his garden; a twinkle of victory lit up his eyes; he lifted his head with a substantial look of triumph and continued,

Do you see that lone prickly cactus in the corner? It doesn't look like anything else in the garden, standing out like a sore thumb, yet it survives on very little and can handle the hottest days that the weather demands. It is undeniably a survivor. The only conventional beauty is the occasional unique bloom. Yet, there is substantial beauty inside, like my parents had, an inner strength they developed. Against all odds, they opened a business, treated people well, and not only survived but thrived. Their courage to reach for a better life fueled me to continue attending school daily. Then, slowly I became brave enough to step out and follow my dreams. The rest I figured out as I continued.

As I prepare to celebrate my 100th birthday in a few months, I know there's a vast universe of information I've yet to discover; disappointments seem to block them. I've read that when anger, disappointment, and negativity are present in your mind, creativity becomes like trying to grab hold of fog; I find that true. So, my day becomes better when I stop being hard on myself. When I take a moment to be grateful, it helps those regrets ease. Ideas and words start forming, maybe not great ones, but as I write, they improve.

I also remember what I like the most about writing; finding better solutions. I've gained satisfaction and recognition for that. Unfortunately, I haven't found a solution for nagging disappointments, but gratefulness is becoming firm in my mind. I have friends who won a Pulitzer, and we were thrilled for them.

We threw a party in honor of their good fortune and celebrated as they acquired more money and a bigger home. But after several months, they confessed that something was missing. They were puzzled, they had achieved the dream, but that feeling of dissatisfaction returned.

Though I still wanted to win an award, their experience confirmed that lasting victories are those intangibles. For example: surviving the challenges in life made me grow as a person, a writer, a friend, and, hopefully, into a better father.

SOL SAKS

Sol concludes,

> Those are the awards that enriched and filled that space inside. They are substantial and have become a part of who I am. I forget this valuable fact now and then, especially when I'm tired, then I must remind myself again. For me, reading books written by people I admire helps me. I also learn from their experiences. So many old classics taught me these struggles had been around since the beginning, and successful people conquered them.

I listened intently to every word Sol spoke as I wrote them down. Each word carried something powerful, somehow different today. Then, Sol suddenly turned his face from me and went into the house. Sitting alone, I re-read each word he spoke, and they were as powerful as when I first heard them. I wondered what it was that made these words more special.

As I was about to return to the office, Sol walked into the garden; his eyes were red and moist. He didn't say a word but began pacing back and forth. I'd learned by then not to react to the awkwardness of the moment. Instead, I reviewed my notes until he stopped and said we would expand on his novel with fresh insight. Sol had dictated more than a thousand new words by the end of the working day and was hopeful of its publication. He entered the house to fix a cup of coffee, and I returned to the office, arranged for the next work day, locked the door, and descended the spiral stairs. Sol was waiting in the front garden; coffee and one long-stem rose in hand with the thorns thoughtfully removed. As he handed me the fragrant, dewy pink rose, he shyly said, "I'll see you Monday, Carolyn; this was a good change! "Lovely change Sol, and thank you; see you Monday."

The Bewitched Barbie Doll

In the dell of our garden, my dolls and I take tea,
and days when I have raisins,
the catbirds dine with me.
—Angela K.

According to Sol, the rights to Bewitched were his, but without notice, a studio sold them with no remuneration given to him. It was a bitter pill that went unresolved, even with the best of lawyers. Sol expounded in frustrated puzzlement,

> *Bewitched* was the only show I created that began with controversy and continued with problems. At the airing of *Bewitched*, people complained, and arguments rose from many corners. Churches and several synagogues complained that to portray witches in a somewhat wholesome way was not wise, not healthy. I remember their loud protests making no sense to me then, and I had lots to say about their remarks. But as we continued, the angry voices diminished to a whisper, and the show gained notoriety. Eventually, a popular spin-off of *Bewitched* was born, along with the beautiful *Bewitched* Barbie Doll; voices rose again! But the *Bewitched* Barbie became a much-loved doll by children and adults. I remember my sisters playing with dolls as a child, and when these appeared on market shelves, they reflected fond memories of those days of childhood play. I did not see anything wrong with them, but many people did.

SOL SAKS

Sol concluded,

> Those first unique dolls in 1965, costing a few dollars, are now a collectible earning anywhere from $325.00 to $3,500.00. Unfortunately, my contract did not include a percentage of the money from the extra cash *Bewitched* generated. At times, the disappointment became burdensome, but I learned to force it to one side and get on with writing. On the occasion of a dreary rainy day or not getting enough sleep, though success was around me, it was not enough. Finding that balance is a hard lesson to learn. The injustices overshadowed what was sitting before me like an unseen war. I tried to find a way to let it go, to keep the enjoyment of writing and discovery alive. Being satisfied with my success yet wanting to do better, I believe, is healthy. However, there are fine lines between wanting to do better, greed, and remaining grateful in the face of a glaring wrong done. It's strange how fuzzy the lines get at times; I endeavor to learn, forgive, and move on, but it's a daily struggle.

6

Alison, Sol, and Hollywood

"Dreams are renewable. No matter what our age or condition, there are still untapped possibilities within us and new beauty waiting to be born."
—Dale E. Turner

In a shady suburb of New York City, a vacant place stands where my dear friend Alison and her husband lived, raised their children, and later died. Since she was a child, Alison read everything she could about Hollywood and dreamed of becoming an actress. However, as she entered the entertainment world in New York, she soon learned that the dream she carried was far better than reality. Becoming an actress was not for Alison, but still, she longed to see the iconic places of Hollywood that continued to fascinate her. The famous restaurants, studios, and stores on Rodeo Drive in Beverly Hills. But one covert stand-out is the famed House of Westmore Salon, reported as the world's most well-known beauty salon. She called to tell me that she was coming to Hollywood for a visit in a month and had arranged a surprise for me. So, was it possible to keep the morning she arrived just for her and me? I agreed immediately!

Alison left the oppressive summer humidity of New York and arrived in the dry, sweltering heat of Los Angeles. However, no matter the weather, Alison was undeterred. She confessed that her childhood dream was at the top of her list, to see a movie star, but first, she wanted to take me for the arranged surprise; an appointment for the two of us at that iconic glamourous mecca, The House of Westmore Salon on Sunset Boulevard. Moved to tears, I shared that I had not been there in years and was looking forward to luxurious, elegant pampering.

It had been a couple of years since Alison and I first met in Paris, and it was lovely to see her and reminisce. On our drive to Westmore's, I shared my surprise with her but held back the location. Dinner at a brilliant restaurant that never disappoints either in food, atmosphere, or the occasional sighting of a movie star. Her eyes widened as she named a few of her favorites, but we had arrived at Westmore's; our dinner destination would have to wait.

SOL SAKS

We pulled into the parking lot, laughing and excited at the prospects ahead. Alison was to experience her first visit, and I hadn't been there since I was a child on a mother-daughter outing. The exterior was the same as I remembered; that charming look of old Hollywood. We walked into the lobby, and euphoric memories rushed through my mind. Then, a woman behind the desk broke through my memories, greeting us with a smile and offering us coffee. Next, she escorted us into a beautifully appointed room. Though Westmore's had retained the old-world charm, opulent décor, and elegance, they seamlessly incorporated their facility with the latest technology; it was glorious to be there. There is an energy of history beyond description, and simply brilliant to experience.

The Westmore family's involvement in Hollywood is legendary and one of Elizabeth Montgomery's favorite destinations. However, a fun secret most of the public didn't know was that most stars never walked through the front door. Instead, they slipped quietly through a back entrance, taken to a hidden room, and the relaxing metamorphosis could begin without anyone knowing they were there.

While having my hair washed, reclining in splendor, the day I spent here as a child began to emerge. My mother and I were in this same situation when we heard a familiar voice from the next room. Mom asked in a whisper if it was actress Betty Davis. You could not mistake her distinctive voice; the beautician nodded yes. Betty was conveying her wishes to the assistant in an exuberant voice, then began a funny but scandalous story. No one in our room said a word. It was like being in the midst of one of her movies for a moment. All were spellbound as each adult listened, wide-eyed to every nuance. Until the woman trimming my mother's hair left for a brief moment to advise Ms. Davis.

Then, sadly, silence fell next door, depriving us of the end of her story. With our hair trimmed and perfectly styled, we walked into the lobby, finding Betty Davis looking gorgeous and bigger than life. She looked at me and smiled; I, beaming, wanted to rush up and ask her about the ending, but mom took me by the hand, and as we said goodbye to Betty, we left. In the span of years, Westmore's wisely included soundproofing.

Leaving the memories behind, I was thrilled to be back again with Alison. One of life's exquisite pleasures is spending time at a top beauty salon or spa; this afternoon was one of those moments. Alison and I emerged from Westmore's feeling quite lovely. A facial, manicure, pedicure, makeup, and hair are camera-ready.

Our next destination was a surprise sumptuous dinner. I drove the famed Sunset Boulevard for wide-eyed speechless Alison. Never taking her eyes off the activity, she reached over, touched my shoulder, and asked if I would mind going a little slower so she could absorb every beautiful site. I slowed down, then Alison suddenly remembered a surprise dinner and asked, "Where are we going?" "Another couple of miles, and you'll see." A wave of joy and anticipation flooded the car to the point of loud laughter. I moved to the slow lane and brought the car to a crawl as we reached the driveway leading to our destination, The Beverly Hills Hotel.

Alison gasped, and for a moment, her breathing stopped. Then, in a voice filled with shock and overwhelming joy, she said, "Oh my gosh, I never thought, Oh, I can't believe I'm here!" Tears poured from our eyes as we turned onto the driveway. For many people, that vantage point still holds a thrillingly romantic and historical presence, even for most Californians, including me.

But, for Alison, it was a breathtaking, long-awaited sight shrouded in Hollywood magic. As we made our way up the drive, she gasped again while wiping the tears from her face. Flooding her mind were years of compiled history, sensational gossip tidbits, and those glamorous movies appearing before her.

At last, we stopped at the entrance between two handsome valets in classic black suits and white gloves. With welcoming smiles, they opened our doors and graciously extended their hands to assist us from the car. Another valet held the hotel door for us as we entered; Alison was in breathless awe as we found our way to the luxuriously appointed Polo Lounge.

Polo Lounge

The lights were low, with tiny lights marking the meandering path within the emerald green walls of this beautifully decorated room. The maître d' escorted us across the luxurious patterned carpet to a side booth lit with a charming shimmering lamp. We chatted a bit as our eyes adjusted to the change in lighting, then ordered a drink. The iconic hotel's glamor, history, and elegant atmosphere consumed Alison completely. The decision of what to eat became a struggle. She looked up at the waiter, almost in a trance, and asked him to please decide for her. I could not believe this was my composed friend Alison. I quickly concealed my surprised smile with the corner of the linen napkin. As our food arrived, she spotted actor Richard Gere seated with a friend not far from us. The attentive waiter served our food while Alison did her best to contain herself. Watching her, I could hardly keep the secret of having dessert with one of her favorite people.

The Polo Lounge serves consistently outstanding and superbly plated food; however, Alison was star-struck and unable to take a bite. With her fork in hand and both draped across her chest in astonishment, she found it impossible to eat while gazing at handsome Richard.

She tried to direct my eyes in his direction, but her efforts were suddenly interrupted. The imposing Sylvester Stallone slowly strolled by our table. Alison froze; her fork dropped from her hand, landing on her plate with a loud clang, sending it tumbling to the floor. Mr. Stallone stopped and retrieved her lost utensil and handed it to her.

With her eyes wide and fixed hypnotically on him, she breathlessly took hold of the fork. I thanked him and said she was visiting from New York. His understanding smile lit up our space as he nodded and continued to his destination. Alison quickly put the coveted prized fork in her purse and asked me if I realized who that was. With a restrained laugh, I called the waiter for a fresh set of cutlery. She took a long sip of wine, a deep breath, then finally took a bite of her food. Returning once more to earth, she commented that the food was outstanding. At last, she was able to enjoy every brilliantly prepared mouthful. At that point, I thought it was best not to tell her that the dessert was waiting in Malibu.

At the end of our star-gazed dinner, with Richard and Sly still swirling around in my dear friend's mind, I announced our next destination was Malibu. The man of the hour was Sol Saks and hosting dessert. Alison, a big fan of *Bewitched*, was over the moon, and I was thrilled she was pleased. Her late father wrote history books, and Alison grew up with a great appreciation of the written word and the brilliantly talented writers who brought them to life.

We drove the stretch of Pacific Coast Highway overlooking our beautiful ocean. Summer in Southern California is the perfect time to linger at the beach, and this night was no exception. As we drove slowly along the coast, Alison was like a kid at Disneyland. She had her window down, captivated by Malibu's sights, sounds, and calming ocean air.

We finally arrived. Alison quickly fixed her hair and asked if she looked alright. She looked amazing! As we left the car, Alison stopped and hugged me, saying thank you for making a dream come true. Now I was in tears and speechless. Emotionally undone, we began descending the wooden stairs. Alison stopped to compose herself, then continued commenting on the flowers in the courtyard below. She was amazed that flowers seemed to grow everywhere in our state. Our host left the front door to his home open, and from that vantage point, we could see the ocean through the glass windows on the other side of his living room. I knocked and called out for Sol. Sol, busy opening a bottle of wine, looked around the corner with a big smile and invited us in. He introduced himself to Alison and asked how we enjoyed our time at The Polo Lounge. Then, he escorted us to the table and chairs on the balcony and turned the railing lights off to give us a unique view.

SOL SAKS

Bioluminescent plankton floating under the ocean's surface flashed intensely like sparkling blue lights within each crashing wave. Then the sparkling water traveled beneath the house, lighting up the sand. It was magical. Overlooking the strange glowing water, Alison shared her love of writing with Sol. Feeling at home and comfortable, she told of the books written by her father that proudly sat on several college library shelves. Having taught in our local colleges, Sol recalled two titles while Alison sat in astonishment. To have a writer she admired know of her father's work was a treasured moment she said she would never forget. Her father died some years prior, but Alison still missed him daily. Her face lit up as she announced that this day's unusual beauty helped wipe away the lingering vestige of grief.

For me, visiting with friends while gazing out over the expansive sea beautifully dotted with sailboats is always glorious. But tonight, as the boats passed slowly through the water with the dazzling blue of the "sea-sparkle," surrounding and trailing them, it was unusually magnificent. The unique waves crashed below us with determined strength while washing away every care. There was something incredibly calming about this home, not just tonight but every time I visited.

Amongst our laughter and ever-present storytelling, the doorbell rang. Sol left for the door, announcing that it was dessert from a favorite restaurant, Wolfgang Pucks. A young man entered, holding two large canvas bags. While placing them on the balcony table, he introduced himself as Jason. Alison and I sat enthralled as Jason unpacked the bags and offered each of us a glass of Champagne. Unfortunately, I had sparkling water because I was to drive the winding steep Malibu Canyon home. But what came next helped ease the deprivation. French Crepe Suzette was being prepared expertly before us!

Sol knew about Alison's fascination with actors, so he arranged a special surprise for her. Another knock at the door came, but Sol remained seated this time. The door opened slowly, and we sat intrigued. Then, while staring toward the front door, a tall, lean man with a cowboy hat pulled down to hide his face walked through the living room and onto the balcony.

First, he said hello to Sol, then introduced himself to Alison and me while removing his disguise. Alison was speechless. It was actor Dennis Weaver and Sol's next-door neighbor. Dennis asked if he could join us, and Sol, pleased with the surprise, laughed and said, "Please do and make yourself at home, great performance, by the way." Dennis smiled, took the seat next to Alison, and I think I heard her giggle.

Jason announced dessert was ready for the final touch, brought his masterpiece to the balcony table, poured brandy on them, and set the Crepes ablaze! What a dramatic, luxurious dessert set within an unparalleled view with friends.

Jason served Dennis a glass of Champagne, then placed a warm, delectable Crepe Suzette before us. This entire night seemed like a page from a perfectly planned movie script, and I was along for the ride.

Dennis Weaver

Dennis, best known for the television series McCloud, had similar endearing qualities to the character of Sam McCloud. A very intelligent, kind, and honorable man. However, unlike his character, he was a more charming guest brimming with engaging conversation. Dennis was an early environmentalist, and we talked about alternative fuels and wind power, which was relatively new to me then. In addition, he once served as president of the Screen Actors Guild, giving him unique insight into the questions Alison asked about Hollywood.

Crepe Suzette never tasted as good as on that enchanting evening. Alison was beaming, Sol was delighted, Dennis was gracious, and I was grateful for a small part in a lifetime gift to my dearest friend Alison. Shortly after dessert, Alison and I left for home. As we stood at the door, Sol pointed to a hidden key and invited us to use his home anytime during that week. So, Alison and I happily return for two fun days.

We walked through the shallow waves as they ran over the soft sand, chatted with neighbors, went out for a morning of fishing, and visited some of the best restaurants Malibu has to offer. Her favorite was Alice's Restaurant, which was also a favorite place for Sol. Throughout the time I worked with Sol, whenever he was not occupying his Malibu retreat, my family and I enjoyed many lovely weekends in the tranquil comforts of his Malibu home.

With his open invitation, the entire property was ours to enjoy. The cozy snug off the living room held a unique round, large comfortable sofa, thoughtfully situated. While resting on this lovely couch, you could overlook the sparkling blue ocean, watch tv, or relax with a good book.

If you were lucky to be on the sofa when the sun rested upon the water at high tide, the reflections it cast throughout the room were a magical wonder. Sparkling lights danced on every surface of the front rooms. One might imagine creation was sending blessings to all present.

In the corner also was an exceptional sound system Sol purchased while in Denmark. A sleek contemporary design filled the house with auditory sensations so clear that if you closed your eyes, you felt like the musicians were in the room. The two bedrooms toward the entrance were lovely, possibly more tranquil, but without that stunning ocean view. I found myself wanting to sleep on the couch instead.

During the two days Alison and I spent there, she, filled with wonder, wanted to sleep out on the deck. It was something she had never done, and she could not get enough of the view. So, she grabbed a blanket and pillow, placed them on a deck chair, and said she lay there gazing at the breathtaking beauty until she relaxed into a child-like sleep.

I also grabbed a blanket and pillow and, from the cozy couch, watched the sailboats gliding over a moonlit sea and the occasional night surfer passing with mesmerizing fascination. A palpable connection to nature enveloped me as I felt the weight of the water crashing against the pylons that suspended the house. Each gently crashing wave dissolved every worry, and sleep was sweetly divine.

The following morning, before my eyes opened, the warm sunlight rested upon my face, gently waking me. The first sight of the day was the incomparable sparkling water. Crashing gently over an outcrop of black rocks a few feet out, then moving lazily across the sand. White Seagulls were landing at the water's edge, searching for food and waking dear Alison. Stretching, she announced she had not slept and felt so relaxed.

A rush to be out in this grandeur filled us like a cup of strong coffee; we quickly dressed, descended the sandy wooden stairs at the back door, and stepped into the warm, soft sand. We strolled and talked for miles through the clear shallow waves and chatted with passing neighbors along the way. The tide was usually out in the early morning, and the walk along the water was exhilarating, calming, and a feast for the eyes. Then it was back for breakfast.

Anne, I suspect, was responsible for the well-equipped kitchen. But, what stood out was the thoughtfulness within every corner of this conservative dwelling. Every pot, pan, and accessory needed to prepare a sumptuous meal was present and available for friends. Moreover, all the comforts of a loving home were welcoming to every visitor. Most guests would bring food and a bit extra to leave for the next person or Sol.

I had grown fond of an occasional yummy cappuccino, so along with my food, I carried a small cappuccino machine and coffee with me. Alison and I prepared a delicious frittata, enough for several people, fresh mixed berries, and cappuccino's sprinkled with chocolate. These fragrant delectables mixed with the sounds of the sea and laughter were near perfection.

After breakfast, we headed to a storage room beneath the house. Games, toys, beach chairs, paddleboards, small pails, shovels, and beach umbrellas were all valued treasures from happy days spent with his family. Sol encouraged all his visitors to use them as if they were their own. Alison and I grabbed beach chairs and an umbrella and settled on the sand to read Hemingway's *A Moveable Feast* and discuss Paris and writing until it was time to leave. I enjoyed every glorious moment.

Knowing Sol was to arrive the following day, we left a generous portion of frittata and berries, plus a bottle of his favorite wine, Châteauneuf-du-Pape. Ahh, life is good.

I carried home the sounds and sights with me that day, and they have lasted these many years. Alison and I continued talking, emailing, and texting, but that was our last face-to-face visit; she died several years later in her home in New York. However, as once said, true friendship never dies; it becomes part of who we are. So, I cherish those days with Alison with such bittersweet gratefulness, my dear friend who added overflowing adventure, fun, and beauty to life.

Alice's Restaurant at 23000 Pacific Coast Highway, perched on the Malibu pier.

Alice's Restaurant is sadly gone, but not the warm memories. As yet, no restaurant can replace the favorite gathering spot for countless people, including Sol.

SOL SAKS

The iconic eatery was within a mile of his home and easily accessed from the beach—Europe's answer to a friendly pub. On occasion, Sol would call and order his lunch to go. Then, with a small pad and pencil tucked in his pocket, he walked the shallow waves to pick up his food while waiting at the bar. Sol remarked that an intriguing, creative atmosphere filled every corner of Alice's and then seemed to drift out along the wooden pier. He could find the often-elusive inspiration just waiting for him there. Night or day, it consistently fed the human soul before a single glance at the menu or an order was given.

For Sol, this day was too stimulating to sit inside. So instead, he opted for an outside bench on the pier overlooking the water.

The wooden planks creaked as each passerby tread the old boards, some glancing directly into his eyes. I wonder if they realized a talented writer was using his gift while sitting comfortably in the sun. Did they know he would sometimes catch a hidden story within their glance? This particular day, it was about to happen. A young family with their new baby walked by, stopping close to the bench Sol occupied, they smiled, and Sol smiled back. As the family gazed beyond the railing to the ocean below, a slow internal narrative began in Sol's mind. He put his lunch aside, capturing each miraculous word on paper. Each word strung together became a captivating story that would later find its way into his play, *Faces of Love*. The family, unaware, wandered further down the pier, talking and laughing. As Sol watched the happy trio, he wondered if they knew how lucky they were, if they could appreciate these fleeting moments. Bittersweet memories filled his mind with the days spent with Anne and his small children. Clutching his new story tightly, he reached for the remainder of his lunch, then strolled the edge of the waves until he arrived home again to return another day.

Over time, Sol, a shy man, developed an amiable personality that attracted people who readily engaged him in conversation. Sol used his conversations as character studies for plays by divulging their points of view on various subjects. Within the cozy walls of his favorite Restaurant, Sol seemed to find the most captivating people. Their experiences and lifestyles were so different from his that he listened intently-fascinated then responded with more questions. His time spent was stimulating for all. Sol said his goodbyes to return home and write down all he had learned with restrained manners. As was his custom, he drew inspiration from them while diving mentally into a new writing adventure. In the early years of his writing, Sol explained,

> I'd wake up in the middle of the night with a clear idea or solution to a problem I had with a scene. Then, convinced I would remember it in the morning, I'd go back to sleep.

Sol concludes,
> The following morning, what was clear, was now muddled. Now, I keep a pencil and paper beside my bed to capture every idea.

Bob Yuro co-owned the beloved Alice's Restaurant from 1972 to 1995. Like Sol, Bob's natural love for people created a home-like atmosphere for everyone who entered through the doors. Sol remembers,
> While sitting at the bar for an evening drink, I could hear people saying how much fun Alice's was, that the candlelight and view of the ocean were dreamy, something was comforting in this place, and fun rolled into one that they couldn't explain. The residents owning boats would tie their craft to the side of the pier, then sit at a table overlooking the water while enjoying a well-prepared meal and cocktail. On several occasions, I saw ships' captains anchor their massive vessels beyond the breakers and use smaller boats to bring deckhands in for a drink at the end of a long day at sea; it was quite a sight. As I watched, I thought these moments seemed like something out of a novel, and I considered buying a boat for a time but quickly gave up the notion.

Dear reader, I'd like to add a few words about Malibu Pier, including a personal invitation to please feel free to drop a fishing line when you're in the area and enjoy the rare atmosphere that fills this anointed space. Then, when you have a moment, let me know about your experience. Next, the Malibu area is a special place holding unique magic, a relatively short distance from Santa Monica and Los Angeles. Second, it exudes a different atmosphere than its more crowded cousins to the east. Before the construction of Alice's, Malibu Pier was opened to the public in 1938 and invited people to enjoy fishing the sea's bounty. Over time, comments, moments, and remembrances from those beautiful souls amid the refreshing ocean breezes were collected and preserved. I've included one from 1938 from a note for you to read, signed by John.
> Today, the endless sparkling Pacific Ocean is unusually active with corbina and mackerel; they're here year-round, but I've never seen such abundance. Halibut, thresher sharks, and bat rays come to swim in the summertime. It's been a lean year; not much work for me. I'm sure feeling sad this morning, but I took a moment to stand on this sturdy pier to relax, pray, and give thanks for the available nourishment swimming just below me. At the end of the dock sits my favorite tackle shop with a friendly sign reminding the traveler and me to enjoy the good life. I take a moment to read, capture, and hold tight to the words.

John concludes,
> I, along with anyone here, earn a holy nudge placing us in a rare moment of opportunity. I can let go of all that burdens me. Fishing becomes something divine as I remain in the moment; God has filled my net with plenty.

Today, PCH (Pacific Coast Highway) is flanked on both sides by expensive, multi-million-dollar estates, and the pier itself seems just a bit out of place. Yet, amid wealth, this 780-foot-long, free-public fishing pier is still open to all. Its creosote timbers continue to be trodden upon by countless thousands. Presidents and many of the biggest names in entertainment have found moments of needed serenity as they walked suspended above the crashing waves. It sits in a small cozy bay once called Keller's Shelter, with the entrance to the pier sitting over a narrow white sandy beach. Nearby, The Malibu Lagoon State Beach and famous Surfrider's Beach are home to the Gidget movies, with a few chosen scenes shot at Malibu Pier.

Malibu Pier remains a favorite location, still used by the TV and Film Industry today. In Sol's time, he saw television crews filming Baywatch, Starsky & Hutch, Happy Days, Charlie's Angels, and Mannix, to name a few. Barbra Streisand and James Caan also were in a scene from *Funny Lady* on this beloved, spotlighted pier. In addition, the legendary cinematographer, James Wong Howe, found the well-used location perfect for a few backdrops in his many projects.

The Rockford Files, predominantly filmed in romantic, secluded Paradise Cove, is just a short drive down the coast. The opening credits roll over a scene of Jim and Rocky Rockford (Noah Beery Jr.) dangling their fishing rods off Malibu Pier. On occasion, they filmed on Malibu Beach to expand the beach scene, then Jim, Noah, and the crew frequented and enjoyed everything about beloved Alice's Restaurant.

Bob Yuro tells one story of many about an employee who would eventually write a film called, *Romancing the Stone,* starring Michael Douglas; he said,
> She used to sit in my restaurant scribbling at the bar, stopping now and then to talk about when she worked there, then walking up and down the pier, returned to resume her story. So a lot of those things happened

Gabrielle, daughter to Bob, worked at Alice's from age 13 to 22, fondly remembers,

> Many servers and bartenders worked there for 15 to 20 years, which was a rarity in our city. They were fun people and part of our family. I remember my years there; it was like being in an off-Broadway show.

Great food, entertainment, and comfort, within this 85-square-foot restaurant. appeared every day, becoming irresistibly popular. Of course, a reservation was necessary at Alice's on a weekend evening. But even with reservations, there were occasions when you had to wait an hour or so for a table. The wait became acceptable, a part of the Malibu vibe. People walked the length of the pier, chatting, gazing, and relaxing in the divine atmosphere. Bob wished he, his family, and his customers could return to those days. He said, "It would be great to be serving customers in Malibu again."

For most people, there has never been a place like it since. For all who enjoyed the home-like fun of Alice's, sentiments run high. It seems like a loss of family, friends, and history tied up in one delightful building.

Indeed, it's just a beat-up old parking sign, and maybe not too friendly looking—but not to a Malibu resident or those who frequented Alice's. However, upon seeing the rusted iconic symbol ready to be thrown away, a particular Malibu resident asked for it. So after officially closing, the parking sign gladly went to this loyal customer.

Los Gatos, John Steinbeck, and Mary

We find after years of struggle that we do not take a trip; a trip takes us.
—*John Steinbeck*

As we begin a brief visit to a snug community 60 miles south of San Francisco, Mary Saks, Sol's daughter, has graciously gifted us with this lovely addition about her memories of the rolling meadows of her Los Gatos home.

Mary writes,

Our family's association with Los Gatos and the surrounding area dates back decades. Dear friends had an egg ranch in the hills above the town, and we spent most Thanksgivings there when my brother and I were growing up. Over time, our friends asked Mom and Dad if they would be interested in buying the back eight acres. The land wasn't being used, and the money from the purchase wouldn't hurt. Besides, Dad always was interested in owning property. For years, that land was leased for various uses; a Christmas tree farm and horse pasturage, to name just two.

It was (and is) a beautiful property: rolling meadows backing onto a deep strip of dark trees, with a knoll at one end and a spring in a declivity at the other. Dad had begun, not long after buying the property, to plant trees around the knoll, and by the time he started thinking of building on the land, there was a lovely blanket of green spread over the rise. Dad worked with an architect (Ben Dengler) to design a cabin. He was influenced by the two-story log cabin next door to our Sherman Oaks house. That house had a single large room downstairs with a single-story kitchen at one end. There was a second-floor hallway leading to the bedrooms.

Dad's cabin was also a large, one-room structure with a second-floor balcony sleeping area which was open to the living space below. A compact kitchen was tucked under the balcony, and a laundry area outside behind the kitchen. The upper and lower rear decks nestled into the surrounding trees with the front of the house and its deck, overlooking the rolling meadow through large windows which flanked a substantial stone fireplace.

Dad owned three houses; the family home in Sherman Oaks, the small, magical house in Malibu, and the cabin in Los Gatos. He said: Sherman Oaks was his wife, Malibu his mistress, and Los Gatos, someone he saw now and again.

Mary concludes,

> The cabin became a refuge for Dad and a vacation destination for the rest of the family. My husband and I stayed there with first one and then two daughters. When they grew older, both of the girls stayed there with their families. My brother lived there while his wife was in law school and various Aunts, Uncles, and cousins enjoyed time spent in that lovely cabin.
>
> –Mary Saks

Sol's old nemesis, depression, hovered nearby as a nagging companion, making the intrepid writer's mornings challenging to move through. Diligently, Sol collected the newspaper on his front porch while Anne prepared breakfast. Then, slowly, turning every page, reading bits here and there, a story about author John Steinbeck captivated him. Sol read many John Steinbeck books but never realized Steinbeck wrote *The Grapes of Wrath* in Los Gatos, California. Sol and his family made many trips to this cozy community, and on occasion, Sol wondered what it would be like to own property there.

But, a day of writing began to form in his mind and interrupted his dreams of owning property. He sat down for breakfast and turned his attention to his family to momentarily quell the rush of words and ideas. Not known to him at the time, that morning, Sol had found his next adventure confirmed between the pages of the Los Angeles Times. The morning challenges of life began to vanish as he enjoyed time eating and talking with his family. Breakfast concluded, and a more relaxed Sol called Jason, a realtor in Los Gatos, who arranged for Sol to see several properties and an overnight stay at a luxury Bed and Breakfast. Sol then prepared for the five-hour drive the following day to meet with Jason, learn where Steinbeck lived, and better understand the housing market.

When Sol arrived, Jason, dressed in the latest Armani suit, welcomed Sol like a long-time friend, then helped him settle into the B&B. Sol remembers wishing he had dressed in more than the jeans he donned with his best red suspenders and a shirt. Before returning to the office, Jason took Sol for a leisurely relaxing five-star lunch and relaxed over a friendly conversation. Sol was now refreshed, energized, and ready to visit the streets where John Steinbeck may have walked. Jason genuinely obliged and took Sol back to his office to begin the tour. A stunning black Bentley was waiting at the entrance to the office. Jason opened the gleaming passenger door inviting Sol to please make himself comfortable. Sol was visibly impressed as he stepped into a world of sumptuous luxury.

SOL SAKS

Jason drove slowly through the sprawling vineyards and dense woodlands, describing the history that lay before them. Jason invited Sol to lower his window and experience the fragrances gathering from each tree and vine as they blended upon the breezes. Sol pressed the interior window control, and the sweet mesmerizing aroma slipped through the open car window—engaging Sol's imagination. Jason told of the intoxicating local reputation of this art colony. So many painters, musicians, writers, actors, and bohemian associates gravitated to Los Gatos over the years. Sol barely touched the window control, and it went up like an effortless breath. Sol said that when the window closed, the entrancing breezes changed to the fragrance of heady lavish leather within the car, giving the sensation of just finishing a glass of wine. This Bentley was the most intoxicating luxury car Sol had ever seen, and he fought to pay attention to the stories. Jason regaled Sol with stories about violinist and conductor Yehudi Menuhin living in Los Gatos as a boy.

Sol turned his head toward Jason in astonishment as he listened, fascinated. Considered one of the great violinists of the 20th century, Menuhin played the Soil Stradivarius, one of the finest violins made by Italian luthier Antonio Stradivari in 1714. Next, they passed Los Gatos High School, where actresses Joan Fontaine and her sister Olivia de Havilland graduated from their quaint but scholarly country school.

Quietly enraptured with this small corner of heaven, Sol committed that moment to the pursuit of a perfect abode to sit and write. Within the month, Sol contacted his friend and architect to discuss the possibilities. Maybe a cabin set within a forest of trees and perched upon a hill. As with his Malibu home, there was a significant balcony, but you could reach out and touch a limb of a tree from this balcony. After purchasing the eight acres offered by his friends, he learned that Los Gatos is Spanish for The Cat and refers to the cougars and bobcats indigenous to the foothills where he would live. Sol said a momentary chill went through him, but he remained undeterred. He determined that this would be the dwelling where his novel would be born.

However, true to his nature, all were welcome when creative writing was not spilling forth within this ideal setting. Just as Sol generously shared Malibu and the ocean breezes, he invited his friends and family to the retreat amongst the relaxing fragrances whispering through the trees. Sol described the cabin to me and offered an open invitation to stay there. It sounded exquisite, with a balcony floating amid the branches, but there was no tv, unreliable phone service, wild cats, and I had a small child at the time. I never made it to charming Los Gatos, but family and many friends did and said it was a bit of heaven. Several writers drove to this beautiful retreat and finished their projects in solitude.

A couple of friends battling cancer and other illnesses found the exquisite seclusion perfect for gathering their thoughts as they walked along the Santa Cruz Mountain paths. One woman I spoke with discovered a remote footpath running alongside a lovely stream. She walked, cried, and left every frustration at the water's edge; she returned stronger, relaxed, and hopeful. Though Sol said he invested in these properties for his family, he never refused a friend's entrance to any of his homes.

As a collaborative writer, Sol generally did not do well in solitude. But he found something out of the ordinary in this cabin that afforded him moments to escape into the creativity surrounding him. Sol did write his novel, a tumultuous fictional story based on fact. Set in the sixties, he compiled his book about a young girl from a middle-class, religious family who inexplicably takes to a life on the treacherous edge of society. A novel told on different levels, first from a middle-aged Hollywood writer—who becomes obsessed with her story, then her. Second, the young girl tells her story through her own eyes.

Next, we hear stories through interviews with intimates of her past: a dropout, consort-in-residence at a movie on location, convict, mistress to a thirty-year-old rock record magnate, call girl for a Mexican gangster in his luxurious apartment in a Puerto Vallarta jail, etc.–until she commits herself to a drug rehabilitation center. Then, his story unfolds through his therapy, his compulsive search for the key to her story, as a successful writer facing a mid-life crisis, with its symptoms of fear of aging, impotence, and dissatisfaction with his ungratifying life.

His novel was a cathartic masterpiece of writing. A combination of an honest look at how a successful writer is facing life, the culmination of news articles he read, people he knew, and most importantly, his artful use of improvisation. Those who read the manuscript gave it rave reviews, but it did not get him an agent or publisher. We sent out masses of letters of inquiry with one lone response that said it was a story before its time. As more letters went out, disappointment escalated as he continued to write; ultimately, Sol put his novel aside. While teaching classes at Pepperdine University and California State University Northridge (CSUN), he told his students;

> The frightening reality is that no one will tap you on the shoulder and ask you if you are a comedy writer. Or, for that matter, are you a writer? So, you must self-start. Then, a more difficult task is to finish. At that point, you stand up and say to the world, here is my work. Take your chances on everyone, telling you that this is the worst material I have ever read in my entire life. It is just possible they won't. Besides, what do they know, anyhow?

SOL SAKS

Sol concludes,

> I learned early in my career that there is no security for a comedy writer. Anxiety goes with the territory. It's the cattle prod toward excellence. The artist without it is mediocre unless they compromise the truth. But, on the other hand, if you write for what is current at the moment, it may sell.
>
> However, to be significant at what you do, like the top athlete, the successful tycoon, the heavyweight champion, the prima ballerina, or the winner of the Pulitzer prize, there will be the fear of failure. Every champion has it because, without that fear, you don't make a champion. But, it is still to thine own self be true!

No matter what life threw at Sol, he kept writing. He felt that the lion-share of creativity resided within his Sherman Oaks home. It remained his ultimate sanctuary. The loving presence of his late wife Anne was there, and when he stilled his mind—he could hear her encouraging words within him. She was a significant part of him and his success. There were palpable lingering memories embedded within those walls. The stories of a life spent with his children, grandchildren, friends, and every vibrant, fun-filled party clung to every space. Sol enjoyed comfortable destinations and a change in scenery that sparked his creativity. Put those together with family and friends, and his mind soared with brilliant ideas and words, culminating in entertainment for the masses. Love, fun, and vacations were in Los Gatos, proving a wise investment that he never regretted, and neither did we.

7

Why Didn't You Write More Episodes for Bewitched?

"The worst thing you write, is better than the thing you didn't write."

I was back working as an actress in Hollywood when I received a call from Sol. His bookkeeper quit, and he needed help. He offered me double the pay, and before I could say no, I heard words he had never spoken to me. They were lovely compliments on my past work and embellishments to seal the deal; of course, I returned to help.

By the second day, his financials were up to date, and he asked me to lunch at my favorite restaurant, Rive Gauche, saying he wanted to discuss a question I'd asked years ago; I was intrigued and agreed. Sol had celebrated his 99th birthday a couple of months earlier and was as healthy and capable as ever. However, he used a cane that day because his back was bothering him. I offered to drive, and he accepted without a thought.

While working for Sol years prior, I asked him why he never wrote more episodes for *Bewitched*. I remember the puzzled look on his face giving way to bewilderment, a shrug of his shoulders; then, we continued working without an answer. But today, it was as if the years in between vanished; we picked up where we left off; maybe today, I would hear the answer to my question. Sol hurriedly brought me up to date as I drove. I wanted to stop the car and listen, but as he began, I attempted to retain every word the best I could.

First, Carolyn, it's strange how your simple question has stuck with me all these years. I searched for a reasonable answer, and sometimes I thought I knew why. But it's not an apparent reason, at least to me. So, when I tell you, I'd like to hear your opinion at the end of my story.

While writing *Bewitched*, I reached a point where I knew I had to stop. I suppose I could have forced the issue, the money was great, but I felt it was not for me. Later, I wrestled with the controversial opinions about the show but blocked them from my mind. Lately, looking back through the eyes of time, the protesting people may have been right. Though I no longer wrote for the show, they did consult me on several occasions, and I enjoyed meeting several cast and crew on and off the set. It subtly began when Elizabeth, or Liz as friends, called her, who was back in New York, for a visit to a department store. Agnes Moorehead, who loved to shop, was at the makeup counter when Liz spotted her and thought *she would be the perfect mother.*

SOL SAKS

Sol concludes,
> After Agnes accepted the job, I asked her if she ever had doubts about *Bewitched* being successful; she paused a while, then said,
>
> 'But, oh yes, I had doubts that *Bewitched* would be successful! When the studio first asked me to read the script for *Bewitched*, I didn't think the show would sell. I also had some reservations about taking the job. I was uncomfortable with the character. However, they made such an attractive offer that I accepted, and when they came back with news that the show sold, it surprised me very much. But then I am always surprised when anything is a big success. I can't tell you why. I don't understand those sorts of things. But once I commit to a show, I have to see it through. I'm grateful for every fun day of work on *Bewitched*, but I hope that the audience remembers me for more than just Endora, the witch.'

Agnes had the talent to make every character she played naturally believable. Her portrayal of Endora is a powerful yet loveable character. After sitting through several hours of hair and makeup, Agnes pinned her favorite piece of jewelry close to her heart. A stunning starburst brooch with 8.5 carats of diamonds that carried memories, bringing her piece of mind.

Agnes Robertson Moorehead

Sol continues,
> In the beginning, while filming *Bewitched*, everyone kept busy learning lines, performing, and keeping up with the pressures of a new show. As the months progressed, a hazy awareness of health problems slowly, almost inconspicuously, began surfacing, mine included. Still, no one talked much about health or personal situations. However, one day while talking to Agnes, she mentioned that no new work offers were coming her way, and she was worried. She said the show's popularity seemed to be trapping her in the character of Endora.

Sol concludes,
> But looking on the bright side, as Agnes did, she was grateful to be in good health and working. But while filming the last season, Agnes was noticeably sick. However, being the consummate professional, she would not let her audience down. The ever-so-talented actress never dropped a line of dialogue and always came to work no matter how she felt.

As Endora, Elizabeth Montgomery's mother, Agnes was magnificent as usual but quite a departure from who she was! Born in Clinton, Massachusetts, daughter of former singer Mary McCauley and Presbyterian minister John Henderson Moorehead. She said she made her first public performance at age 3 when she recited the Lord's Prayer in her father's church. Agnes recalls,
> I think I learned the happiness of being with people from my father. He was so warm and outgoing. He did not believe in just being a Sunday morning preacher sermonizing to his congregation.
> No, he went to their homes frequently and invited them to ours. Even as a little girl, I shared social activities with my parents. No one else in our family had ever been in show business, but there was something about entertaining people that enriched me. My father was a kind, understanding man; I always valued and wanted his opinion. At an early age, I told my father that I intended to start dancing lessons and enter training to be an actress. He looked at me with such love and said,
> 'Agnes, if this is what gives you happiness, go ahead. What you learn is sure to impart pleasure to others.' He was a very unusual minister, especially for the times. I still miss him every day.

On several occasions, Agnes met Sol in the commissary for lunch and consistently commented how grateful she was for the work. That is until one day, on their walk back to the set, she casually shared with Sol that a strong sense of uneasiness was growing and becoming distracting. But the trooper Endora pushed the distraction aside, remaining cheerful as the show's puzzling difficulties and her life grew more stressful each day. Finally, Agnes began showing signs of fatigue. Not long after her conversation with Sol, Agnes received a call from her doctor. Agnes had uterine cancer, and he could not say how long she would live. She shared the news with the producers, who asked if she wanted to quit. Agnes refused to stop working or give up, though sometimes in terrible discomfort. She continued working until the show closed. She died two years later, still youthful, at 74 years old.

SOL SAKS

Elizabeth and Family

*"I think everyone should become rich
and famous and do everything
they ever dreamed of, so they can
see that it's not the answer."*
—Actor Jim Carey

We arrived at Rive Gauche, found an out-of-the-way table, and prepared for work over a lovely lunch. The chef was from France, and everything he prepared was exquisite. We continued our conversation until the first masterpiece from this talented chef arrived; Salade Nicoise, a true national treasure of France. With my first taste, I was back dining in a Paris cafe. Sol sat looking at me with a conservative grin and asked if I had momentarily left the restaurant. I laughed as I explained my love of Paris and my dream to return one day. Unimpressed, Sol took a bite; his eyes lit up with understanding as he tucked in for a yummy lunch while regaling me with more of his fascinating stories. Moving on to the star of *Bewitched*, in between bites, Sol said,

> Then there is Elizabeth Montgomery, but let me start with her parents because it has much to do with her choices. Her mother was actress Elizabeth Bryan Allen and her father, Robert Montgomery, the legendary film star of the 1930s and 1940s. Elizabeth Brayan Allen was very talented and could perform comedy and drama. In addition, she appeared with some of Hollywood's best actors. Her sister Martha-Bryan Allen was also an actress. Magic and witchcraft began finding their way into Hollywood and fascinated actors.
>
> **Robert Montgomery,** born Henry Montgomery Jr., was an American film and television actor, director, and producer. Robert began his acting career on the stage, but MGM soon noticed and hired him. Initially assigned roles in comedies, they saw he could handle dramatic ones too. The couple met in 1924 when they appeared in the Broadway play *Dawn*. They were married on April 14, 1928, and unfortunately divorced in 1950. They had three children: Martha, Elizabeth, and Robert Jr. She lost her first child, Martha, at age 14 months and, according to Elizabeth, turned to the comforts of magic and never fully recovered.

As Sol continued his story, he gave me small insights into Robert Montgomery's background; it matched what I had imagined as a girl.

BEWITCHED

As a young adult, I heard a commentary Steven Spielberg gave on black-and-white movies. I became fascinated with the creativity of shading, lighting, and new camera angles of the times. I discovered I loved any movie Robert Montgomery was in, and I believe I developed a secret crush on this charming actor.

Robert came from a life of privilege and elite society, but I was about to find out he had hidden strength. His father lost the family fortune, became inconsolable, and committed suicide by jumping off the Brooklyn Bridge. Though the family was horrified, his mother firmly believed in the truths she found in the bible. Sharing them with Robert gave him the skills to survive, take care of his family, and thrive in life. I think that depth of character was the compelling force, the magnetism the audience saw in his eyes; even in the days before his passing at age 77, he retained a youthful, boyish charm.

Elizabeth Allen with John Wayne in *Donavon's Reef*
and
Robert Montgomery

Elizabeth Montgomery had what most would imagine as an enviable upbringing and career. She had learned the entertainment business from two of the best. Elizabeth entered her career knowing how to maneuver through the studio system and most Hollywood pitfalls.

SOL SAKS

She enjoyed a career spanning five decades that happily began in 1951 with a role in her father's television series, *Robert Montgomery Presents*.

Elizabeth With Her Father

In 1955 when Elizabeth decided to marry at age 20, it looked like the end of a promising career. Her socialite husband, Fred Cammann, opposed her acting career and urged her to quit. In those days, a woman's profession was usually a housewife, which seemed a standard request for those times. However, Elizabeth wasn't satisfied with this life and wanted more; she left Fred and moved to Los Angeles. A year passed, they divorced, and Elizabeth soon became a household name.

In 1956, she won a Theater World Award for her Broadway debut in *Late Love*. However, Elizabeth is best known for her leading role on *Bewitched* and reported a hit comedy show invited into homes every week, garnering top ratings for eight years. Her work on *Bewitched* earned her five Prime Time Emmy Award nominations and four Golden Globe nominations. After *Bewitched* ended its run in 1972, she continued her career in numerous television films, including *A Case of Rape* (1974), as the character Ellen Harrod and *The Legend of Lizzie Borden* (1975), portraying Lizzie. Both roles earned her additional Emmy Award nominations. In addition, Elizabeth continued tirelessly volunteering in various forms of political activism and charitable work throughout her career. However, Sol has more to say here,

> Carolyn, did I tell you that before meeting Elizabeth that fateful day at Screen Gems, I met her second husband, actor Gig Young. During the summer months, theater productions were in full swing. Gig loved the theater, and we had several conversations over lunch about him appearing in one of my plays. I thought he was an exceptional actor but a troubled and somewhat tormented soul.

Sol continues,

> Remember when I told you about meeting Elizabeth in late 1963? That windy day at the studio, when she and her third husband, William Asher, were ushered through the studio doors by the wind? What I forgot to say was when I discovered who she was, my mind raced back to meeting her husband, Gig, just months earlier, and I thought they were still married.
>
> I was puzzled and distracted as I listened to their glowing comments about my latest script. But, it wasn't the time to ask questions about Elizabeth's personal life; it unfolded in time. I also discovered that we had a similar dislike of sticking with one character for too long. But that information didn't surface until 1972. She confessed she was tired of the series and wanted to move on, which I understood. I commended her for her resolve and helping make the show a hit.
>
> With each passing day, she remained stunning. Amazed, I asked if what people were saying about her was true, and she gasped in horror. 'What are they saying?' People wonder if you use your special powers to put a spell on yourself. There was a long pause. 'I don't understand.' They say you grow more beautiful, almost as if you know some secret anti-aging magic. Her smile lit up the room in relief; she bent over in laughter without a word. Like her character, the nose-twitching Samantha, her beauty continues to live. Elizabeth said in an interview given by our local newspaper;
>
> 'I had never considered a television series. I would rather play a character for an hour and move to a new script, a new character. But when my husband and I first saw Sol Saks pilot, we were intrigued and felt it would be a new adventure. I also thought his writing made acting a breeze. Though Sol didn't continually write for *Bewitched*, he was consulted, and his standards were followed. I think if they hadn't, I wouldn't have lasted a year.'
>
> For many actors, when they're on a television show for many years, it does not matter how amazing the show is; they will most likely get tired at some point, and it happened to Elizabeth. Weariness set in by season 5; she was ready to quit. When producers heard about this, they offered her a substantial raise in pay. So much so that she absolutely could not turn it down. She ended up staying on the show, but sadly her passionate performance lessened. I was at a meeting at ABC when Elizabeth asked if I'd like to have lunch in the commissary when I finished. Of course, I agreed, and we met and ordered. The room vibrated with excited and energetic talent, everyone talking at once.

SOL SAKS

Sol continues,

> It was a great place to be, and I smiled while overhearing a few new actors' stories. Then, I turned to say something to Elizabeth and saw the deep sadness behind Samantha's character, which only appeared off-screen. Liz kept primarily to herself on set, but she shared many stories with me away from the camera. Today was one of those days. I saw a more profound sadness than ever before. Unusually quiet, I asked how she was doing. Then, amid surrounding laughter, torment began to appear on Liz's face. She didn't say a word but gazed off into space. Concerned, I asked if she was okay. 'I never found what I was looking for.'
>
> Puzzled, I said, 'what are you attempting to find?' She breathed in as if desperate for air and said, 'I don't know.' Disturbed, Liz pushed her half-filled plate of food to the center of the table, grabbed her coffee, and consumed the entire cup. Then, appearing drained of all energy, she slowly returned to the set to resume her character. Like plugging in a lamp, Liz walked before the camera and lit up brilliantly as if every care was gone. In this scene, it was time to create some magic; Liz raised her arms to suggest the illusion of a magic spell, and stood frozen, then the stagehands rushed in to complete the effects. The fantasy took longer than expected, so they gave her a device to assist her arms until the director called action. The development was masterly completed, and everyone left for the day knowing they had given their best.
>
> The only times I remember seeing her face light up off-screen was when she blew through the studio doors on our first meeting and during a conversation about animals. Though it is difficult for some of us writers and actors to stay with the same character year after year, there is a measure of guilt and panic that comes with this decision. However, when you are in the entertainment industry, you have to resolve that you are doing the right thing for yourself, and there will be more work as you let go of a sure thing.
>
> Though the ratings for *Bewitched* were dropping, they had a contract with ABC for two more years, which the studio honored. But, the demands for the lead of a series are considerable. So, with problems at home and her waning interest in her character, Elizabeth opted to leave. Liz and I were to meet again months later for lunch when I received a phone call from her. Liz attempted to say something about lunch that I didn't understand. Her voice was quietly strained and solemn. There was an uncomfortable pause until she broke the silence with a heartbreaking sob.

Sol continues,

> I remember being shocked. Liz was trying to hold back the tears while explaining that she could not keep our appointment but asked if we could meet when she was better. I agreed but was upset to hear her crying and asked if there was anything I could do. The silence on her end of the phone was troubling. Finally, without responding to my question, she gave me her new number and explained that she had left Bill, remarried director Richard Michaels, and now trying to find the legendary Blue Bird of Happiness she read about as a child.
> Richard was the director for a few episodes of *Bewitched*, and they fell in love, married, then went to Europe for an extended honeymoon. But the legendary bird was not to be found. I told her I was a phone call away if she needed anything. She thanked me, apologized, told me how much she cared and admired me then we said goodbye. For days, I had the uncomfortable, helpless feeling that she was in trouble and there was nothing I could do. I called and left a message inviting her and her husband to spend as much time as needed at my beach house, but no response came.
> I decided to drive to the beach and rest in the calming atmosphere. I walked the beach and thought of my friend's enviable childhood. I had no reference to a life that afforded anything a person wanted; I wondered what had happened. I remembered again that happiness is a choice, and I'm beginning to suspect it's true except for a medical condition. Most of us only dream of her lifestyle, and yet, having everything a child could dream of and attaining stardom as an adult, she said she was never happy. I was unable to understand completely, and she could not explain. Liz was part of an elite society. She wore beautiful designer clothes, dined with President and Jacqueline Kennedy, traveled the world, and met many dignitaries; I could continue filling pages, but sadly, she never found her elusive Blue Bird. Liz was never well enough to meet again for lunch and explained she had colon cancer but was hopeful. We had a few brief phone visits, and during our last one, she asked me questions about Anne's final days. She died later, in 1995; my friend was only 62.
> In 2005, a bronze statue went up as a tribute to Liz in Salem, Massachusetts. As you know, Salem was the location of the Salem Witch Trials, which seems fitting to them that they put up an enormous statue of Elizabeth Montgomery playing the role of Samantha. Thirteen years after Liz died, in January of 2008, the Hollywood Walk of Fame honored her with a star. The star award was for her work on TV, but she was so much more than just an actress.

SOL SAKS

Elizabeth's Legacy Lives On

Sol continues,

> While Liz may have been private about her personal life, she was vocal about her political views. Elizabeth used her Celebrity Status to bring awareness to causes like women's rights; she stopped wearing a bra at the end of the filming of *Bewitched* to support the women's movement. Liz was one of the very first celebrities who openly supported gay rights and was a huge advocate for people living with AIDS. She consistently volunteered in Los Angeles for the AIDS project; her support was monumental to the gay rights movement. Her unwavering support was right on time; people then didn't know much about AIDS, so Liz stepped up to enlighten and help them understand the disease.
>
> Even after she passed away, she continued to help needy people. For example, an auction featured all of her clothing which Erin Murphy (Tabitha) modeled for the auction and raised a substantial amount of money for AIDS research and patient care.
>
> She was a frequent volunteer at the Los Angeles Unit of Learning Ally. She also recorded their bestselling poetry book, *When We Were Very Young*. In addition to recording the book, she produced TV and radio PSA (Public Service Announcements) for them. The organization is known for recording books, CDs, etc., for people with disabilities.
>
> Then, she bequeathed an extraordinary gift to New York State after her passing. Her beautiful summer home in Patterson, New York, a sprawling 794-acre estate. The land is now an 1145-acre Wonder Lake State Park with almost 9 miles of hiking trails and one scenic trail that lines an entire lake! The park also helps to protect parts of the Great Swamp.

I sat in amazement at Elizabeth's accomplishments and contributions as Sol concluded,

> Elizabeth is in the company of others on the show who died the under age of 65, such as Alice Pearce, Paul Lynde, Dick York, and Dick Sargent. So, what do you think so far, Carolyn?

Frankly, I was a bit numb. At this point, I reserved my opinion. We had finished our salad and were both saddened by the story. I asked Sol if Elizabeth felt any satisfaction in her accomplishments, giving people hours of entertainment. He shrugged his shoulders in uncertainty, but he thought maybe she had moments. I shared that I had a wise friend who also told me that happiness was a choice.

As a highly decorated Navy SEAL, he learned that no matter the tragedy or disappointment in life, we needed to be grateful for what we had, continue to hope or work toward dreams, but choose happiness in the meantime. It took me several years to implement his sage advice, but I acquired a grand key to life. As Sol listened to my story, his brow furrowed as he began to stare off in thought.

We discussed that Samantha's magic was just the stagehands at work. CGI and illusion technology did not exist back when *Bewitched* first started. However, Samantha created her witchery in a particular manner. The production team had stagehands who worked tirelessly to conjure up all of the magic. Let's say, for instance, Samantha wanted to clean up a messy room quickly; Elizabeth would stand there, throw her arms up, and then the director would cut the scene. At this point, stagehands would come on set and remove everything that her magic was going to remove. Then they would roll again, looking like she had made everything disappear.

Neither of us had a definitive answer to Sol's nagging puzzle, but the story about my friend refreshed a memory of something his mother told him years ago. Sol said,

> When my mother left Poland, her mother hugged her and said that lasting joy was unattainable unless gifted by God. Her parting words to her daughter were, 'ask for this, Sarah.' My grandmother understood the unbearable pain of war and what it would take to have a good life. But my mother said she never asked, thinking it unimportant and unrealistic. She knew moments of happiness but confessed, never abiding joy.

Feeling the weight of answers to mysteries unattainable, we took a deep breath as our main course, seafood crepes, arrived. Sol then began remembering Dick York and his admiration for his talent, gracious personality, and loving concern for people. He stated that the role of Darrin first went to actor Richard Crenna, who passed because of his commitment to *The Real McCoys*, a popular tv show at the time. Dick came from a lovely family in Fort Wayne, Indiana. His mother, Betty, was a seamstress, and Bernard, his father, was a salesman.

SOL SAKS

Bernard taught his son the art of selling, then Dick used those principles as an actor, finding a place in humanities-heart long before *Bewitched*.

Dick York

Raised in Chicago, Dick sang in the choir, and a Catholic nun first recognized his talent. Dick was only 15 when his career began. He earned the starring role on the CBS radio program *That Brewster Boy*. After that, it was non-stop from there. But it was while filming the movie; *They Came to Cordura* in 1959 with Gary Cooper and Rita Hayworth that Dick suffered a permanent, disabling back injury. While on the show, he had a role in the classic film Inherit the Wind. Known for being quite handsome and a total heartthrob! Dick aged very gracefully and continued to be attractive, charming, and loved by all.

Nonetheless, while on Bewitched, he had a role in the classic film Inherit the Wind. The pain never diminished his handsome face; he was considered a total heartthrob! Dick aged very gracefully and continued to be attractive, charming, and loved by all.

Our impressive dessert arrived, and Sol was immediately impressed. After the first mouthful, his story stopped. Then, in silence, he reached across the table to give me a copy of a newspaper interview on the career and struggles of Dick York. Dick said,

> Gary Cooper and I were propelling a handcar carrying several wounded men down the railroad track while filming *They Came to Cordura*. I was on the bottom stroke of this teeter-totter mechanism that made the handcar run. I was lifting the handle as the director yelled, 'Cut!' One of the wounded cast members reached up and grabbed the other side of the mechanism. Now, instead of lifting the expected weight, I was suddenly lifting his entire weight off the flatbed- 180 pounds or so. All at once, the muscles along the right side of my back tore. Then, they just snapped and let loose. That was the start of it all: the pain, the painkillers, the addiction, the lost career.

His injury didn't immediately end his career, Dick continued appearing in dozens of movies and television episodes, but the pain was ever-present from that day in 1959. When the call came that the studio was interested in casting Dick York as Darrin in *Bewitched*, Dick rose to the occasion and won the part. He put the pain aside and learned his lines. Rehearsals for the pilot began November 22, 1963, with the cast assembled on set in raised anticipation. But before shooting began, a solemn-looking gentleman entered, walked to Director William (Bill) Asher, and leaned close, whispering into his ear. Bill closed his eyes with a furrowed brow, then lowered his head. His eyes filled with tears as he announced to the cast the heartbreaking news. It was the assassination of then-President John F. Kennedy, which happened only moments earlier.

Bill was deeply affected as he knew President Kennedy; and produced the 1962 televised birthday party where Marilyn Monroe sang "Happy Birthday, Mr. President." The cast and crew sat in silent disbelief. Then, the phone rang with a call from a studio executive. He suggested that everyone take a break for a couple of hours. Sadly, the rehearsals and possible filming had to resume because of the deadline.

When rehearsals finally resumed, it was as though a dark cloud rested upon each professional on the set, first because of the unspeakable tragedy and second because someone mentioned the studio might cancel the show. Finally, with worry and depression taking center stage, someone on set loudly commented with frustration, "We haven't even begun filming!"

In hopes of changing the studio's mind and acquiring a spark of brightness to the production, William, a most formidable director, secured Academy Award-winning actor Jose Ferrer to serve as the pilot's narrator; the investors voted to continue with the show. Mr. Ferrer served brilliantly as the episode's narrator, starting with the words, "Once upon a time..." Mr. Ferrer did not receive credit for this role but was graciously happy to help. Historically the entertainment industry has delivered when faced with hardship. The show must go on is more than a mere phrase to them. *Bewitched* met the deadline, and the pilot aired on time, bringing a bit of laughter in a sad and challenging time. A sigh of relief found its way throughout the set on the last day of shooting. The cast and crew could now mourn John F. Kennedy, and Dick could get a much-needed rest.

This photo of Darren and Samantha, taken during the pilot, was about the occult destabilization of the conformist life of an upwardly mobile advertising man, Darrin.

SOL SAKS

In the picture, Dick is in considerable pain and struggling to stay in the character of Darrin. Samantha Stephens promises her new husband, Darrin, not to use her magic. A promise, initiating a pattern that would continue into each subsequent episode. Again, the conflict in each episode surrounds Samantha's failed attempts to keep her promise. Dick, the consummate actor, seamlessly hid his pain within Darrin's frustration.

Almost immediately, letters of protest arrived regarding the content of this new pilot and this particular scene. And, once again, there was talk about canceling the show. Yet, the head studio executives laughingly said, "No, I think the audience felt sorry for Darrin."

The investors were thrilled, and Darrin received congratulations on his performance. The show continued, and Dick York appeared faithfully once a week before his now welcoming audience within their comfortable living rooms. The tide was turning with letters received by the studio stating that Dick became a treasured family member that the audience looked forward to having in their homes; he became the champion against the onslaught of witchcraft. They made popcorn, set out drinks, made hot chocolate, and got ready to be entertained by their friend. Unknown to his faithful viewers, hiding quietly behind the camera, Dick was in agonizing pain. Carpenters working for the studio built Dick a slant board to lean on in-between takes, which helped ease his pain. Halfway through the third season, the pain relentlessly grew worse, and Dick needed help to walk. Our dutifully gracious entertainer spent his off-times following his doctor's advice; he rested. But health was not to return; by the fifth season, Dick became ill.

In an interview, Dick said,

> I was too sick to go on. I had a temperature of 105 and was full of strong antibiotics for almost ten days. I went to work that day but was sick; I should have stayed home. After being in make-up, I lay in my dressing room, waiting for my on-set call. They knew I was feeling pretty rotten and tried to give me time to rest. I kept having chills.
> It was the middle of the summer, and I was wearing a sheepskin jacket and chilling. I was shaking all over. Then, while sitting on a scaffolding with Maurice Evans, being lit for a special-effects scene, they set an inky—a tiny spotlight that was supposed to be just flickering over my eyes. That flickering, flickering, flickering made me feel weird. So as I was sitting on this platform up in the air, I turned to Gibby, who was just down below, and said, 'Gibby, I think I have to get down.' So he started to help me, and that's the last thing I remember until I woke up on the floor. I'd managed to bite a large hole in the side of my tongue before anyone could pry my teeth apart; that's about all I remember of the incident.

While Dick was in the hospital, director William Asher visited him and asked, "Do you want to quit Dick?" Dick sadly knew the time he dreaded had arrived; it was time to make the daunting decision. "If it's all right with you, Billy."

A painful silence filled the room as Dick and Billy clasped hands in a long endearing handshake. As Billy left, anguish rose, flooding Dick's thoughts at leaving the sitcom and possibly the end of his career. Quickly with resolve, he determined to devote himself to recovery; maybe he could salvage his career. He never again returned to the set of *Bewitched*.

In his memoir, *The Seesaw Girl and Me*, published posthumously, he describes the struggle to break his addiction. Also, candidly expressed within his book is the coming-to-grips with the loss of his career. But, most of all, the book is essentially a love letter to his wife, Joan, the seesaw girl of the title, who stuck with him through the hard times. He then quit drugs without medical help, which led to six months of painful withdrawal and recovery. Dick recalled in an interview,

> I had a band playing in my head, bagpipes night and day. It just went on and on and on and on and on. The fans whispered to me, the walls whispered to me, I looked at the television, and sometimes it flashed in a certain way that sent me into a fit. I knew that my wife had put her hand in my mouth so I would not bite off my tongue. I couldn't sleep. I hallucinated. I used to make a tape recording of rain to listen to the rain lying in bed at night to drown out those damned bagpipes.

SOL SAKS

Along with mediation were other habits of the time. For example, in the early days of movies, drinking and smoking in abundance were everyday occurrences, also the use of uppers and sleeping pills. While filming television shows, many situations in the sixties were a carry-over from the movie days and would not happen today. One example was that cast members would often drink on the set. Many of the *Bewitched* cast, including the lead actors, were all heavy drinkers and smokers; alcohol and cigarettes in abundance were available on the stage. Erin Murphy, who played Tabitha, said she remembered her parents telling her that smoking was not good. Still, she didn't understand why it was terrible since everyone around her at work was doing it nonstop—definitely confusing for a child.

Not only did they drink a lot on set, but they also continually mentioned various bars or clubs on the show. Some of the bars and clubs mentioned in the script were Joe's Bar and Grill, The Diamond Slipper, Hearthstone Bar, Happy Times Bar, and Dundee's Bar referred to as the best in town!

A little sidebar here: The Dundee's Bar, they referred to belonged to my family. Located on Colorado Blvd. in Glendale, California; and is named after my Uncle, Vince Dundee, former New York State middleweight champion of the world. Dundee's was a favorite hangout of boxers and people in the entertainment industry.

Dick eventually beat his addiction and, in the early 1980s, tried to revive his career. His last two credits were on two primetime television series, *Simon and Simon* and *Fantasy Island*. However, Dick was a three-pack-a-day smoker for much of his life, spending his final years battling emphysema. By 1989, he was using an oxygen tank to help him breathe. While bedridden in his Rockford, Michigan, home, he founded *Acting for Life*, a private charity to help the homeless and others in need. Dick motivated politicians, business people, and the general public to contribute supplies and money while using his telephone as his platform. Despite his suffering, York said,

> I have no complaints. I have been able to work at a job I love; I consider it a blessing. It is an honor to entertain people, give them a break from their daily routines, and maybe even a few laughs. People on the radio, on stage, and in motion pictures and television surrounded me and loved me. How blessed I have been. The things that have gone wrong are only physical.

Sol ended his remembrance of Dick York, lowering his head in a brief moment of sadness, saying,

> Dick remained a terrific salesman—a gracious and entertaining artist through all his struggles. Everyone who worked with him retains the fondest memories; what a gift to leave. But, when talent that gives such pleasure to people is no longer in the world, there's an irreplaceable void.

Sol shook his head and smiled as we agreed that this was an epic lunch. The restaurant was quiet that day, and the kind proprietor invited us to stay as long as we wanted. I had pages of notes, and it sounded like Sol had much more to say. To go to Rive Gauche and not have their Crème Brûlée is missing a treasure. Because, again, the chef was from France and brilliant. We decided to splurge and ordered one each! While waiting, I settled in as Sol remembered a tragedy before Dick York left, then Dick Sargent's brave entrance.

The tragedy struck during an episode of *Bewitched* entitled "I Confess," which aired on April 4th, 1968. The show was interrupted by ABC news to announce the assassination of civil rights leader Martin Luther King in Memphis, Tennessee, earlier that evening. Sadly, America had been dealing with high tensions and race riots for years; this became the boiling point!

Sol wasn't sure if the episode continued after the news announcement or if they just saved it to re-air at a later day. The atmosphere in town was dark. On the roads drove angry people, fighting escalated, and pressures and uncertainties filled the *Bewitched* set. At this point, Dick Sargent enters.

Dick Sargent

Dick was born Richard Stanford in a favorite place of mine, the quaint town of Carmel, California, on April 19, 1930. His mother, Ruth McNaughton, daughter of John McNaughton (who founded Los Angeles's famed Union Stockyards), was an actress in several films. She appeared under the stage name of Ruth Powell, playing minor parts.

SOL SAKS

His father, Colonel Elmer Cox, served in WWI and, as reported by Dick, stayed until the bitter end. The Colonel later became a formidable business manager to such Hollywood alums as Douglas Fairbanks and Erich von Stroheim.

After discussing Dick's heritage, Sol paused as he recalled replacing Dick York, saying,

> The studio hired Dick Sargent to take Dick York's place in season six. Sargent seemed thrilled, and the studio was pleased he was on board. He was a well-prepared actor, very professional, and had no illusions about the business. He was someone all could count on to get the job done. Unfortunately, the ratings began to drop when the audience discovered York had left the show. At this point, Elizabeth wanted out too, which created a more challenging atmosphere.
>
> Sargent, a likable fellow, bravely stepped into the part; knowing the possible opposition ahead, he made the character his own while making the best of the situation. But well into his role, he began feeling unwell. Great days became good, then moved to not-so-good. Dick never complained but joked and joyfully stated that people would forever link him to Bewitched.
>
> He was true to his reputation and continued until the close of season eight in 1972. Sadly, he never regained his health and died several years later of prostate cancer at age 64.
>
> Elizabeth showed me a copy of an interview she gave regarding Dick. It read that Dick was a great friend and that she would miss his love, sense of humor, and remarkable courage. It was her experience that you never get over losing a true friend. You do get past it, but never over missing them. Watching the demise of her talented and caring friends is one difficult challenge after another. They each left a space in her life. They were great friends, but especially Dick! Unfortunately, it was only a year later that Elizabeth herself died of colon cancer.

Sol finished his story about Dick Sargent, saying he wondered why there was so much tragedy around that show. Then, changing the subject, he thanked me for introducing him to Rive Gauche Cafe. I smiled, and before responding, the legendary Crème Brûlée arrived with silver spoons and crisp linen napkins, as if on cue. Sol took one bite and sent compliments to the chef. He commented that the food and atmosphere helped ease the pain of so much loss.

The waiter arrived with our coffee, and Sol solemnly gazed into his divinely made Cappuccino; as he gathered his thoughts.

Then, slowly picking up his cup, he took a sip; a smile of approval appeared, and he said, "What a perfect combination to a Crème Brûlée! David would have loved this restaurant."

David White

David White was his next story, but before he began, he lingered a while over dessert as he thought back to happier days spent around the pool with David, drinking a glass of wine and reading the latest *Bewitched* script, then said,

    David played Larry Tate, Darrin's boss. He was an impressive actor on film, stage, and later television and worked with several top stars of his day. We were thrilled to see him cast as Larry Tate. David served in the Marines during the Second World War, which I believe brought admirable strength and an enhanced point-of-few to each character he played.

    We shared many great times at Theatre West. We would go over scripts and discuss various topics that always included a reference to *Bewitched*. David had a gift for conversation and the uniquely impressive ability to maintain simplicity in the face of the surrounding chaos. Unfortunately, within months of starting the show, David began having a few health issues, but despite them, he always arrived on set with terrific performances and helpful ideas. For example, when David read that the characters Larry and Louise Tate had a son, he requested the studio name their on-screen Jonathan, after his real-life son, and they agreed.

    David had raised his son Jonathan on his own. Sadly his wife passed away due to pregnancy complications with their 2nd child. Unfortunately, this was not the only tragedy that David would endure. His beloved son Johnathan left for a much-needed vacation.

SOL SAKS

Sol continues,

> Happy for the rest, Jonathan hugged David goodbye, kissed him on the cheek, boarded Pan Am Flight 103, and waved another cheery goodbye through the small window. Then, while over Lockerbie, Scotland, an onboard terrorist bomb exploded. No one aboard the plane survived; his beautiful 33-year-old son was dead. Hitting David square in the heart, he said it was as if a bolt of lightning struck his soul, leaving him devastated, his emotional balance lost, and unable to cope, his mind turned off for a time.
>
> A month after the death of his son, David called me and needed a change of scenery and asked if I would join him for lunch at a local restaurant. As you can imagine, David looked tired, and his face held a pain I had never seen there before. While we ate, he explained the bombing to me. I tried to change the subject for his sake, but intense anger and a sense of helplessness took over his thoughts and conversation. David imagined his son in the plane and couldn't turn off the horrifying image. Maybe he needed to talk it out, so I sat and listened. He did seem more relaxed at the end of lunch and even managed a smile.
>
> We continued meeting for lunch over the months, and I attended a few grief counseling sessions with him, but sadly, nothing could penetrate the heavy veil of sorrow. David never fully recovered from the grief and shock, he was declining, and I felt powerless.
>
> The next time David wanted to meet for lunch, he asked if I would pick him up. I met him at the door of his home in North Hollywood; illness was evident. Though visibly weak that day, David and I enjoyed a few laughs over lunch, and he surprised me by ordering a decadent chocolate soufflé for dessert. Before that afternoon, at no time when we dined together did he ever have dessert.
>
> David finished every bit of his soufflé, then slowly walked to my car.
>
> When I left him inside his front door, I had a strange feeling it would be a long time before seeing him again. As I walked back to my car, David was still standing at the door, looking at me. I waved goodbye to my friend; it was the last time I saw him. After that, we shared a few brief phone calls until November 27, 1990.
>
> David died of a heart attack at his home; he was 74. I miss him every day.
>
> There were many tragedies with the *Bewitched* cast and crew members. Unfortunately, I also had my share of health problems; some linger still with me.

My lunch with Sol ended on a somewhat sad note that day. I felt that history was repeating itself, but I was the observer this time. Sol and I walked to my car, still talking, while in my hands, I clutched a stack of stories. On the drive home, Sol overwhelmed me with compliments and gratitude for the years we worked together. That was a first, and I was speechless. Until that day, I only heard words of correction spoken, but I became more proficient because of them.

That strange sadness lingered in the car as I watched Sol safely to his door. I still had no definable answer to my question so many years ago. We concluded that it was prudent to follow that knowing that resides inside us. I believe it was wisdom speaking, safety cautioning, and love directing. I needed to clear my head and thought I would take a walk in the park near my home. The shadows gradually left my heart with each step while strolling beneath the sun. I stopped by my favorite tree next to the horse trail. It has one sturdy low-growing branch that is perfect for sitting. Under the canopy of leaves, I wrote down more of the narrative Sol shared with me. The park was quiet, the warm breeze drifted through the tree, and the leaves seemed to applaud as I tried to capture every moment. While sitting there that day, I never dreamed while enjoying the words of a seasoned writer, a spectacular lunch, then the serenity within the branches of a tree that I'd be writing his story to you, dear reader. Life is simply an unequaled and undefinable adventure. But certainly not for the faint of heart.

Well, at this point, our travel back to the busy early days has concluded as we end these chapters. It's time to move forward from the days of writing for television to special moments within a secret garden. I must say, I have so enjoyed having you here with me on this flight into the past and the sheltered glimpse of the heart of Sol Saks through the written word.

8

Within the Secret Garden

*"Gardening simply does not allow
one to be mentally old, because
too many hopes and dreams are
yet to be realized."*
—*Allan Armitage*

In the magnetic town of Hollywood, where personal struggles find their way into gossip columns, dreams often become a nightmare; a garden sanctuary rested behind the Saks home. Returning to the late eighties, it was mid-summer, my third day on the job, and a sweltering 103 degrees in the San Fernando Valley! Lovingly planted behind the secluded home of Mr. Sol Saks, a shaded garden lies. With no air conditioning in the office and the humid air clinging to us, Sol suggested we try writing by the refreshing swimming pool. Grabbing a yellow legal pad and a few pencils, I gladly agreed. Sol stood on the stair landing, directing in a fatherly tone that I leave one hand free while descending the spiral staircase. Adhering to the same protocol, Sol proceeded before me, glancing back to see if I was following directions. We entered a small, raised, shaded courtyard and down a few more steps leading to the hallowed park-like sanctuary.

On the left side of the garden lay a rich-velvety green--mini-pasture, artistically surrounded by various textured plants, fragrant flowers, and delicious fruit trees dotted here and there. A massive Cherimoya tree sat in the center with sturdy, sprawling branches full of ambrosia-tasting fruit. At the end of the workday, Sol suggested I gather fruit and flowers to take home, which I happily did. My daughter Jennipher continues to say, "It's the most delicious fruit ever!"

On the right side, the rectangular swimming pool sparkled with the reflecting rays of the sun, bouncing onto the side path near the fence dotted with dark purple and pink flowers. For an instant, the garden reflected diamond-like lights dancing about the leaves, capturing the attention of a bright electric blue dragonfly. This gorgeous creature skimmed the pool surface leaving a trail of scattered lights dancing behind him; one could easily believe in breathtaking enchantment.

Well-tended gardens, glamorous Hollywood, and political parties within Sherman Oaks are prevalent, but Sol and Anne's garden held a defining gift, setting it apart.

BEWITCHED

It was the generous, unselfish love bestowed upon all the talented people that traveled through this fragrant garden and dined at tables lovingly placed throughout the grounds. Nothing was required, no distinction made as to status, simply an invitation to share their home, food, and success, and a sincere request to enjoy yourself. The generosity of his heart made room for a deposit of hidden, brilliant energy surrounding every blade of grass and flower.

Entertainment was born amongst family and friendships in this space. Unexplainable creativity settled on the canopy of the trees, flowing down to each well-loved plant, and remained. Sol continued strolling through the breeze, gazing at his dreamed-of-pool as if walking through palpable memories. Finally, recovering from the oppressive heat, he laughingly told me about an early dream, saying,

> Living and working on the east coast, I often read about Hollywood agents, actors, and writers having meetings around their pools. So I cut out glamorous pictures of people swimming while making million-dollar deals and thought how great it would be to be part of that scene. I remained intrigued with the vision into adulthood and determined to have a pool and a beautiful home for Anne and my family. Maybe even seal a deal or two around the pool. When the dream became a reality, we couldn't wait to open our home to friends. The entertainers working in the area would arrive with their children for a swim, and inevitably stories, jokes, and laughter filled the garden.

One such friend was actor, comedian, and dancer Buddy Ebsen.

(Left) Buddy in Beverly Hillbillies

We worked on several of the same shows, always took a moment to say hello, and, if we had time, catch up on each other's lives.

Buddy also had a strong work ethic which I admired and liked to think we had in common. My friend is best known as Jed Clampett of the *Beverly Hillbillies* or as the title character in the television detective drama *Barnaby Jones*.

SOL SAKS

Sol continues,

> But I first met Buddy before actors worked on television. It was during the legendary era of glamorous Hollywood films. Buddy was a generous, fun pal. On a day when he could stop by with his family for a swim, he'd ask me to tell Mary not to cook; he'd bring the food. It was one of the few times Mary could relax with us.
>
> Stories around the pool were always great, charged with energy, and many unprintable. Buddy began his career as a dancer in the late 1920s in a Broadway chorus. He later formed a vaudeville act with Vilma Ebsen, his sister, and they appeared on Broadway. In 1935 Buddy and Vilma went to Hollywood, where MGM signed them for their first Eleanor Powell movie *Broadway Melody*.
>
> I loved hearing about those early days. Buddy was a wise man and knew how to navigate his way in Hollywood. I learned a lot from Buddy. He later danced in *Captain January* with child star Shirley Temple. Then Hollywood chose him for the Scarecrow in *The Wizard of Oz*. Before filming began, the studio reassigned characters. Buddy would play the Tin Man. If you remember, the Tin Man's face beamed with silver makeup. This aluminum dust in his makeup caused severe illness to Buddy during filming, making it impossible to continue.
>
> However, not long after, our fine friend was back working again. Buddy portrayed Doc Golightly, the older husband of Audrey Hepburn's character Holly in *Breakfast at Tiffany's*. He remained kind, approachable, and professional throughout his long and fascinating career. It's rewarding to see his bright talent embedded forever in film. For those blessed to know him, he captured our hearts and will remain lovingly there. Those moments spent with friends and family around the pool were some of my fondest memories. Eventually, those meetings I dreamed about took place poolside, similar to those seen in a magazine when I was a boy.

Sol possessed a wealth of fond memories that sustained and encouraged him to continue to reach higher, well past societies deemed retirement age. His friends would linger for the feeling of welcome and the wonderful unseen embrace of a lovely intangible with Sol and his family. I understood their sentiments as Sol turned his attention across the lawn to a lone tangerine tree and motioned for me to follow. We moved to the shade beneath the massive limbs of the Cherimoya tree until we arrived at the dwarf Tangerine tree. Sol reached into the small tree, picked a few ripe tangerines, then headed for a cozy-looking outbuilding in the back-left corner.

He slowly opened the creaking wooden door to reveal a few neatly placed garden tools within a shed transformed into a workshop. Sol explained that one Tuesday evening a month, he and his friends gathered to work on their particular hobby while visiting simultaneously. Sol pointed to the tools and adoringly conveyed how his late wife Anne loved working in the garden. Sol's eyes teared as he told how Anne tamed a squirrel who somehow knew when she passed the Cherimoya and flowers. The young squirrel would rush down the trunk expecting to sit on her shoulder, and she gladly obliged him.

She had a way of bringing love to her children, friends, animals, flowers, the food she prepared, and, best-of-all, to Sol. He hesitatingly closed the door while gazing at Anne's favorite tree. His voice lowered as he explained her gentle insistence on planting a Tangerine tree. Sol didn't care for Tangerines. He shook his head no, then vocally protested. Anne stood her ground and was confident he would grow to enjoy them one day. Sol shrugged his shoulders in frustration, then asked the gardener to plant the tree.

Sol ran his hands across the leaves in wonderment at her insight, then picked several more beautifully formed tangerines while breathing in their unique sweet scent. He hesitantly disclosed how much he now enjoys them, though he doesn't remember when this change occurred. Sol often walks out at night across the moonlit lawn to pick one sweet tangerine and swears the sweet fragrance of Anne's perfume is within reach of his heart. He pointed to the flower beds explaining how she tirelessly worked in each area throughout the beautifully landscaped yard. He saw her so vividly in his mind as he told his story that I strangely felt I could see her too.

Sol and Anne Saks

SOL SAKS

Sol smiled as he remembered,

> Anne didn't pace herself well; she'd start a project and determined that she had to complete it no matter how long it took. So, when my beautiful wife returned to the house, she was exhausted and awoke the following morning in pain. With a slight groan, Anne pushed past the discomfort while beginning her day, then stood by the Cherimoya tree, making this funny squirrel sound so as not to disappoint her adoring friend. Eventually, the squirrel chirped back, ran down the branches, then leaped onto her shoulder. She loved that squirrel, and he loved her; she was a remarkable woman.

We returned to a table and chairs by the pool, and Sol invited me to enjoy the tangerines. He removed his shoes and socks, rolled up his pant legs, and dangled his feet in the water while looking deep into the beautiful, almost Olympic-size pool. Sitting pensively, Sol confessed he could be too independent in those early days. The producers' impression was that Sol was a man of great wealth, which brought their respect.

However, the truth was that he didn't have the money to join them during meetings over an expensive lunch, and the misunderstanding was becoming a burden. The realization was clear, nothing good could come from a lie. With this growing misinterpretation, he could not excel as a writer or see his dreams come to pass. Anne once again helped him out of his dilemma. Sol continues,

> You know, Carolyn, Anne was very frugal. When I got a thirteen-week contract, I'd explain to Anne that we had to save enough money for a year, and she never failed to manage my request. She made it possible for me to quit a job if a producer wanted to compromise my writing. A quiet gift that gave me more confidence to tell people, with conviction I was not rich, but they still didn't believe me, so I let them say it. I told the truth, and the burden was gone. I remember how much clearer my thinking became after that incident. Even my appreciation for the simple fact that Anne loved this home improved. I grew to appreciate the talent Anne had. How she'd be downstairs on a day like this cooking something for lunch; I realized it was no longer a simple task but a gift to be treasured.
>
> Anne Chaddock was an old-fashion girl with beautiful auburn brown hair and big kind eyes. I met her in the early days of my career in Chicago. She was a Christian, so I didn't mention that to my family until after we were married. Though my family was a bit miffed when they uncovered our secret, they loved Anne by that time and laughingly figured they could live with the difference.

BEWITCHED

Sol continues,

> We had a small furnished apartment and were on the go most of the time. But when we were home, Anne enjoyed cooking for my family, and they loved her cooking. If I had a job close to home, I always looked forward to her meeting me for lunch. I would not have achieved this much without her if I were honest. She had a calmness about her; she found joy in making a home where I could relax.
>
> The day we bought this home in sunny California was a significant one. Anne was thrilled with the possibilities of life within these walls and gardens, and it remained a joy for years. However, life is a series of changes. Women began wanting more from life and independence, as did Anne. When the children were grown, a restlessness developed that never left her. She wanted a job and paycheck of her own, besides just taking care of our home. It was difficult for me; I did not adjust well to the changes in our lives. She landed a few jobs but never seemed to like any of them.
>
> I understand better now that every human being has talent and dreams that need nurturing. My generation had safe categories to place each person within. To stray from the organized formula was frowned upon and strongly discouraged. Selfishly, I admit, I preferred her to stay at home; it was lovely for me. Sadly, my Anne died a year or so later, but if she'd had time, I'd like to think she would have found a fulfilling career and that I would have helped her find one.

Anne died in 1972, around the time *Bewitched* ended. However, she did find small jobs, brought home a paycheck, and found a bit of satisfaction. Sol said, toward the end of Anne's life, she thought it was her destiny to take care of him and their two children, and at that, she was a terrific success; Sol heartily agreed. He took one more longing gaze at his garden, then announced with an energetic rush that it was time to write.

Writing began with the energy of a flash flood while he relaxed into the flow of his creative process. While his feet lingered playfully relaxed in his pool, Sol brilliantly edited his play, work on a novel began, and a decision to purchase a computer with accompanying lessons for me were all completed before noon.

I had a unique rollercoaster of a job and many more memorable mornings sitting beside his realized dream. Throughout the frustrating times of working with a man of driven perfection, I wanted to quit, but something inside urged me to stop, breathe, and learn valuable lessons from those I met on life's journey. I often reminded myself of those inner instructions as I focused my attention when Sol spoke.

During those moments when he was sad, I would hear him say that childhood impressions of ourselves can linger, sometimes all of our lives. Therefore, it is vital to see ourselves in a better light. He was no longer that skinny kid with glasses and a big nose that could not get a girl. Though Sol continued to wear glasses, he struggled to change his image on the inside. Finally, it began to show in his confidence. His glasses were now a studious look, his nose perfectly proportioned to his face, he reached a healthy weight, and he did get the girls.

Sol frequently shared his lofty dreams and poignant memories with me over the years I worked with him. I always thought it was part of his process, and maybe it was. But as I sit here writing his book, it may be more complex than I thought. Whispers remind me of his final lesson: never to stop attempting to dream new dreams and set new goals. Up to the day he passed at age 100, he wrote regularly and remained a complex prism of a man, a focused, fiercely determined writer who lived as if he would never die.

Warning…Lunching with Comedy Writers

It's December 10, and today is the birthday of writer Sol Saks. Though most of the United States is cold, it is warm and sunny in Los Angeles, California. Sol has decided he would like to work by the pool again today. So, we gathered the essentials and made our way into the warm sunshine. Sol was preparing a play for Theatre West, and it was my job to make all the necessary changes to his masterpiece. We worked until 1:00 PM and were preparing to stop for the day when Sol heard the doorbell.

It was a surprise visit from two friends, Sherwood Schwartz and Bill Froug, who wanted to take him to lunch. I didn't realize it at the time, but there, standing at the entrance to the garden, were three of the most prolific writers in Hollywood. The writing accomplishments for Sherwood are enormous and would take a book of its own. In addition, he is the creator of many shows that continue to entertain millions. So, to bring this to a minimum, I will only mention *Gilligan's Island* and *The Brady Bunch*.

Bill is also a prolific writer, producer, and tenured professor at U.C.L.A. Bill, at that time, was instructing students worldwide on the art of screenwriting. It was his passion and joy to be teaching future writers. College records show a long waiting list for the advanced screenwriting seminars taught by Professor Froug. According to former students and colleagues, they were the most popular and inspiring courses at the time.

Writing credits for Bill are too numerous to mention here and are still being viewed by audiences worldwide: *The Twilight Zone, Charlie's Angels,* and he worked with Sol on *Bewitched.*

Sol asked his friends to join us at the poolside and introduced me. The three immediately invited me to join them for lunch, then helped me bring everything up to the office while telling hysterical jokes with every step. As we entered the front yard, there in the driveway sat a gorgeous black Bentley with a mirror-like finish. Having borrowed a chauffeur's cap from the wardrobe department, Sherwood quickly placed the hat on his head, then ceremoniously opened the car door for Sol. Sol, stunned, began to laugh as he stepped into the leather and Burlwood-clad paradise. Though the drive was short, it remains an incredibly memorable drive to Sol's favorite Deli, just blocks from his home in Sherman Oaks. Over lunch, I learned that Sherwood and Sol met and worked together in Chicago sometime in the 1950s. Curios, I asked Sherwood how he began as a writer. A broad smile lit up his face, and he said,

> I was studying to be a doctor while my older brother was having fun writing jokes for the popular radio program The Bob Hope Show, so I decided to write jokes instead!

Stunned by his answer, I thought, *What a decisive, brave man!* Then, when I composed myself, I asked if he had ever doubted his decision, and he confessed that it had happened many times. He also battled the thought that he'd disappointed his family. Sol and Bill nodded in agreement—they understood.

Sol announced congratulations on the success of Bill's recently published book, The Ultimate Writer's Guide to Hollywood and Screenwriting Tricks of the Trade; Sol confessed it was one of the best he'd read. The three highly talented men worked together over the years and shared many cherished adventures and childhood memories.

I marveled as I listened intently to their interestingly similar family backgrounds. The day was remarkable, and I had a cherished glimpse of the enormous talent each of them possessed. At that point, I was unaware of the full extent of their credits, but I would later learn with astonishment.

We took a brief moment to order; then, stories flew through the air at an alarming rate. I was and am admittedly captivated by how these men struggled through painful adversity, made their lives excel, and brought delightful entertainment to the world. With that epiphany whirling through my mind, the waitress returned with four enormous pastrami-on-rye sandwiches. Amid jokes circulating, they watched me attempt to eat.

SOL SAKS

I endeavored at the edge, thinking of working toward the center of the sandwich. Thoroughly amused, Sherwood lit up with delight as he pointed at me and said he could use my struggles in a sitcom. By now, the crowded Deli was looking in our direction, and my face flushed with embarrassment. In a raised voice, Sherwood asked our waitress for more napkins for this Italian girl. Though embarrassed, I couldn't stop laughing while Sherwood got up from the booth, walked over, and tucked a large napkin around my neck. Bill sitting next to me, leaned in to assist him. Suddenly someone across the room applauded, encouraging more customers to join his applause. Sol and Bill prodded me with their fingers to stand and take a bow, but all I could manage was to put my hand in the air and wave. I was way too light-headed to stand.

They were kind, honorable men, embodied with unique life struggles, giving them a different vantage point than most. They had learned to take the pain in their lives and use it to make the world a kinder place, to realize a better life for themselves, their families, friends, and strangers. The jokes made over lunch that afternoon were inclusions into their rare, inviting sphere, not meant to be cruel and demeaning. I saw an expanded thinking pattern for a moment and wanted to learn more. The opportunity arose a few more times, and each joy-filled moment was a priceless addition to my life.

Our next meeting was at Il Pastaio (The Pasta Maker) for an early dinner. I arrived with a better understanding of the mind of the comedy writer. I heard it said if you want to be wise, spend time with someone of wisdom. I indeed found that to be true and applicable to almost every endeavor. Destiny allowed me to grow further while seated in one of our popular restaurants. The Sicilian Drago family's culinary dynasty sits prominently on North Canon Drive in Beverly Hills, and the atmosphere can be intimidating. However, it is one of the best kitchens in the city, distinctively serving people from all over the world. Many in our entertainment industry consider themselves regular customers. A top New York executive and faithful customer, David hosts many business and family parties.

David consistently orders two gallons of Ill Pastaio red sauce and extravagant desserts. Shipped and delivered the day before the party, David and all invited look forward to dining together over sumptuous food. This practice is not an uncommon occurrence among many loyal customers.

Food preparations vary from region to region in Italy, and I grew up with recipes from Naples and am admittedly biased. However, Sol and Sherwood knew of my preference and assured me I would enjoy this well-prepared meal. Though not convinced, I was speechless with delight upon my first bite. Sherwood again called out for the waitress. This time he requested the chef. Again, Sherwood and Sol encouraged me to confess his food was the best while the entire restaurant looked on in anticipation.

With a more seasoned attitude, I complimented his food as decidedly exquisite. Then, I apologized that he came second only to my grandmother from Naples. The chef and all seated around me roared with laughter, then this talented chef reached out and kissed my hand in acceptance of a quality-second place. I was only slightly embarrassed this time, while Sol and Sherwood unabashedly enjoyed my every uncomfortable moment.

One of the onlookers that evening was a gray-haired man sitting alone in a dimly lit corner. I couldn't see his face but heard him say in a familiar voice that his roots were in Naples too, and he was a frequent customer. I smiled and had a brief conversation with this stranger. Moments later, I learned that gentleman was singer/actor Dean Martin. He enjoyed a simple dish of freshly made pasta and a glass of red wine. Sherwood, knowing Dean, went to his table to say a quiet hello, then returned with a new story idea; the travels of celebrities in Hollywood.

The stories Sol and Sherwood spun were intoxicating through dinner, wine, and dessert. It was a fascinating evening over delicious food in an unparalleled atmosphere while watching two talented, highly inspired writers and great friends working together. At one point, Sol got up and walked through the restaurant, just like he did in the office, out the front door and back again. I felt like joining him as the entire experience was almost too brilliant to assimilate.

When coffee and biscotti arrived, they had pages of notes. Sol took a deep breath, then paused for a moment looking in the direction of the now-vacant shaded corner. Sol turned his head toward us and said,

> The subtleties of attitude lay within the subdivision of drama. I think what we saw tonight, the notes we've made, are more in line with drama. There is nothing funny about a man, visibly sad, dining alone in the shadows at the end of his career. I hope to always use good taste in writing comedy. I know the argument of good taste varies from person to person, but I have to go with my concept.

Neither man could give an exact definition of comedy when I asked but explained that any form of embarrassment is usually a good source of amusement to others and, hopefully, in time to the victim. Lenny Bruce calls comedy 'remembered pain.' Sol and Sherwood agreed not to use the notes for a new show. However, bits and pieces of observations about that eventful evening linger respectfully in plays they wrote for Theatre West.

By looking deeper and learning more that evening, the beautifully written drama, *The Faces of Love,* written by Sol, took on inspired and expanded sensitive moments. The last time we spent together was to see *Rockers*, a comedy/drama written by Sherwood and performed at Theatre West.

The evening was in honor and celebration of the 90th birthday of Mr. Sol Saks. Sherwood later confided that the evening at Il Pastaio helped remove some rough edges in his thinking.

It was no secret that as Sol entered his nineties, he was not too interested in writing for television. At this stage of his life, he was not finding television engaging enough to hold his attention. However, his love for the theater remained as strong as ever. Sol spent hours at our local and beloved theater, Theatre West, in creative bliss.

Sol was in his element. His writing flowed, and some of our brightest stars read his lines. One such bright star was Betty Garrett. Betty & Sol first met when Betty worked with Danny Kaye, and Sol wrote for the talented comedian. Throughout the years, their creative paths continued to cross while working. Betty had a formidable career in movies working with top stars like Frank Sinatra and Dean Martin and was full-to-the-brim of captivating stories. Her brilliant movie actor husband, Larry Parks, was best known for his starring role in The Al Jolson Story.

Betty Garrett, Frank Sinatra, and Larry Parks

One afternoon, years prior, the Parks couple received a summons from the House Un-American Activities Committee regarding the Communist Party. Life suddenly became a painful pursuit, and work abruptly halted. Betty, pregnant at the time, did not have to testify. However, Larry remained before the committee, the prying camera, and news reporters while answering their every question.

Larry admitted to Communist Party membership from 1941 to 1945 but refused to name names; this caused his name to immediately appear on the dreaded Hollywood Blacklist, drastically reducing the couple's ability to work.

Suddenly, they were shuttled from excellent paying film jobs to meager wages singing or performing comedy acts at nightclubs and appearing in legit plays. Although Parks never quite shook off the Blacklist incident, he did win a role in John Huston's 1962 film, Freud. Betty went on to appear in roles in many television series.

The struggle through this time was close to shattering for the couple; many longtime friends quietly stopped seeing them in fear of association. But Sol and Anne offered a non-judgmental hand of thoughtful friendship through it all. They invited the couple to several home-cooked meals, unending conversation, and much-needed laughs.

Between Sol and Betty was a wealth of experience, knowledge, and information from old and new Hollywood. Most in the industry knew that inspiration would find you if you were around either of them for even the shortest time. The two Hollywood veterans were a force of unparalleled creative energy.

Director Stu Berg commented that Sol was the group's elder statesman at Theatre West and an amazingly creative man. Stu directed several plays Sol wrote and confessed that he was fascinated with the incredible amount of energy Sol had. How sharp he remained well into his 90s and constantly marveled that Sol was always busy. He reported in an interview that 'Sol was working on new things and sharpening dialogue on old things.' Sol struggled with life complaints and issues like all of us and would have liked to have complained and explained them away at times, but he chose to spend his energy wisely honing his craft.

Theatre West remained an artistic home to Sol and many of our most talented people. Residing within this haven were such luminaries as Betty Garrett, Lee Meriwether, Richard Dreyfuss, Carroll O'Connor, Beau Bridges, Martin Landau, Dick Van Dyke, an occasional visit from Angela Lansbury, and dozens of brilliant entertainers new to the industry. Productions from our cherished theatre toured through the United States, Broadway in New York, and across the pond to Edinburgh and Dublin Festivals.

Moments with Marvin Kaplan

Marvin Wilbur Kaplan

Winter was upon us this workday as we sat in the Sutton Street treehouse. The fierce rain pounded against the windows as the driving winds blew through the treetops. This scary vantage point was unsettling as debris hit the windows, then sailed recklessly through the yard. Cold, and my clothes damp, I put the kettle on to boil, made a cup of tea, and prepared to work.

The rain, thankfully, was short-lived that morning, and we were well into Sol's new play when Marvin Kaplan arrived. Sol and Marvin were old friends from their days in Brooklyn. Sol cast Marvin in *A Day in The Life of An Actor*, one of the four segments of his play, *The Faces of Love*. Marvin stopped by to visit with his long-time friend and lend a hand with the script wherever he could. Sol introduced us, and I felt I'd known him all my life, an adorable, immediately likable character actor who performed on stage, screen, and television. Katharine Hepburn discovered this gem-of-a-man in 1947, opening the door for further work with many top stars over his 47-year career.

Marvin and Sol edited and talked for the rest of the morning about the play, changing lines, and sharpening dialog, and I typed the results. One of Marvin's talents was to add a dimension of quirkiness that was unique to him alone. I was still busy entering the new dialogue when Marvin bent over my chair and hugged me goodbye before leaving for lunch, saying he hoped I'd be at the performance. Pleased with such an invitation, I accepted wholeheartedly. How could I miss such a presentation? So, of course, I attended, and it was an hour of pure bliss to watch a play I'd seen written and then unfold through such talented and inspirational actors. I later saw him practicing his craft at a San Fernando Valley neighborhood theater with veteran character-actor Orson Bean.

Orson, at the time, was working as store owner *Loren Bray* on *Doctor Quinn Medicine Woman* starring Jane Seymore.

It was lovely to receive an invitation to a closed session and a rare treat to watch; they were brilliant and hysterical professionals.

Sitting with the creator of *M*A*S*H*, Larry Gelbart

Larry Simon Gelbart

Larry was an American television writer, playwright, screenwriter, director, and author, but most importantly, the best of humankind. Best known as the creator and producer of the television series *M*A*S*H* and as co-writer of the Broadway musicals, *A Funny Thing Happened on the Way to the Forum* and *City of Angels*.

Larry and Sol met while working together for *Danny Thomas* on his radio show. Larry was 18 years younger than Sol, and both were from Chicago. Both men had similar backgrounds and interests and would talk for hours. According to Sol, Larry was a gifted writer from birth. He was just a kid when they first met and wrote great jokes. His father was a barber to Danny Thomas and, being proud of his son, showed Danny a few of the skits his son Larry wrote. It opened doors that never shut. Larry wrote for Jack Paar, Bob Hope, Neil Simon, Woody Allen, and numerous others.

When Larry and his family moved to Los Angeles, they contacted Sol, and the two families joyfully reconnected. Sol remembers the day as something like going home. But for Sol and Larry, those occasional times they could work together were the best. Today was to be one of those rare occasions. Larry came to the office to go over ideas for a new sitcom. It was his first visit, and Larry, enthralled with the unique space, told Sol he must have a place to write like this one.

SOL SAKS

I sat in captivated splendor as these two masters worked, an experience I shall never forget. The two hours they brainstormed were more educational than a college semester in writing.

From Jewish immigrant parents from Poland also, Larry knew painful prejudice firsthand. However, he learned to take each thoughtless word spoken over him, each denial of an entrance, to build instead of tearing down his soul. Their jokes and sitcoms had roots in otherwise heartrending sneers and comments. However, stepping stones were made from every insult, leading them to success with their compassion and generosity intact. Unlike some, they did not waste their energy seeking revenge. Though there may have been a lingering pain waiting to get out, they chose to leave the payback in the hands of God. They pushed through the unkindness and made people laugh, cry, and sometimes shout for joy. They had a wealth of material stored and ready for use at any given time. Their parent's upbringing and mannerisms were different than what I've known, but the pain caused by diminishing words directed at us is universal. Everyone, if honest, has felt not quite good enough at some point in their lives.

Larry and Sol compared a few similar incidents from their youth and concluded that being young and singled out because you're not like others causes scars. Larry looked at Sol with a sudden revelation at the irony. They realized that going through the early injustice made them fearless in a den of lions, and they faced many. There are devouring lions in the entertainment industry, but when these gifted men wrote, the lions sat at attention, signed a contract, and sent them out with silver and gold.

Larry said these lovely sentiments in an interview about his dear friend Sol Saks. So, I present them in his own unedited words.

> Some people can do something that is very difficult to do. They can write comedy. Others can do something that is even more difficult. They can write about comedy. Either Sol Saks is very different, or he is two people because he can do both brilliantly.

–Larry Gelbart, *M*A*S*H*

9

Applause, Disappointments, and His Last Writing Class

> *"As we express our gratitude,*
> *we must never forget that the*
> *highest appreciation is not to*
> *utter words, but to live by them."*
> —John F. Kennedy

Sol Saks braved the rough times of his profession. Always, he carried, tucked securely beneath the ever-changing tides of life, his secret garden. While away, Sol could close his eyes momentarily to retreat to this nourishing sanctuary in his mind. Then, he stepped out into the reality born of his determination, skills, and beliefs. Buoyed by the past, Sol moved forward to make new memories and set new goals. He learned that the mind of a writer is a fascinating and sometimes troubled place. There is a channel of inspiration where creativity only comes to people gifted for the task. This information download takes many forms, and its outward aspect is beyond the usual thought process. It can be elusive, stunning in its quiet presentation, of another realm, or brilliantly filled with promise; the list is endless and can be exhilarating or daunting depending on what you're bringing to the audience. However, the gift comes at the price of remaining sensitive to the giver of the talent, leaving the recipient vulnerable at times. Sol had his share of this fight for balance but found stability by giving to students. Sol said,

> It was a gratifying and insightful time for me. While sharing information with the students and teaching the class, I'd think—I didn't know that! I realized the insight given to teachers was a gratification I had not known before. I greatly respect teachers and would like to have been a teacher. If only teaching paid a living wage. Anyway, I gained an insight that led to expanded thinking.

Sol never fully experienced the release of disappointment over a few choices he didn't like. So he decided to share his wealth of information with his eager college students. Maybe he could help them better navigate the politics and hidden pitfalls of the profession. During the last writing class to be taught by Sol, his students asked him what his childhood was like and did it influence his writing.

SOL SAKS

Sol paced the aisles, then sat on the corner of his desk, looked out over his young students at the beginning of their careers, and said,

Crime, violence, prejudice, and societal suppression, have been around since the beginning. When I was very young, no one told me this fact—and—to be fair, I do not think people fully realized it then. As a result, I adopted unhealthy-defensive attitudes and opinions about myself. These were back in the days when I was a small boy. I couldn't understand why people spoke hateful names about me, my family, and my religion. My parents, familiar with the harsher treatment of war, developed the habit of focusing on and pointing out the good we had. We kept busy serving customers while making a living. Eventually, we made enough to help others less fortunate than us. As we succeeded financially, persecution in the form of jealousy soon arrived. We were now called cheats, sneaks, and words I will not repeat.

I am Jewish—and my family is from a long line of Polish immigrants; this fact appeared to give most people the freedom to say and do anything that came to mind. No matter how kind and generous my parents were, some people had to throw verbal stones. I learned it was ignorance on their behalf, which helped a little. It was not long before I also learned to keep my head down, work hard, ignore them, and learn everything I could to realize my dreams—much like my parents did.

The hypocrisy at the time was confusing and painful to me. I didn't know—even as a teenager, about the conflicting value systems my mother and father had to endure during their childhood. I later learned that mental and physical abuse during that war era was a tortuous common occurrence. Unfortunately, my parents and grandparents were part of those horrors. Many of my maternal grandparent's possessions were stolen or destroyed during the conflicts, and they saw atrocities that still burned in their minds until the day they died. In those days, Post-traumatic Stress Syndrome was not widely known. Yet, in retrospect, I believe they all suffered, to some extent, from this affliction. Many of the symptoms were evident. Yet, help for the type of trauma they endured—at least for them, was unknown then.

But even in their darkest moments, my parents were determined to provide a better life for us, and they used their unspeakable pain to take them to success they may not have reached otherwise. They talked about a few experiences when I was grown up and married. Some, however, my mother said with tears would never be spoken.

Sol continues,

> Though a covert form of prejudice resides in this beautiful land of America, it is better than their childhood life in Poland, and she prefers to focus on the freedom offered in her new country. A country where she and my father could work and raise a family. During the years of World War 2, my parents continued working hard, smiling through the day, serving customers, and taking care of us. But at night, I could hear my mother crying. When I asked her the next day, she would say she had a painful headache. Years later, she told me she had friends and family members taken to concentration camps. She and my father tried several possible solutions but could do nothing. They struggled with conflict, helplessness, and at times guilt. The irrational thought that my mother had abandoned them somehow hovered over her like a plague. Periodically—the unimaginable emotional pain eclipsed so much of the remaining beauty surrounding her. Of course, as a child, a couple of unintentional mannerisms my mother had could be confusing to me. Whatever the secrets my parents held—the burdens occasionally spilled out in confusing and disturbing ways that I still don't understand but have forgiven a long time ago.
>
> There are brief moments lately when I think of their pain and suffering, but now with a clearer vision of admiration. From a vantage point of living and observing for many years, I can more fully appreciate the strength, love, and compassion they fought to keep. When bitter struggles war within our minds, the words of truth bring clarity and peace. But, enough said, I am older now, and some of those harsh experiences have served me well. They have made me stronger, wiser, and, like my parents, more determined than I might have been, and yes, they influence my writing considerably. However, life for me remains a mystery unsolved, and so many adventures I have yet to understand. I hope you will appreciate this fair country and strive to improve it, but without hatred. Read, learn, pray for wisdom, then apply for a change. I will leave you with these great words of Abraham Lincoln; that government of the people, by the people, for the people, shall not perish from the earth.

Every student stood with thunderous applause as Sol was still seated on the edge of his desk; now stunned, his eyes began to tear. Gaining his composure, he slowly stood to thank his students, but the applause continued to roar. Overcome, Sol thanked them with a gracious slight bowing of his head and exited the room. The applause continued to follow him down the hall and out the door.

SOL SAKS

The bittersweet sounds and faces he would carry with him until his last day. Although according to Sol, these were the treasured awards he could take with him when he left the earth.

Sol Saks...late nineties

"What would you say is the proudest writing achievement of your career?" An interviewer asked Sol, now age 99 years old. Closing his eyes as he paused to think, looking down, away from the camera, Sol said in a contemplative voice,

> There were a few proud achievements. None of which were published or produced. If you ask a successful novelist what his favorite book is, you'd expect him to name his bestseller; he doesn't. He always mentions the one that didn't work well because he wants to know that one was good. For me, I would think it was something in writing.
>
> There was a show called *Cameo* on the radio by Sherman Marks. It was an hour show featuring drama. I had been on the air for four or five years on several popular shows then, and I always wrote things but seldom sold them. I assumed because my family was so busy, they did not have time to listen to my work that did sell. But this one time, I wrote about my boyhood in Chicago. I submitted my work to *Cameo*, and they liked it, and it aired on their radio show. It's the one thing I'm most proud of and the one thing my father said to me that meant the most.
>
> To my surprise, my father listened to *Cameo* the night my script aired. When I saw him next, he looked at me smiling and told me it was a good script I had written. So, it returns to what I was saying, tells the truth, and will serve you well. Also, many students said that I helped them with their careers. So, I have to include that as a most rewarding achievement.

BEWITCHED

"Did you have a mentor who showed you the ropes?" This question seemed to take Sol by surprise; he looked away and, in a quiet, barely audible voice, answered,

> No, no, I think it is my attitude. I believe I don't take advice or help well. I've seen cases where somebody takes someone under their wing, but that was not the case with me. But there is another thing you can get lost that way. Unless the mentor has no regard for anything for themselves, you can lose yourself in them. You become an adjunct to them. That is a position I could never take. No one has given me advice as many people do, especially movie stars. Like Ida Lupino and Joan Caulfield, they would like you to be their friend and buddy. They were approachable in that respect. They were open to help, maybe because they were confident in themselves.

"What is the most significant advice anyone ever gave you about writing for TV?" Sol, answering with a conservative laugh, said,

> I don't remember ever getting advice. As I said, I think I am not the kind of man people would advise. I'm too bristly, and as I said before, the best advice is the advice I've given myself. Learn your craft and tell the truth. I've learned by working hard and watching people.
>
> People from the Danish TV network asked me to be their consultant, and though they came to me for advice, I learned valuable lessons from interacting with them. Age does not seem to be an issue there as it is here. If you are past the retirement age of 65 and a writer in Hollywood, it varies from difficult to impossible to get work. I'm generous with the age level also. The Danish working environment and government situation make it easier to work as a team. They take a more realistic look at life. They include all ages, types, religions, and upbringing in their entertainment. Their tv production hours are regulated. No one would have worked my hours, mainly because it would not have been necessary. But in saying these things, I have been able to amass more money than they can. I've had more freedom of choice. On the other hand, their programming holds to a stricter standard. So, there are many things we can learn from each other.

"Tell me about your days at CBS and if you have any regrets." Sol took a deep breath, put his hands up, leaned into the camera, and said,

> I was the fair-haired boy at CBS and wrote pilots for a time. With the first five written, the studio used them immediately. It worked because one of the suits would get an idea, and all they needed was someone to write the script.

SOL SAKS

Sol continues,

> As a writer, you hear the line, 'This idea would be a great show if you could put in the jokes. You're the writer.' Well, you don't put in the jokes, they grow in, or you don't put them in. Ida Lupino had a show written by her ex-husband, which wasn't good, and they needed a producer. So, CBS suggested Freddy de Cordova to Ida. These were the days before he produced for Johnny Carson. So, Ida, who was great, one of the best, told CBS that they had to pass it by Sol. That was an unusual and brave approach! Hearing Ida's exception, Freddy called me; he wanted to meet me for lunch in Beverly Hills, but I never went into town for a meeting. I didn't shave or get dressed up very often. Undeterred, Freddy said he'd come to the valley, which he did, and we met at my home. He had read three of my scripts and commented that they were the best scripts he'd ever read. He told me that this is the kind of television he wanted to do; all of his life, he wanted to work on a show like this. How could you say no to a guy like that? So I enthusiastically recommended Freddy to CBS! The arrangements made were to work at the Desilu Studios. Freddy wanted to show me his office on the first day of shooting.
>
> He led me into a big beautiful office with wood paneling, old English etchings, and an antique desk; it was luxurious. He gets a call on a phone that lights up like a beacon, so his assistant finishes the tour. The second office was not as big but still had carpet on the floor and no etchings; that's the associate producer's office. Then we come into a room, which is the size of an efficient kitchen in a condo. That's my office. It has a desk with carved initials, two chairs, and a typewriter. I'm standing looking at this in shock, and Freddy de Cordova comes to the door and says, 'Sol, I've reread your three scripts, two we can't use, but the third I think I know how we can fix.' I turned from the old beat-up desk and told him I was not writing three new scripts and that the three scripts I submitted were good. Immediately upset, he got in his car and went to CBS. He said those dreaded words I had heard all the days of my career, 'I'm the producer. I can screw up this whole script because I'm the producer!' He told them he was having trouble with me, and they said, 'Let him alone.' Because they knew Ida was on my side. Freddy, till the day he died, I believe, hated me.

"So, what happened next?"

> Then, I became an Executive Producer at CBS, which was new for me. I was not responsible for a script belonging to someone else, I was now one of the suits, and my gosh, it was delightful!

BEWITCHED

Sol continues,

> I was Executive Producer of all comedy shows for CBS, including; Gilligan's Island, Beverly Hillbillies, Dick Van Dyke Show, Andy Griffith, and others. There was no resemblance to being a writer where the day has gone by, and you screwed up the whole day and sharpened your pencil like Larry Gilbart said, until it has a surgical point. So, by 5, or 5:30, I went home. No waiting around until Hunt Stromberg went home as everybody else did. Because, again, there was no pressing need for me to create a winning script. I could enjoy, more fully, the fact that I had a wife and two small kids, and I could go home and be with them. It was wonderful.

"What can you tell us about your involvement with Gilligan's Island?"

> I can tell you about one of the producers, a friend of mine, who I do not think would mind if I told this story. I'm not sure if he knows what happened even to this day, but here goes. Gilligan's Island was a show that Sherwood had conceived, invested money in, and worked long and hard to make the pilot. Sherwood was to produce Gilligan's Island here in the San Fernando Valley, and he was underway when his producer quit. His producer was also a partner with Sherwood on Gilligan's Island. They were close to production time and did not have one foot of film. The stress was fierce. As you can imagine, a great deal of invested money and time was on the line. The CBS meetings were for new shows and about the suits blasting the writer. This one with Sherwood was no different. First, they pointed out everything wrong with the show, then ended the meeting and dismissed Sherwood. Then, behind closed doors, they concluded that everyone liked Sherwood, but he was not doing the job, and they had to let him go.
>
> These thick contracts state that they could fire him whenever they wanted. First, however, they had to pay him a specified royalty. Bill Froug, another friend, expanded the story by telling me about the suits putting him in charge. He would take the place of Sherwood because Bill was more experienced; he had already produced a show. They set up another meeting with Sherwood and Bill, and Bill would tell Sherwood as diplomatically as possible that he was to leave the show. After doing a bit of research, Bill called Hunt Stromberg to give him his findings and a suggestion about that meeting with Sherwood when Hunt abruptly interrupts and, with a raised voice, says,
>
> 'Look, I told you that you are going to tell Sherwood on Tuesday!'

SOL SAKS

Sol continues,

> Bill said, 'Yeah, yeah, but did you see the new ratings? Gilligan's Island is number 4!' There was a slight pause, then with an even louder voice of frustration, Hunt hollers, 'Cancel the meeting, cancel the meeting!' After that, Sherwood hated the network because they tried to ruin the show, pushing him around considerably. It was a mess. Sherwood and I had the same agent, George Rosenberg. George told Sherwood to go to Hawaii, take a two-week vacation, and get away from the show. Sherwood wanted to go to Hawaii but rested at home instead. Within a few days, he received a call from the studio to come back and produce his show. Sherwood was writing Louis B. Mayer stories, which appealed to the audience. He has the same talent as the Warner Brothers, Goldwin, and Mayer. However, Sherwood wasn't the most literate—not his strong point. But when he heard a story that he liked, it was usually popular with the television audience. Sherwood could sit down and write a show tonight that the critics would love. He was also sure they would cancel it within four weeks because it wasn't necessarily what the audience loved. Sherwood wrote and produced for people, not for critics. He had great talent and knew what people liked. After all that, I say this reluctantly, but I didn't care for the show as presented. Nobody liked the script. It wasn't well-written. But I did say I wished I had the idea. I liked the thought of different people on an island, a perfect TV concept. It gave you a foundation for a lot of stories. So, Sherwood was right, and I was wrong because his show was successful. Except, as I said, I wish I had that idea. To answer if I had any regrets, yes, my stint at CBS because working with them did me no good. My time there was non-creative, though restful, pleasant, and an outstanding experience. I think that's one thing that happens in all the arts, the experience, something new to try. I said I was the fair-haired boy until the guy who replaced Hunt Stromberg came along. I can't remember his name. For some reason, he didn't like me, my work, or both. So, I left and probably should have stayed. The guy who replaced me, Larry Gelbart, got M*A*S*H. Which, as you know, was a successful play and television series. If I'd stayed, it would have come to me. But Larry was a friend, and I was happy for him.
> M.A.S.H was ahead of its time. They wrote for adults, not telling jokes to kids. I also see theater plays I wish I'd written every once in a while, which isn't a good feeling. I'd wonder why I didn't write that play.

Sol continues,

> But then, I've often thought, what if I'd gone to New York and not California? I would have loved to be a playwright. I have no doubt I would have written plays. But a book that Neil Simon wrote about himself helped me in many ways. Simon commented in his book that he did *The Sid Caesar Show*. The show eventually went off the air, and all the writers went to California, where there was work. His wife didn't want to leave New York, so they stayed. What do you do in New York as a writer? You write plays. So, If Neil Simon had gone with the other group, he might never have been successful. Alan Jay Lerner, who wrote *My Fair Lady* and *Camelot,* owned shoe stores. He tried out for Duffy's Tavern, and the producers thought he wrote too light, so they didn't hire him. Now, if Alan had written a little stronger, they would have taken him to California, and today, Alan would be a successful comedy writer. But instead, he stayed and wrote these beautiful musicals. I saw this way of thinking when I wrote my first five-minute piece; it was for the Chicago radio *Duffy's Tavern,* for which I got $35.00. Anne and I were just married, and we had been planning a weekend away when I got a call. The producer wanted one of those writing pieces right away. He sounded rushed but assured me I would get my usual $35.00. That was the only job I did then, and I became torn with the decision. First, *I should take that piece, write and not go on this vacation.* Then, I started to feel uncomfortable with that decision and thought, *no—I'm going on a vacation. Someday I'll have a swimming pool, and I won't be sorry I didn't do the script.*
>
> So, it took me until I was in my nineties to realize there was always a plan and guidance, like my wife Anne said, and I shouldn't use my energy on regrets. She was correct; our vacation is a memory that has helped me through difficult times and has stayed with me all these years, a priceless memory with Anne.
>
> By the way, those moments also become invaluable to a writer. They add dimension to the words you string into sentences. Listen, we all have regrets. But I read a line that has stuck with me, and I have seen it come true in my life, 'Our lives, filled with misfortunes, most of which never happen.' If I genuinely regret anything, it's having plaguing regrets; they stunt creativity. Like, why didn't I go to New York? The truth is that when dramatics fell in New York, and we saw nothing but musicals, I would have been out of work. I'd be out of work now. With television, I was never out of work. Also, I am now writing plays performed at several theaters in town.

Sol concludes,
> *Faces of Love* recently presented again at Theatre West in Los Angeles and received excellent reviews calling it a long-overdue success. The enjoyment of working with everyone involved is beyond money for me.

"What were your other responsibilities at CBS at that time?"
> Just overseeing the other shows, I was the guy in charge. Bob Sweeny, a friend of mine, had a show I was responsible for called Baily's of Balboa. By this time, I found that other writers resented me in my new position. They didn't resent the other guy with the necktie because he was supposed to do it, but not me. I called Bob and asked him if he could come to my office, and he said he was busy. I said, well, okay, I'll meet you there. Bob asked if I'd mind having his head writer, Arthur Julian, attend, and I said no, that's fine. I arrived with their script in hand. I began to explain that there was a problem with the script.
>
> I attempted to explain, but they seemed offended and sarcastic. Both writers were sure I wanted what they called a jokey show. So I went on as kindly as possible to explain the problem and solution but to no avail. So, I said, I haven't made myself clear. The script stinks. 'Why?' Bob and Arthur shouted. Then I told them that it was the third act; it was not working. So then they tried to fix it. I went home to my wife and told her I knew how to be an executive producer. You tell them that the script stinks and tell them they need you. Nope, I don't want to be that guy. I don't want to do that job. I was exhausted, unfulfilled, and miserable. When I started writing, I wanted to write stories that people wanted to hear. A friend of mine asked me what I had to say. What information did I have to enlighten the world? I told him that I had nothing to add in that way. Then he insisted there was no chance I could be a writer! Well, I found that not to be true. Someone said a man has an insatiable appetite for entertainment, which is the truth. That means those of us, from a hooker to Beethoven, are in that business of satisfying. Whoever the writer is closest to, I will leave it up to you, but I know the best and worst of us are sometimes close to one or the other. Storytellers are what we are, the descendants of the man who first sat by the fireside and told stories. Storytellers write documentaries now seen on television. Years ago, they went from camp to camp, telling good stories.

Sol concludes,
> My daughter wanted a story every night. I was to read her a story, make up a story, or tell her a story about when I was a little boy. So, I believe storytelling is a noble profession.
>
> Similar to a chef who caters to the appetite of people. The better the chef, the harder he works to present the best possible food. Then a man or woman comes home from work and may want to sit down to watch a basketball game, as I will do tonight. Maybe they want to go out with friends, listen to music, or go to the opera; each wants entertainment. A diversion often refreshes the mind, offers a time of rest, or introduces a new way of seeing the world around us. The only thing wrong might be if you're lying or bad with your abilities.

Hollywood Ageism

"There is a fountain of youth: it is your mind, your talents, the creativity you bring to your life and the lives of people you love. When you learn to tap this source, you will truly have defeated age."
—Sophia Loren

A passionate topic of discussion was and continues to be ageism in Hollywood. It hampers actors, but it covertly shuttles writers to the side. So, Sol Saks, Norman Leer, and friends became staunch human rights advocates between writing projects. One of several examples of ageism for Sol was his beautifully written and meticulously edited novel. Written in his late seventies, he asked trusted, respected industry friends to read and comment on his work. Each enjoyed his relevant manuscript and encouraged him to get his work published. Sol, confident that his work was good and before self-publishing became popular, gave me the task of writing to literary agents. Then, Sol scheduled meetings with those agents to promote his book on his days off. Two kindly-crafted rejection notes came out of hundreds of queries and numerous meetings; the remaining were silent.

Nevertheless, the agents widely admired Sol's brilliant reputation as a writer. Sol also had one book published. So, what was the problem? He persisted for several years and re-wrote portions of his novel, but the defining, deafening silence continued. Finally, he decided to investigate. He learned that he was considered too old and had been so for years, much to his dismay. He had slipped silently into one of the foreboding unseen cracks in our beautifully tolerant Hollywood. Being an active member at Theatre West, several writers suggested Sol hire a twenty-year-old to promote the book for him. Sol considered their suggestion but found the prospect intolerable.

SOL SAKS

Through the help of a couple of Hollywood unions, he found several actors forming a group to protest this injustice.
He met with longtime friend and beloved actress Doris Roberts, best known for *Everybody Loves Raymond*.

Doris May Roberts

Sol and Doris had many enlightening talks and considered various solutions when they discovered a young friend in common; the late-actor James Dean. Doris lived in a home she once rented to James, and Sol regaled her with a story when he lived next door in the early days of James' career. James would ask Doris and Sol many questions about the industry, listen intently, consider what they said, and then act upon his gathered answers. James had impacted their lives, leaving them with a sense of family, much like a younger brother. If James had lived, he would be in his 70s at that time and probably considered too old to work. This revelation was an empowering moment, lighting an unquenchable fire in them both.

Doris shared that she had many extremely talented actress friends in the humiliating position of asking if they could borrow money from her. Some would quietly say they would take even the smallest part on her show in desperation. Those cruel circumstances and the thought of James fueled the anger that took Doris to Washington on September 4, 2002. Driven by her loyalty, she began a strategy for justice for women and everyone in the industry. She made international headlines when she testified before U.S. Senator John Breaux's Special Committee on Ageism in Washington. Doris gave a scathing summary of the cruelty women of a certain age can face later in their careers. Though not mentioned, she told Sol that James was always present in her thoughts while in Washington. In a People magazine interview, she said,

> No photograph in any magazine I can think of, other than The AARP Magazine, shows a woman over 45 unless she's ill or selling Viagra. They like to airbrush us out of existence. So, I hold Madison Avenue at fault for dismissing us.

Doris then became a Cultural Ambassador for the U.S. Department of State, traveling to underdeveloped countries worldwide to speak about hope. As most people in Hollywood's writing community knew, Sol was a fierce advocate for the rights of humankind and was known in this group for taking a stance. But now, out from the shadows, word emerged to the public, sighting that Saks was the first to secure a writer's on-screen credit and was looking forward to the challenge of making another significant change. He stated in interviews that producers, agents, and executives prefer young assistants, preferably those just out of film school. Actors and writers were the most brutally hit. Even notable talent and friend Cary Grant began slipping into the abyss. However, while Cary was still marketable, he signed a contract to become a spokesman for a celebrated face cream. When Elizabeth Taylor experienced this Hollywood phenomenon, she went with perfume. Neither acted again, which was difficult because they enjoyed their work. In separate interviews, each stated that they decided to remain grateful. Both maintained a humble yet confident self-image and managed to rise above prejudice. But the humiliation was devastating for many without a saleable name and spotlighted by the Hollywood media.

Without divulging names, some actors lost their lives because of that deep, unseen cavern in our town, turning to alcohol, drugs, and, eventually, suicide. One particular well-known actor in the 1960s was nearing forty when jobs became scarce for him. Approached by a group that offered him a large amount of money for helping with something illegal, he desperately said yes. Unfortunately, if he received the money remains unknown, and his murder still goes unsolved.

Sol felt we could learn from the people of Britain and Denmark, who make a place for the full range of talented people until they want to leave or are physically unable to work. Britain's writing includes a broad spectrum of ages, and they brilliantly use their country's history to convey compelling stories. Sol, Doris, and friends would gratefully see a few changes in Hollywood, making life in our city a bit easier. Avenues of work opened slightly to accommodate more realistic storylines and a broader spectrum of humanity. Debbie Macomber, a brilliant, beloved writer, wrote Mrs. Merkle. The book became several movies for television, and dear Doris starred as Mrs. Merkle.

Submissions from a talented minority of writers once denied were becoming accepted, but of course, with mandatory publisher revisions. However, still not impressed, Sol did not pursue the publication of his novel. Instead, he went back to his first love, writing dramatic plays. The steady pursuit of justice slowed as Spring arrived in Los Angeles, California, bringing lovely sights and sounds of promise.

SOL SAKS

The fight for change subsided to a dull roar while the creative process in town escalated with a new sense of hope. Sol and I were again in the quiet office amongst the treetops preparing to sharpen his plays, and I wondered what new adventures lay ahead. His boxed novel sat on my desk with a note, *put away for now*. So, sadly I put years of hard work on the office shelf and closed the door. I must admit that I was and am sad that Sol didn't pursue the publication of his novel. But, I think as I write these many years later, there sits in a dark closet somewhere, a brilliant piece of writing waiting for wings.

But for now, I must return to that particular day in the office. I had a momentary daydream of better times ahead while preparing for that day of writing. Sitting immediately outside the expansive windows, birds sat singing as if full of expectation. Their tiny feet gripped tightly to swaying branches while cool breezes brought a peaceful atmosphere entering the entirety of Sutton Street. There was a lesson before me. Though the wind blew strongly, buffeting them about, they didn't appear anxious about anything. I opened the windows, letting the cool breezes rush past me, carrying with them the cooing sounds of Doves and the lesson of restful thinking. I relaxed, breathed in the fresh air, and returned to thoughts of work. When I returned to my desk, I saw a review in The Hollywood Reporter about Sol. I was surprised and perplexed by his unusual candor.

I asked him what he would like me to do with his article. Gazing only at the publication in my hand, he began pensively speaking without ever taking his eyes off the magazine; he said,

Because I spoke up and caused a tumult, a partial print of my background is now in the public eye. It is a vulnerable position. I have seen entertainers fold under the politically driven scrutiny of exposure. But, I have learned a few valuable lessons from Cary Grant and Ida Lupino. While continually under scrutiny, they said it is essential to be secure in who they were, no matter the bias or the half-truths written; I'm doing my best to let it go. What is important to remember is where we came from and to remain grateful. I now see that one can lose sight of possibilities when the opposition is loud. Expectations are constantly increasing to be better, more cutting edge, and more controversial, all to grab the attention of more viewers. As a result, you can lose your way.

There was a sense of poignancy in his words, and I knew I must remember them as Sol continued.

No matter our background, the environment we grew up in, or even how we feel about ourselves, these things don't have to kill our dreams. Ageism does not have to stop us. We have a choice.

Sol rose from his chair and paced the room with determination. He took the article from my hand, waving it in the air as he continued,

It's a matter of decision, Carolyn. Listen, being born to poor Jewish immigrants in New York was no easy life back then. We were an outcast practically everywhere. But, no matter what people said, my father opened a business. House Paint was a product everyone needed, and he kept it affordable. As a result, people found our store, and my parents remained gracious even if the customers were rude. Though the words hurt, they believed God heard them and would rectify the situation. I thought their decision was weak at first, but their wisdom was undeniable after time passed; my parents were wise beyond their humble education. I could write a book just about that subject alone.

Remember when I mentioned that I worked on the radio as a child? My parents asked if I could be happy doing that. When I said yes without hesitation, they encouraged me to try. I got the job, but it was short-lived, albeit a good experience. I enjoyed making my own money, contributing to my family, and gaining much-needed confidence. But I don't think I often thought about being an actor when I started. I wouldn't do it if people did not like me. There was nothing I could do about people's opinions or control. I decided I wanted a better life, to follow my dream no matter the cost. I have better now. I am still Jewish, but now I am old, and Hollywood does not use old. Society now says you cannot because you are too old, I will not buy it, and neither should anybody. I would like to see this advice in printed form one day.

Stopping abruptly, he took a deep breath, then placed the article back on my desk. He turned and walked to the window overlooking his back garden. A sadness seemed to envelop him, and I, a bit overwhelmed, had to hide the tears beginning to form. Now calm, he looked at me and said, "Oh, well, maybe I'll do another interview. Or, someday, you might write it for me.

Do you write, Carolyn?"

"Oh no, not me, Sol!"

10

"What Better Teacher Than Sol Saks?" –Norman Leer

*"There's nothing I believe more than this,
that laughter adds time to one's life."*
—Norman Lear

Sol and Norman Lear, both comedy writers, had several things in common that brought them together as allies in a harsh business. Both parents came from humble beginnings and experienced the devastation war brings. In addition, the father of Norman Lear was of Russian-Jewish heritage, and his mother was from Ukraine.

All in the Family, one of many television series Norman created, was a huge success then, and Sol asked how he came up with the characters. Norman laughed and said that his father was a rascal. When Norman was nine years old, his father went to prison for selling fake bonds. Though he was not a white Protestant, his father was the inspiration for Archie. His mother, in part, inspired Edith, but from that point, the characters took on a life of their own.

Sol and Norman had a wealth of inspirational family life to draw from, and both used painful anti-Semitism to succeed. They found a healthy way to view criticism that made them rich beyond monetary gains. They found a wealth of social acceptance and mental freedom unknown to their parents. They were also consummate editors. Sol was adamant about editing, editing, and editing again. Throughout my nine years working with Sol, his editing skills remained brilliantly consistent, but much to his distress didn't always end with his writing. Though he possessed a coveted gift for writing, frequently in conversation, the ingrained editing skill mentally edited long redundant phrases from the person attempting to explain a situation. If it was a woman he was dating, that might have been their last date. The process became abundantly stressful to this writer of brevity. His doctor warned Sol against stress, so, often in a business situation conducted by phone, it was my job to take the call, listen, take notes, edit, then pass them to Sol. After he spent a moment of relaxed reading, he responded via a letter he would dictate to me.

However, student or media consultations were enjoyable moments for Sol and done with relative ease. Below are notes from personal chats and the last media interview given by Sol seven months before he died; he was 99 years old.

Sadly, a noticeable cough from bronchial congestion interrupted the proceedings several times. But Sol soldiered on and generously continued to share his wealth of information.

"How did you earn a living at the beginning of your career, Mr. Saks?"

> Many of us in our early days earned much of our living switching risqué jokes. We would replace the offensive sexual references while leaving the rest intact, like root-canal work. Thus, we got a double laugh. One from the revised humor of the old standard. Then another from those who recalled it in its original form.

"Can you explain comedy to me?"

> Comedy, I believe, is built on hostility. The exception may be a clown who has a painted happy face. Otherwise, if you examine comedy, you find hostility; there is where the fun comes in. You can make fun of someone, saying that I have a friend that is so dumb, etc. You are creating characters. I don't buy the saying that there are five ideas or maybe seven. I believe everyone is different. Somebody can write the same script as I did and the same plot, but they are uniquely different. The level of conflict, drama, and hostility is different. What is most important is what appeals to you, what is funny to you; that is the only thing you should trust. It fails if anybody tries anything else, like writing above or below it! If I write a story where a husband has a mistress, but I never had a mistress, and try to make a joke, it's just okay and eventually becomes tiresome. Truthfulness and honesty are most important!
>
> It's been my experience that someone who doesn't know the language becomes more interesting; they're not building the lines up with unnecessary phrases. They can say simple words like hit me. That phrase may take a writer four pages to say the same thing. I like the question, what do you know for sure? Like when someone in the Midwest asks you, what do you know for sure? It's a subtle way of saying I don't want gossip or theories. I want to know just the truth behind what happened. That concept has worked great for me. Stories for children are reality-based, but I don't want to say too much here. Today's reality shows are less genuine than the shows we did years ago. Then, we wrote about how people lived. Practically, with differences, with polish. On the reality shows of today, they make up situations. That's not reality. It's the opposite.

SOL SAKS

Sol concludes,

> The quote in Shakespeare where Polonius makes his statement stands the test of time. It reads,
> 'This, above all, to thine own self, be true and, it must follow, as the night the day, thou canst not then be false to any man.' This quote is a masterful key to successful writing.

"What advice have you followed?"

> Thoreau writes a line, never take a job where you must wear a costume. A costume today is a shirt and tie, and I hate to get dressed in the morning. Salinger, one of my favorites, writes just what happens—F. Scott Fitzgerald also is admirable.
> On tv, if you remember some of the comedy shows when they'd have a kid, or several people of a different nationality enter, that creates a new environment; and a place for new jokes. I never liked the average tv comedy because you didn't see husband and wife working together. They also didn't argue. Or where the husband has screwed up the plumbing under the sink and flooded everything. Then the wife calls the plumber who repairs it all. She then looks up at her husband adoringly and tells him how smart he is. These are clichés. The audience knows she is the bright one.
> Lying offers no advantages, except if you're a bank robber. If you're the bank robber and asked if you robbed the bank, you say no, though you did. So, if you're not a bank robber, there's very little reason to lie. Lying makes your life difficult. I have one problem with saying all of this. I consider myself a relatively honest man, but there's one place where I can't beat it. It's when someone invites me somewhere I don't want to go. So, I say, 'Oh, I'm busy that day!' When the truth is, I don't want to go. One time I was stuck. I found myself adding to my excuse that I was busy. 'Oh, my mother's coming in that day, and we've made plans.' The other person says, 'Oh, I have the date wrong. It's the following week.' Now I'm stuck. I have to go.
> Tell the truth, plant your feet. It's the best thing. I wrote a book called Funny Business, The Craft of Comedy Writing. The head of the writing department at California State University was a non-writer. He was a producer. But he talked like a writer and wrote a book on writing and then gave it to me to read. It was dreadful, so I decided to write a book about comedy writing. I put down everything I could think of that I said in lectures, and I had forty pages and sent it off to a publisher. They sent me a letter saying they liked it and would like to publish my work.

BEWITCHED

Sol continues,

> They requested I send them the following 200 pages by September. I was shocked. I thought, *200 pages! I wrote everything I knew in 40 pages!* So, I padded it. I thought of anecdotes and attitudes that I put in a script. I did what I'm telling you not to do, but I wanted to get the book published.

The above photograph is of Sol inside his treehouse office, his secret garden in the background, holding his newly published book, *Funny Business—the Craft of Comedy Writing*, published in 1985 by Writer's Digest Books and is used in many universities.

Sol continues,

> Writing is simple, but it's not easy. It's when you complicate it that it becomes a problem. A good example is, if you want to tell a story about how you fell at the doorstep of your house, then your face fell into a piece of the pie, write the story the way it is. Or, if you're going to San Francisco, your audience wants to hear about the trip. You don't have to tell us why you were there. You don't want to hear that you stopped into this place and bumped into an old schoolmate; keep it simple. I've received letters, phone calls, and questions from students about the dreaded block writer's experience. It sounds harsh, but I do not believe in the writers-block, mainly because I found a way to discredit that illusion. In radio and television, there was no such malady for a writer. You could not do a half-hour of dead air on NBC Tuesday at 7 in the evening; something has to fill that space.

SOL SAKS

Sol continues,

>With writers-block, you may think my ideas are not good and get stumped. So, I figured it out. Start the piece the way you would if you were writing badly, the way you would not turn it in. Then, as you put the words down, your writing improves because you tackle the subject as soon as you start writing. Also, step back and take an objective look. Typically, it is because you have improper ingredients. Almost every time, the missing ingredient is conflict. Conflict is what makes the wheels go around. In humor, the struggle is more crucial than in drama. When I came from Chicago to California, I was without a job and hoping to get one.
>
>As I recall, I came by coach, sleeping on the seat for three nights. I would daydream that a guy would stop me when I arrived in California. He asked me if I was Sol Saks. I, of course, would say yes. The guy told me that he was a talent agent for Bob Hope and would like me to work for them. Now I would start to write my daydream and write that Bob Hope walks into a hotel to book a room, and then what? While sitting there, I tried to make this funny in my mind. After all, this is Bob Hope, and he always says something funny. What could he say that would make me laugh; I would like a room. Finally, my writing came to a stop. I was worried. I thought I better get off this train at the next stop and return to Chicago. Then it occurred to me. No, if Bob Hope asks for a room and the receptionist tells him they only have one room left, and he has to share it with a kangaroo, or that six chorus girls are dressing in there, I have something.
>
>You put in a problem, an objection, which makes room for comedy. If there's a room and no problem, there's no comedy. I had two funny buddies growing up, and I was their audience. I would laugh at their antics. But when I became a writer, they looked at me and wondered how I did it. They always said that I was never funny. They would shake their heads in frustration and ask me why they could not write funny. But, I looked at something and thought of what was amusing about that or what could be funny. So that's what I wrote about, what amused me. My very first writing was in the 8th grade. We had an auditory paper to read in front of the class. An overweight boy in the class named Franky was struggling with the assignment. In those days, anyone overweight was considered genetically unfunny. So, I gave him a joke I heard on a Vaudeville stage. It goes like this;
>
>'Carl came to Nancy's house and called to her. Nancy, I'm here. She called back. I'm upstairs taking a shower.

Sol concludes,

> He said, Well, slip on something and come down. So, she slipped on a bar of soap and came down.'
>
> It got good laughs from the kids; it was a hit. Now, I'm on the side watching while Franky is getting all the laughs. Then I noticed the teacher standing at the head of the class, attempting to get our attention. Finally, frustrated and a bit angry, she slammed the corner of her desk with a ruler and excused us for recess. That was all except Franky; she singled him out, kept him in, and told him never to do that again. In addition, he should never, ever recite any off-color jokes. So, he came out to the schoolyard to find me, then punched me out. That day, I found my first truth about writing. When it works, you're anonymous. When it doesn't work—you're fired!

"What do you find the most problematic aspects of comedy writing"?

> As I said earlier, we didn't have the laugh machines when we started. You had a live audience. So, your scene endings should always be a joke where the audience laughs out loud. It was a requirement for a good show. That was the hard thing, the most problematic. On that line, you would get stuck very often. So, I'll quote a line from Mel Brooks that I think is apropos. 'Tragedy is when I cut my finger. Comedy is when you fall into an open sewer; what happens to me personally is often not funny.'

At His Desk Answering Questions

SOL SAKS

"What do you find is the most rewarding aspect of comedy writing, and what changes have you seen in that feature?" There was a long uncomfortable pause, then, in a quiet tone, Sol said,

>The laugh, definitely the laugh. Which is like the girl that you like the most can hurt you the most. When the laugh fails, as it sometimes does, it's tough. But then came an invention that made a considerable difference for a comedy writer. It was called *The Laff Box*. After that, life became slightly more comfortable for us. If people heard others in their area laughing, it would stimulate laughter. That was the thinking in those days. Primarily, it was an enhancement for existing footage filmed before a live studio audience. Now producers could cue every outrageous moment and resolve every audience reaction at the level they needed. If a joke didn't land live, a little extra juice from the machine punched it up. While filming a live show, a man was in a room behind the scenes. Then, unlike today, this sound engineer would put in a live laugh or applause. Today, they would add it to the tape. There's a true story here I'd like to tell you. The room was full of studio executives viewing my show on a giant screen on one particular day. Excited, I positioned myself to the side next to the man with the applause machine.
>
>The words written by Sol Saks appeared in big letters across the massive screen before us. It was my thrilling moment, so I nudged the guy and persuaded him to give big applause. The room suddenly filled with thunderous applause, and everyone jumped, thinking it was real. Returning to the changes, when the introduction of videotape appeared, it moved television away from a 'live performance.' Instead, behind-the-scene work was more composed. The same scene would be shot multiple times from different angles and pieced together in editing. There was no way to control the volume and enthusiasm of audience reactions between takes. Canned audiences are primarily a thing of the past. But it is incredible to think how this invention changed the way the world laughed.

"How do I know if my writing is funny?"

>Well, you never know for sure. There are three tests. One, and most important, is it funny to me? Second, is it funny to the one who will use it? The third, and again most important. Is it funny for the audience? But a note of caution. If your work does not make you laugh, forget it, no matter how many people laugh. Using comedy lines—you are not reacting to it's like having a teetotaler choose the dinner wine.

"How did you sell your first script?"

> Well, I was very optimistic and slightly naïve. I also happened upon a similar buyer—a rare combination I would not recommend. Although, if you believe in God—give it a try. I first learned my craft. Then I knocked at every door. I checked every possible market and designed my writing to fit what the people were buying. It sounds simplistic, but it still stands the test of time. Everyone told me I must have an agent, but agents did not want to see me because I was not working. I believe I said this earlier, but I went to the company buying shows and pitched my idea to them. They liked my story, bought it, and then the agents bent backward to get me to sign. It was and still is crazy.

"One of the many things I learned from your book is a quote you stated from someone else." 'There are no good-comedy writers, just bad parents.'

> Ah, yes, Bob Schiller. He is the one who said to his father, 'How do you want to be buried when you die?' His father said, 'surprise me!' In my book, I also referenced a story about a caliph who asked the Jewish scholar to explain the Talmud. But he insisted that it be no longer than he could stand on one foot. He said, 'Do unto others as you would have them do unto you. The rest is commentary; go study!' So I decided to ask a few outstanding writers of comedy, all award winners, a similar question on the subject, only slightly less incomprehensible. I ask them, 'How much can you tell me about comedy writing in no longer than I can stand on one foot?' The following are their unedited answers.

BOB SCHILLER
Television: *I Love Lucy—All in the Family—Maude*

> When I asked the late Ed Gardner (*Archie of Duffy's Tavern*) how he found comedy writers, he always answered, "I look for people who think crooked."

Sol comments,

Now, if you think Bob Schiller was referring to criminal minds—you'll never be a comedy writer. In truth, Bob referred to the ability to turn a simple thought into a humorous one. Or, to put it another way, thinking funny. When you say hello to a comedy writer, they immediately try to find a response that isn't the normal one. They think off-center. Off-center is a blessing or a curse depending on how successful that person is in capitalizing on this quality.

SOL SAKS

Sol concludes,
> The point is a person is born with it. There's no teaching it—and you can't acquire it.
> So, if you haven't thought of a dozen or more hilarious responses to this paragraph, read no further. Give this book to the class clown and go into the buttonhole business. There are lots of openings. Okay, okay, so sometimes we miss; nobody's perfect. There are four essential steps to writing comedy: Pick something readily identifiable, zero in on the conflict, take an unconventional point of view, and surprise us! Then, I must tell you the three indispensable attributes of the comedy writer: motivation, courage, and a high tolerance for suffering.

ART BUCHWALD
Syndicated Columnist
> You don't write humor. You think humor. Then you write that funny bit. Nobody can teach you. This secret of thinking in a funny way goes from one generation to another, and I will not tell mine except to my son.

LARRY GELBART
Television: *M.A.S.H*—Features: *Oh God*—*Tootsie*.
Musical: *A Funny Thing Happened on the Way to the Forum*.
> To write comedy is to view life through a particular prescription, reminding us of what we already know, feel, or refuse to admit, and hopefully illuminating those truths, emotions, and denials in an altogether entertaining way. And the reward is laughter, the outward expression of a nerve well-struck.

NORMAN LEAR
Television: *All in the Family*—*Maude*—*Mary Hartman, Mary Hartman*.
Features: *Divorce American Style*—*The Night They Raided Minsky's*—*Cold Turkey*.
> The best advice anybody ever gave a writer was to write. And if you believe you see life through the end of the telescope that finds the humor in the most austere situations, write out of your own experience. I promise you, your mother was funny. So were your uncles and aunts. Use them. And use yourself. Assuming you are human, you are foolish. That is the human condition. Write it.

I.A.L. DIAMOND
Features: *The Apartment—Some Like It Hot—One, Two, Three.*

The disparity of a situation is the basis for most humor, especially the differences between the way man sees himself and who he honestly is. Treat our self-delusions as tragic, and you get *Death of a Salesman* and *A Streetcar Named Desire* and *The Iceman Cometh*; treat them as comic, and you have Moliere and Chaplin and Lenny Bruce.

HAL KANTER
Television: *Chico and the Man—Jimmy Stewart Show—Julia.*
Features: *Road to Bali—Loving You.*

Writing comedy is a mysterious process that begins long before establishing the craft. One sees the world through a prism that distorts the truth and, equally, puts sham and pretense into recognizable perspective. When that sight is recognized, and one learns to commit vision to paper, deftly imparting his way of seeing something to the reader (or director or player of the piece), the difficulty begins for the comedy writer. But, of course, that comes with the ongoing struggle to convince others that what you've written is, indeed, funny! In commercial theatre, alas, comedy is not necessarily what makes you laugh; it's what makes most people laugh. But few things in life provide a richer reward to the author than the sound of most people laughing at what he, too, thinks is funny.

BOB WEISKOPF
Television: *I Love Lucy—All in the Family—Maude.*

To be a professional comedy writer, be ready for a great deal of rejection, plus lots of advice and "help" from those least qualified to offer it. Everyone knows better than the writer, but only after writing something. As Fred Allen so aptly put it, "Where is everyone when the paper's blank?"

EVERETT GREENBAUM
Television: *Mr. Peepers—M.A.S.H—Andy Griffith Show.*
Features: *Angel in My Pocket—Good Neighbor Sam.*

Local radio and possibly even TV broadcasts each day, often with comedy, and is full of people. It is possible to arrange to write material for them without pay or credit of authorship. The point is that you can learn how the material sounds and what works and what doesn't.

SOL SAKS

Greenbaum concludes,

> If you have a hometown (where you can live with your folks) and can't get a foothold in the big city, it might be a good idea to find a station back home. Mine was Buffalo. Trying New York again, I thought, *Wow! Here's another suggestion coming up, ethnic stations.* Big cities have stations catering to all nationalities. So, I worked my way into a station that catered to the Jewish population. I not only wrote but also performed for fifteen dollars a week. It more than paid my rent. When watching Public TV or listening to Public Radio, I often think how lucky a beginner is to have that as a training ground. Most of the people in these facilities work for nothing. They would probably be more than happy to see you.

"How does the writer, Mr. Saks, adapt to the new comedy?"

> He goes for the jugular! As I have said before, in other words, it is safe to repeat and cannot be over-emphasized. A writer must plant his feet, look em' in the eye, and tell the truth. And the truth will set him free and make you money. All the new comedy is, very simply, moving and getting closer and closer to the truth. One of my favorite quotes is by George Bernard Shaw. He clearly states that his way of joking is telling the truth. It is the funniest joke in the world. In all my writing, I have found the statement of George Bernard Shaw solid, which has led me to success. Also, I should mention that there is a need for passion. That is if you want to be one of the best. It's not essential to being a successful writer but indispensable to being a good one. Perhaps that is the definition of a hack—one who has no passion. So, it behooves you to find something that gets your adrenaline pumping, motivates, and makes you more captivating. But then, of course, you must know how to channel that passion—what to do with it, how to use it best. Second, remember that comedy writing is a craft. If you have chosen it as your profession, learn more.

11
"Cary Grant Did A Lot for Me" —Sol Saks

"Sweet is the memory of distant friends!
Like the mellow rays of the departing sun,
it falls tenderly, yet sadly, on the heart."
—Washington Irving

"I know respect and admire the work of Sol Saks. We've worked and filmed together, and I happily advise anyone interested in writing comedy to read his book. You will find, as I did, Sol Saks' thoughts on the subject wonderfully amusing and his advice of immeasurable help." —Cary Grant

On the Set of *Walk Don't Run'*
Left: Cary Grant, Samantha Eggar, Sol Saks, behind Sol is English actor, John Harding, to his far right is Jim Hutton.

Sol comments,
> I've never taken posed photographs with celebrities. However, I found this one taken while on the *Walk Don't Run* set. Cary was one of the few guys who insisted I be there on the set with the actors whenever I chose—a first for me and a dream come true! This favorite photo of mine encapsulates those fun and beautiful moments.

SOL SAKS

"What about *Walk Don't Run?*"

During the run of *Bewitched,* I became an executive producer with CBS in Hollywood. I oversaw comedy programming. For a writer, this is an attractive job, very attractive. I sat in my office, recommending and passing the scripts forward for the studio to use. Then, I'd go home at 5 p.m. without further work. For three months, I loved it, and I enjoyed being home with my family at a reasonable time. But then I started to get bored with my job and, at the same time, torn with the thought of ending the regularity of dining with my family. I knew I belonged back in the trenches and had to follow that. So, I left CBS and began writing again.

I was offered a writing position for the feature movie *Walk Don't Run*. Writing this particular script was a formidable experience for me in many ways. There were three characters, an older man and a young juvenile couple. The studio set up a meeting with Spencer Tracy and Katherine Hepburn at producer Sol Siegel's home. We read through the script, and everyone loved the screenplay. While a maid served coffee, Spencer took me aside and asked why I wanted him to play the part. I was speechless, as I had never mentioned his name to the producers. They just told Spencer that the writer wrote it for him. I was in an embarrassing dilemma and abruptly said that I thought he would be perfect. I think my face turned red. Spencer smiled, then looked to see where Katherine was. In a low voice, he carefully told me that his wife liked the script too. At the time, he was married but living with Katherine Hepburn. The awkwardness was a bit consuming for me. Not sure what to say to him, I stood silent, all the time struggling with the thought; *he brings screenplays to his wife!* The concept was unsettling. Then, Spencer asked me another question. I forget now, but I remember my answer. 'I'd like to be as good a writer as you are an actor.' Thank God he smiled. I must have answered correctly. Then, he and I sat and drank our coffee. It was a long and somewhat stressful day, but we all got along fine, and they agreed to do the show. We happily concluded that we would do any necessary rewrites on the boat to Japan. Despite all the awkwardness, I found the thought of taking a boat trip to Japan with Spencer Tracy and Katharine Hepburn crazy but exciting. In the meantime, the producers also sent the script to Cary Grant, who said he was too old to play the romantic lead but would play the older man. To have Cary was a big plus for the studio. I received the information that Cary accepted the part offered to Spencer. I knew pictures with Cary

Grant never lost money, and he realized the studio would not turn him down.

SOL SAKS

Sol continues,

I went to the producer to ask what Spencer thought of this development. The producer gave me a wordless blank stare. No discussion, nothing. I also remained silent and left the office. This situation helped me to stay off the psychiatrist's couch. I realized this decision was not personal; money was the motivating factor. Spencer Tracy is a man who is the best in his field, attracts the most desirable women in the world, has all the money he needs, and is doing what he loves, but at this moment, he is unhappy. Someone will come to Spencer and inform him of that picture he decided to do Cary Grant is now doing. It became clear there was no security in this business. I don't think it's just our business, but it is predominant in this industry because it moves faster than most. The haven of security must be inside yourself, not in a big car, a yacht, or anything else.

I went home and told my wife that Cary Grant had replaced Spencer Tracy, but I was still going to Tokyo and had no clothes. Anne's eyes lit up at the news of Cary Grant, but she realized we needed to go to the exclusive Carroll & Company in Beverly Hills to find suitable clothing. Anne loved to shop and was on the phone immediately to book an appointment. We were off to 427 N. Canon Dr., Suite 114, in The Courtyard Beverly Hills, within days. I found a hopsack suit that was perfect for me. The material doesn't wrinkle, always looks great, and comes in light grey, dark grey, and blue. I asked Anne which one I should get, and she said to take all three. So, I bought all three and was happy I did. The tailor at the store made the necessary alterations within the time I needed, and I felt confident with my choice of clothes. I packed my bags and boarded another dream. Though I'm sad my trip with Spencer Tracy and Katharine Hepburn never happened, getting to know Cary more than made up for the disappointment. We were close in age, which was an eye-opening experience for me. We had dinner together every night at the hotel, and I learned he couldn't leave the hotel because he'd get swarmed. On the first night, he asked me where I was dining before I knew about his situation. I told him about a restaurant down the street I'd like to try and invited him. He said he would love to but couldn't leave the hotel. The hotel had seven restaurants, so we stayed and dined in style. His secretary would call for reservations even within the hotel; she specified that the table must be in the corner because Cary sits facing the wall. The following day, we returned from the dailies and stopped at the entrance to the hotel to say something. Within thirty seconds, a crowd of people surrounded Cary to the point he could not move.

BEWITCHED

Sol continues,

> I was stunned. People were so excited, and they kept touching him, patting him on the back, and asking questions simultaneously. Cary learned a few words in Japanese, but they continued to swarm him no matter what he said. Cary was taller than most in Japan, so he stood out even more. Finally, the hotel security saw what was happening and immediately came to his rescue. It took a group of security personnel to separate him from the crowd and bring him inside the hotel; then, they returned and brought me in. Cary apologized that I was pushed and shoved almost to the curb. He explained that he experienced the same reaction where ever he traveled. I learned that day what a celebrity goes through. It was not glamorous as I once thought. He said it was the most difficult on those closest to him and overshadowed so much of life. I now knew what I was in for and adjusted my thinking accordingly. I prepared myself and thought, *this is a short-lived experience for me; I can handle this.* If you can, for a moment, imagine you're Cary Grant, and every time you lift your head, all eyes are on you. He couldn't stand still for thirty seconds without being mobbed—it's not pleasant, and he didn't need that kind of attention. Maybe as a young actor just starting it was exciting, but even then, there were times when it became a bit frightening. With experience came the knowledge that the excitement people were feeling was for the character on the screen, not him. At that time of his life, he remained grateful for his success and honored by such widespread acceptance, but the price was higher than he had ever imagined. We talked about my job at CBS, and Cary pointed out a similarity. The job looked like a dream at first but became almost a nightmare. Cary was terrific company, an intelligent and talented person, and, except for being mobbed, we both enjoyed being in Japan. The people were kind, the culture intriguing, and the food delicious. Through the days, I noticed a priceless sense of compassion developing, helping me personally, and expanding my perspective as a writer. But let me tell you of a special moment that says much about Cary. In my mind, he was the epitome of a well-dressed man, and I was not. My closet in the hotel was in a dark corner of my room, so sometimes in the restaurant with Cary, I'd look down and see that I got the wrong coat for the pants I was wearing. When I got to know him well, I asked him if he'd spotted that sometimes my jacket didn't match my pants. Cary leaned in and said quietly, Sol, on you, I only notice when they do. He made me laugh. He was a sweet guy and greatly added to my comedy material and life.

SOL SAKS

Sol continues,

> When my wife Anne flew to Tokyo to visit me, she made sure my clothes matched before meeting Cary for dinner. I could see him smiling when we walked in. When we got to the table, he said he noticed my clothes matched and wondered if this could be because of my wife. We laughed as I introduced her and admitted it was. We all sat in the corner, sheltered from the rest, and Cary asked Anne how we met. Anne, nervous, took a sip of wine while calming herself. She explained that we met in Chicago and briefly told our story. Cary listened intently and was amazed that she had married me before I was a success. Cary could be bravely open and make you immediately comfortable, and he did so that evening. Anne didn't need another sip of wine as she smiled and said yes, that when we were first married, we had very little and needed everything. Anne, feeling comfortable, leaned in and laughingly professed of an afternoon in a local cafeteria. She looked at Cary hesitantly, wondering if to confess such an act, then blurted out that she had taken some of their silverware home with her. Cary just leaned in with no expression except deep compassion. Anne told him that she brought it back when we left New York. Cary was astonished, sat back, and said he was delighted to be sitting with us. It was not often when he heard the truth so beautifully revealed and thanked us for adding a fresh normal to his life. She reminisced that our mothers were also friends and had a favorite Chicago Deli they loved. The two met there often for lunch, shared stories, and caught up on the neighborhood news. Cary seemed captivated by every word Anne spoke. His well-manicured hands rested on the table as she told of our early life together. Then, suddenly a look of sadness, a moment of envy, appeared on his face as he took another quick look at my matching suit. The idea that Anne didn't marry me because I was a big-shot celebrity with money and we were still in love was his elusive dream, a dream he realized would never come to pass. We talked for a long time that evening, and I learned that we all have empty places in our hearts. All have dreams that seem impossible. Cary built an intriguing life for himself that was the envy of most, but deep sadness persisted, and many unresolved haunting issues clung tightly. Yet, surprisingly, we had much in common, and I could appreciate that his high profile kept him a prisoner of sorts. Anne returned to America after our wonderful week together with a revised mindset. The movie-star admiration of her favorite actor that she arrived with grew to mind-expanding deep respect and understanding of his journey to fame.

Sol continues,

> Through all the ups and downs of Hollywood life, he remained the kindest and most talented person in the business. Cary also did a lot for me, but I never had the chance to tell him. Sometime after my wife died, I began missing the company of women after being married for so many years. Eventually, I started to receive invitations to parties. I was shocked when I realized I didn't know how to talk to women when I'd meet one; I didn't know what to say. Then I thought, *I write lines for Cary Grant; I will create something for me!* So, I thought of myself as Cary Grant, and then I found myself giving her Cary Grant lines—and it worked! It was great! Then one evening, I went for a drink. I worked writing lines all day, was tired, and bumped into the same people. Drowsy, I smiled—and they expected something interesting from me—and I had nothing to say. With their expectations not met, a look of disappointment was visible as they turned and left. So being Cary Grant was not easy. Cary was also my idea of a perfect blind date. So, the imagined idea goes: The girl who has a blind date hears a knock at the door, and when she opens it, there stands just outside her door Cary Grant! That was a dream come true for women at the time. So, I thought I would try that scenario when or if a similar thing happened. A long time passed after my dream scenario when my friends set me up with a blind date. I was nervous and had trouble finding her address, making me 25 minutes late. My heart was racing, and my mind a blank as I approached the door. She furiously slammed the door in my face while hollering her resentment of this happening with men before. I left speechless for my favorite restaurant; this was my last blind date. My excuse would be more acceptable if I could have thought like Cary Grant back then. I would have brought flowers, complimented her, then apologized.
>
> There were so many things Cary did for me. By being candid about his life, he helped me with many painful memories from the past. So many memories I thought would never have happened if I had been more of this or that. I only wished I could have been as much help to him. Once back in the states, I attended a couple of Dodger games with Cary. He wore a hat, dark glasses, and a bulky overcoat, but still, it was difficult to hide his presence. It was the only time I dressed better than Cary. Once he entered his private Dodger suite, he could relax, get rid of the bulky clothes, and then he was smartly dressed again.
>
> I wonder, now and then, what it would be like to have traveled with Spencer Tracy and certainly Katharine Hepburn.

12

The Fair-Haired Boy At CBS

"Truth is like the sun.
You can shut it out for a time,
But it ain't goin' away."
—*Elvis Presley*

"Would you say your style is more character-driven versus joke-driven?"

I hate to say it this way, but I'm not saying I was the best writer but the most responsible. I write for myself, and they can be sure they will get a suitable script on the day needed. *Bewitched* wasn't the best television, but it was the newest. I think of people in situations first. The jokes come later, woven into the scene If they're appropriate.

"Were you still at CBS when the television landscape changed from simple comedy to more complex shows like *All in The Family* and *Mash*?"

Yes, I was still there and saw many changes after a while. But I must admit, I was distracted by a comfortable workplace. They immediately gave me a privileged parking spot next to my office—a new prestigious experience. I had a secretary and a button on my desk to call her, I could close the door if I wanted to say something confidential, and I read scripts and analyzed them; it was a great job. When I left the office at the end of the day, I had no guilt that I had no pages completed! But when I finally came out of the euphoric spell with my new job at CBS, I realized the changes were a shift in the audience, who demanded better and were tired of the same old scripts. The people at CBS thought shows like *Seinfeld* and *Mary Tyler Moore* were going to be a flop. They canceled Star Trek in its infancy, but the people saved the show. The consumer is the one who decides. If consumers see a particular line of quality goods in a store, it is not the store that says it is better. The people who, though it costs more, want to buy it because it is of better quality. They have better taste. I agree with George Burns, who once said there is no place to be mediocre on television. I don't watch many shows, but I do like Seinfeld. It's a well-written show with great comedic timing that brings big laughs. But, again, though this job gave me a great vantage point and, I believe, added to me personally, it got to be a bore.

Sol continues,

> At the end of the year, I let the studio know I was done and did not want this job anymore, and they asked me why not. I thought for a moment and realized I had to be honest. I told them the job was good, but I did not want to work in an office daily. I am a writer. I feel like a writer and more so than ever since my CBS days. I am not a good producer. I am a fair director, but I am a good writer, and it is what I like to do best. Strange, but as I told them, I was now comfortable continuing to be as good a writer as possible; I entered a great sense of freedom. So, I thanked them for the opportunity, and I left. The studio called me the next day at home and asked if I would consider working for them from home. I figured I could write and analyze their story ideas without a problem. So, I sat at home and wrote, and once or twice a week, a messenger would show up with a script. I spent half a day on it, which was my job and rewarding. Each one was something they wanted to make into pilots. I took the job seriously and, with careful consideration, noted my analysis of them. However, they never took any of my well-thought-out advice. Not one script idea that I told them was great did they do. The ones that I noted were lousy; they did. It was a strange and frustrating position, and the freedom I experienced was gone.
>
> My wife kindly suggested that maybe I was stealing the money! I laughed as I told her she was probably right, but watch; they would still pick me up next year. Because, again, they do not know what to say to the sponsor. Anne gave me a cup of coffee, sat beside me, and began a simple story. It was of a time, years prior, when I left the Ida Lupino show. I got along with them; Ida and Howard were our friends, but I was tired of writing the same episodes and stopped thinking of the premises. Anne was great at telling stories too. She reminded me of a day I came home from writing for Ida and Howard, and she was distraught. Our dog had puppies and became sick. Anne had to take the dog with the puppies to the vet, and we had people coming to dinner that night. She relays this story to a snobby aunt of mine who was the first to arrive, and my prig of an aunt says to her condescendingly that she should relax. My aunt sat down as Anne prepared for the rest of the company, then, without taking a breath, babbled to my now frustrated Anne that we had all been in this position. Anne listened to her patiently, and with each word my aunt spoke, Anne became more agitated.

SOL SAKS

Sol continues,

> Suddenly, in the middle of her story, I remembered that there was always some jerk announcing that you should relax. Of course, you should rest, but what if you are unable? As I listened to Anne, I formed an idea in my mind that was a great premise! That's who a writer is! That's where he gets his material. I had to be honest. Though I was well-paid and treated great at CBS, politics precluded my position. I could not do my best under those conditions. As soon as I took steps to follow what that small voice inside me was saying, my energy and sense of freedom returned. When I look back, I find that reading all those scripts, three-fourths of them were by people who didn't know their craft. If trained in the art of writing, you already out-script 75% of the competition. Look, it is not always easy to follow what you know is right. It is, however, essential if you want to succeed. When I was a boy, my parents told me about a destiny for each of us if we were brave enough to follow the quiet guidance inside, but I did not believe it completely. Now in my nineties, I see that to be an unparalleled truth. I have always liked to spend my time writing short stories, essays, and plays. However, the theater is different—the writer is king, and I enjoy the immediacy of the theater. *A Dream of Butterflies* is a play I wrote. The title comes from something I read from Confucius. 'Last night I dreamt I was a butterfly; today, I do not know if I am a man who dreamt he was a butterfly or a butterfly who today is dreaming he is a man.' Near my home in Universal City is an unassuming theater called Theatre West. My play recently performed there and received excellent reviews; the entire process was incredible. Because of the Writers Guild, life for the writer in television has improved, but for me, though the hours are long and the pay minimal, my heart is still within the hallowed walls of the theater. It's more than just the roar of the grease paint and the smell of the crowd. All kidding aside, being part of an indescribable creative process is special for me. The atmosphere in the room is immediately palpable. But, most of all, my heart still skips a beat when the lights go down.

With a look of sublime contentment filling the eyes of a man who is nearing 100 years of age, Sol held steady in the love he found, as he professed,

> I love the theatre! Though I'm grateful for the good-living television has afforded me, there's an energy from the audience seated in the theater, immediate magical moments about a stage of actors working before an audience. As a writer, the fun begins with devising a plan—building characters—giving them words.

Sol continues,
> Artists and storytellers live in a world of 'what if.' We improvise and continue with improvisation, changing and discarding until we get a usable line.
>
> We pick our character by the 'what-if' method. We were thinking, *what if I were timid?* We choose the situation; w*hat if he looked exactly like a member of the Mafia who was a womanizer?* I know I've 'what-ifed' myself into a cliché, but that's how improvising starts, and a good 'what-ifer' improvises his way into something fresh and surprising. With persistence and luck, we may find a usable sequence. Similar to a few grains of gold on the bottom of a pan for mining. And then, if that shiny stuff at the bottom of the pan assays out, and we can find someone in the marketplace who knows the genuine article when he sees it, maybe the reward is ahead with enough money to buy a pair of boots.
>
> In my later years, when I was no longer writing for television, I had the great pleasure of continuing to work at Theatre West. My dream of writing dramatic plays came to fruition among the newcomers to the arts and several of our most valued and talented actors. There is always something to learn from everyone I meet, and my Theatre West experience was no different. This local theatre reportedly has served as a green-house for artists, a place to grow and explore work they can do nowhere else, to experiment in 'the laboratory of themselves.'

"How would you like to be remembered?"
> Well, on a personal level, it's a whole different story. I imagine we're talking about a professional level, and being a good writer, would be a good remembrance. But, on a personal level, that's a hard one, a big question I've not honestly considered. I think I'm a fair man. Whether that's the most important thing, I'm not sure. I believe I made life better for my family and many friends. I shared what I could, and it seemed to bring enjoyment. I know it was gratifying for me to have something to share. Even with people who have been my adversaries, I think I've been fair-minded with them. I hope my work brought moments of enjoyment, maybe escape, or added a different perspective to the audience.
>
> When people watch or think of *Bewitched*, maybe they may think of me.

SOL SAKS

"Well, unfortunately we've reached the end of our interview. Thank you, Mr. Saks, for your time and for candidly sharing your thoughts, experiences, and insightful stories. I've enjoyed my time with you and am certain you have added greatly to lives. I know you have added considerably to mine."

The commentator ended with a quote from Sol and a five-star review from *Time Magazine*.

- "If you can make people laugh, you'll find an audience. As soon as you can write funny, your services will be sought-after."—Sol Saks.

This quote of Sol's was a favorite repeated like a mantra throughout his university days, and it still stands the test of time.

- 'Saks dialogue on the film *Walk Don't Run* bristles amiably from first to last."—Time Magazine.

(Printed also in every Trade paper, including the New York & Los Angeles Times.)

Not long after his concluding interview, I drove Sol back home from our last lunch together; he said there was something important he wanted to tell me.

There is a secret I would like to share with you, Carolyn. Look around and enjoy what you have, even if it's meager. I've found that when an opportunity arises for me to be of help, I listen inside first, then, if it's okay, I take the step. There is so much good in this life that we can fail to see. It is a matter of focus and determination.

Each word became penetratingly charged as he spoke with unusual sincerity. Captivated, I intently listened as he continued,

Within this beautiful sphere we live in is hidden darkness that slips unnoticed into the minds and hearts of people that make them say and do unspeakable things. But, if we turn from it, don't fight it head-on, and focus on our destiny, on what good we can contribute; that action alone shines a light and dispels that awful darkness. Those are the unseen stepping stones to success. It is not an easy task; it's a struggle, sometimes heartbreakingly painful. But a determination to stay on the high road is paramount if you want to find a victory that fills every part of your life and the life of others.

BEWITCHED

I remember those moments in my car with Sol like it was yesterday. Only one other time, years prior, did I experience the intense immediacy of thoughts when everything around me disappeared, and only the words before me seemed to exist. I am so grateful for those spoken words.

SOL SAKS

13

Inspirations Last Journey to the Silver Screen

*"The cinema has the power to make you not feel lonely, even when you are.
As a young man, even if I was going to see a play or a film by myself,
I didn't feel like I was alone. There was something that was unfolding
up there that brought me into it. And I recognized that.
For those two hours, it made me feel
like I belonged to something really good."*
—Tom Hanks

As a young girl, one of Anne's favorite weekend getaways was going to the movies; when she married Sol, it became one of her passions. An evening at their favorite restaurant and the local theater were moments of heaven. As Sol regularly did, he set an evening aside and took his beautiful Anne to the movie of her choice. They kept a date night in their marriage before it was popular. When Sol suggested a newly released film filled with action and progressive ideas, Anne would answer, "No, a movie, movie!" That meant the type she could enter into and dream. A magic carpet of entertainment sweeping her up and away from the limitations of ordinary life.

Sol leaned back in his comfortable tan leather chair and reminisced about their last time together at the movies. There was something different about that evening that he could not describe, but it has remained vivid in his thoughts. Then, almost reluctantly, Sol closed his eyes as if watching the evening unfold and began his story.

I took Anne to her favorite restaurant for dinner. We spent a leisurely time dining, talking, and laughing. There were no thoughts of work for those moments with her. I was always captivated by her beautiful eyes, but that night as they reflected the flickering candlelight, they were beautiful beyond words. It seemed impossible, but I felt closer than ever to Anne as we went to see the motion picture she had talked about for weeks; *Fiddler on the Roof*. Having been nominated for eight awards and winning three, Anne was thrilled at the prospect of seeing this film. Anne laughed when I told her I thought it was a chick flick, a romantic movie. We entered the hallowed walls of the dimly lit theater. Anne breathed in the atmosphere as her shoulders relaxed. I didn't mind attending what I thought was a non-progressive film; instead, I decided to attempt to enter the dream world with Anne. She could set a most inviting atmosphere that was always a haven for me.

Sol concludes,

> As we walked, that comforting, familiar aroma of popcorn drew us to the counter. I bought two bags of buttered popcorn, candy, and drinks, then found comfortable seats; in the center of a row in the middle of the theater. It was always special when relaxing with Anne, something I still can't explain. Settled while waiting for the movie to begin, I thought, *how would my television series Bewitched look on that massive screen before me? How could I adapt the tv series into a big-screen film?* As the movie began, so too did a premise form in my mind for Bewitched, the Movie.

However, on that evening, joy and sadness rose together in puzzling wonderment. Feeling uneasy, Sol decided to keep his newly formed premise to himself without interrupting Anne's pleasure. He was unaware that they were beginning a new journey. As "The End" appeared on the screen, Anne, in a state of sublime euphoria, nudged Sol to wait just a moment as the theater slowly cleared. She wanted to hear the brilliant ending music. After all, it had won an Oscar for Best Music. Even Sol commented that it would remain a memorable and beautifully made film for him.

One by one, people stood to leave. Wondrously entertained and enthralled with the exciting performance, Anne slowly returned to earth with each musical note surrounding her. Finally, landing enraptured, she was ready to go home. Trailing behind the crowd, Anne took the arm of her beloved husband, leaned close, and whispered, "I would love to see a movie of yours on the big screen one day." Sol clutched her hand in his; she had touched his heart and confirmed his dream. Speechless, his eyes suddenly welled with tears as he kissed her cheek and walked like a newlywed to the car.

Anne died, leaving his side only months after their memorable evening together. Sol, grief-stricken, was to continue his journey alone. He wished he could return to that night at the movies. To have paid more attention to what his adorable wife found intriguing within the story. He regretted his preoccupation that kept him from being in the moment with Anne and remembering more of the storyline. Anne died, leaving his side only months after their memorable evening together. Sol, grief-stricken, was to continue his journey alone. He wished he could return to that night at the movies. To have paid more attention to what his adorable wife found intriguing within the story. He regretted his preoccupation that kept him from being in the moment with Anne and remembering more of the storyline.

When the grief subsided, the feeling that he could have done better remained a deep sadness. Nevertheless, Sol threw himself into work more feverishly than before while *Bewitched* continued flourishing.

SOL SAKS

Sol read that the series entertained hundreds of thousands of people sitting in their living rooms with popcorn, drinks, and candy as they dreamed and laughed; how bittersweet those words sounded to him. The thought of a *Bewitched* movie drifted quietly aside while he learned to live without Anne.

Bewitched the Movie

Sol, emerging from grief, began hearing talk about producing a Bewitched movie based on the TV series. Shaken, he began working on his dream premise and submitted them. After several attempts at contacting the studio, the comments returned were that *Bewitched* was considered a brilliant tv series but needed relevant ideas for a successful movie. Relevancy was easy for Sol, and many contemporaries deemed his premise appropriate.

However, Ted Bessell (Donald on *That Girl*), an actor/director, earned an attempt at a remake. In the mid-1990s, pre-production began with producer/director Penny Marshall and her team at Paramount. Penny first hired former *Laverne & Shirley* staff writer Monica Johnson to develop a script. As time passed, Richard Curtis (*Four Weddings and a Funeral*) took a crack at the story, as did Broadway playwright Douglas Carter Beane. After the sudden and unexpected death of Ted Bessell in 1996, all *Bewitched* feature film plans halted.

The development of the *Bewitched* movie took nearly a decade, and Sol was approaching his nineties. He realized the substantial age bias was something he couldn't break through, but he still hoped for at least a consideration, maybe a consultation.

Eventually, Penny Marshall joined with producers Lucy Fisher and Douglas Wick's Red Wagon Entertainment at Sony/Columbia Pictures; but Sol's hopes went unrealized. Over time, considerations for the coveted role of Samantha Stephens went to actresses Cameron Diaz, Kristin Davis, Lisa Kudrow, Gwyneth Paltrow, Alicia Silverstone, and Reese Witherspoon. However, the Sony *Bewitched* project remained locked in limbo with a pile of rejected screenplays from a few more talented writers, including Ellen Simon (*One Fine Day*) and Laurice Elehwany (*My Girl, The Brady Bunch Movie*).

Then, in 2003, Oscar-winning actress and life-long *Bewitched* TV show fan Nicole Kidman expressed genuine interest in the long-shelved *Bewitched* film. News of Nicole's interest reached Amy Pascal, Sony/Columbia Pictures chairman. Reportedly, Amy contacted her friend Nora Ephron (When Harry Met Sally and You've Got Mail), and successful romantic-comedy producer/director/writer Nora signed up to head the project.

BEWITCHED

Amy pleaded for a pitch, a plot, anything to ensure that Nicole Kidman would finally commit to the Sony film.

The creatively brilliant Nora, and writer favorite, decided on an original approach, far removed from the traditional retread or parody-style remakes. Nora devised that Nicole would play a new witch looking for mortal love. The new witch Nicole gets cast in a *Bewitched* television show remake simply because she had a nose resembling Elizabeth Montgomery's famous twitcher! Nicole loved the idea and signed a "play-or-pay contract" for $17.5 million. The contract ensured Nicole that even if the film stalled again for any reason, she would still get her star salary.

Nicole Kidman & Will Ferrell in Book Soup Bookstore
Will is waiting to see her nose twitch.

Filming began in the late Summer of 2004 on the stages of Sony Culver Studio. Shooting locations were: The Sunset Strip, Book Soup Bookstore, Pann's Restaurant in West Los Angeles (known for its food, history, role in movies, and distinctive architecture,) Bed, Bath, and Beyond store in charming Pasadena, a gorgeous home in Hancock Park, Los Angeles, and the serene ocean walk in Santa Monica. It was unanimous that these were dream locations.

As if the locations were not enough. The cast and crew enjoyed lovely and comfortable working conditions in the Fall months, including gourmet catering for everyone and weekend dinner parties hosted by Nora, the beloved director and ex-food-critic. In addition, by the arrival of Halloween, the local media received a brilliant marketing idea to heighten audience interest in Sony's upcoming summer comedy, a promotional gift-wrapped broom from the members of the new *Bewitched* movie.

SOL SAKS

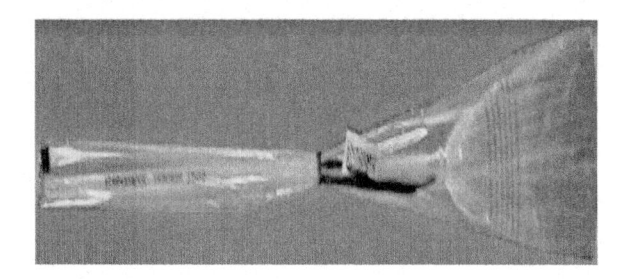

Next came a teaser trailer that appeared in late Fall 2004 and read Coming Summer 2005. The trailer highlighted Nicole Kidman flying on a broom, wearing a red sleeveless dress and a heart necklace. She twitched her nose like TV's Samantha in a full close-up. Then flew through the sky with Will Ferrell comically holding the end of her broom while dramatic new cues from the old TV theme played. However, Sony's film posters were the traditional Samantha/Darrin motif.

Played was a rough cut of the *Bewitched* film to test audiences in early Spring 2005. The comment cards revealed that audiences wanted "more magic" and "scenes with magical family members." So, the studio flew Michael Caine back to Los Angeles from London for re-shoots and added scenes. Sony then launched an official *Bewitched* movie website, followed by movie tie-in promotions; then, products began a lively online emergence. By late Spring 2005, systematically released full trailers hit the media. The trailers gave U.S. audiences previews of the plot. They also revealed that this was not a classic remake. Instead, it featured new stories and exciting characters.

June 13, 2005, during the morning hours, Nicole was preparing for her red-carpet premiere duties when she received heartbreaking news. Her long-time makeup man and friend, Robert McCann, had unexpectedly died the prior evening. Distressed and grieving, the ever-professional Nicole put on a brave face and arrived at Manhattan's Ziegfeld Theatre to honor her commitment.

BEWITCHED

However, immediately confronted by a belligerent photographer, Nicole became visibly upset. Unfortunately, a photograph of her scolding the paparazzi appeared later in the news.

In the meantime, across town, Sol received an invitation to be the guest of honor at the *Bewitched* premiere. It was a thrilling honor and a bittersweet appointment shrouded with a hint of disappointment. Yet, with this invitation came a rush of heartwarming memories: Anne wrapping her arm around his. Whispering, hoping to see a movie written by him on the big screen one day. The memories were immediate; they hit his heart like a tidal wave.

For a moment, he was sure of the fragrance of her perfume; it took his breath away. His eyes, flooded with tears, wandered around the room at the vacant space before him. He stood motionless as an unexplainable reassuring calm filled with a peaceful warmth entered his soul. Then, with a gasping breath of air, Sol slowly regained his composure. Something quite tranquil, yet a presence almost within reach, assured him that Anne, somewhere in time, would still see her dream on the big screen.

Though Sol could not see Anne with his eyes, he remarked that her love was always in his heart, along with words spoken only to him. Still, her love made room for him to be happy again and though many years later, to marry again. Sol had continued to move through life one day at a time until a sense of fulfillment returned. Strange, he thought that he would find a caring companion and remarried a short time before the premiere.

The evening of the awaited premiere arrived, and Sol entered the theater with his new love. Upon entering, memories of his evening with Anne filled his mind. She was most certainly traveling with him on this momentous occasion. He found his requested seats in the center of the theater and noticed an empty seat beside them. Sol discreetly reached over and touched the arm of the empty chair; it seemed like it was waiting just for Anne. He felt an indescribable, momentary pain of loss; until, just then, a massive man squeezed past Sol and plopped down in the seat, shocking Sol back to reality. Sol quickly removed his hand, quietly laughing as he realized he was being over-sentimental and would never write a scene like that.

As the lights dimmed over the packed theater, the movie began, with every head turned in anticipation toward the screen. The audience enthusiastically cheered for the opening title. When the film featured the TV series familiar font, applause again erupted. Viewing the original television series clips on the big movie screen was sensational, especially for Sol. Thoughts returned to the days he dreamed of being a writer. It reminded him that no Laff Box was needed this night, no encouragement from the stage manager off to the side. The live audience's applause and stomping feet filled the room this night.

SOL SAKS

Sol sat in a bittersweet fog as the memory of Anne filled his head. No popcorn, candy, and drinks tonight, but he could feel her delicate hand in his and knew she was there with him. Contentment rested on Sol, replacing the disappointment at not having a chance to write for the movie. He held on to thoughts of gratitude for having the original TV idea and that this premier would not have happened if it were not for Anne. Sol experienced the carpet of dreams Anne so often visited; just a tiny moment of heaven.

A surprisingly cool breeze brushed his cheek and brought his thoughts back to the movie playing on the expansive silver screen. He watched with delight, knowing Anne would have loved this evening. Maybe she truly could see from where she was. Sol sighed and sat in a euphoric state of mind as the movie ended, and a featured dedication to the late Ted Bessell appeared on the screen. Still feeling Anne beside him, Sol watched as each person slowly left the theater. To rise from his memories and return to the life remaining tugged at his heart, but looking at his new love, Sol knew this was not an option.

They made their way across the empty and dimly lit aisle leading to the entry while following the last person to leave. Sol heard a cheery voice calling his name through the door's blinding light. It was the delightful and gracious Will Ferrell. Will introduced himself and complimented Sol for his genius writing of the TV series. Expressing his love for Sol's brilliant creation and stating he was a big fan, Will continued enthusiastically commenting on how grateful he was to have played the part of Darrin. Then, calmly leaning toward Sol, Will asked what he thought of the remake. Sol's eyes adjusting to the light and still having Anne clearly on his mind had difficulty answering. At the height of his career, Will, a young comedian, stood bravely waiting for a comment from Sol. Not seeing much of the movie, Sol congratulated Will and the cast's superb performance. They shook hands, and Sol reluctantly left for home.

The next day Sol read that the movie garnered mediocre reviews from critics. Eventually disclosed were the figures. At the cost of 85 million dollars to make, it achieved a worldwide gross of 131.4 million and was considered disappointing. However, it regained favor globally in countries familiar with the original TV series. A comment made in an interview was that it would have been prudent to have hired Sol Saks to write the script. They wondered why no one had thought of that simple remedy. I heartily agree with the comments.

An Honored Visit

Toward the end of his life, Sol was still writing, striving for creative ideas, and reaching for excellence in his chosen craft. He continued his walks, swimming in his beautiful pool, spending time with his family, and driving his gleaming grey Mercedes, albeit short distances.

He was the only one in his circle of friends enjoying marriage again with a lovely woman, a welcomed companion. She assisted in the many tasks that make up this writer's creative mindset. Sol casually admitted that he thought a dedicated writer like himself could be a bit of tedious work. If this was true, his lovely wife, a helpful companion, seemed a perfect choice: a patient, intelligent woman who was someone to admire as she juggled life around Sol.

The three of us were to meet for lunch a few months before his one-hundredth birthday, and I was looking forward to spending time with the newlyweds. For reasons unknown, sadly, it would be just Sol and me. I drove to the Sutton Street home to pick Sol up, and we went to one of his favorite restaurants, La Frite Cafe in Sherman Oaks. On the drive, he seemed preoccupied and slightly irritable. I asked him if he was okay, and he told me he had a dream a week prior that continued to bother him.

We arrived, ordered lunch, and asked if I could do anything. Sol wanted to share what happened last week and give him my opinion. I hesitatingly agreed, and as our food arrived, he began. Sol dreamed an angel came to his bedside. This magnificent-looking angel took Sol's hand gently in his, asking him if he wanted to go home. The word home resonated through his being like nothing he had ever experienced. As if the word itself had power. Love, youth, and joy surged through Sol like electricity; all pain was gone. He had never experienced health like that in his lifetime. Sol said he wanted to leave immediately and agreed but realized he needed to say goodbye. The angel stood silently by his bed, his arms raised as an opening in the room appeared. Sol saw lifelong friends who had died, young again and living in beautifully vivid surroundings. They were smiling and so happy to see him. Sol was shocked, thrilled, and speechless as the opening slowly closed. Then, lovingly brushing his hand over Sol's, the angel clothed in brilliant white slowly turned and left the room. Sol said his sleep that night was the best in years.

My mind felt sadly numb. I sat silent and was unable to offer my thoughts. We quietly finished our lunch, glancing up now and again as our eyes connected. The moments were most profound, with the word goodbye swimming before my eyes.

SOL SAKS

With the dream now shared, Sol appeared more relaxed than I had ever seen him, but I, filled with emotions, was restless. There was, however, a sense of honor to experience these particular moments, this information, and this responsibility. Conflicted, I wanted to linger yet run, but something in me said this was my appointed time to say goodbye. Sol sensing my distress asked if I was alright. Did I want a glass of wine? My first thought was no. A second later, I declared I would have a crème brûlée with a brandy float and a cappuccino. I was surprised that I said that. His face lit up with contagious joy and laughter while motioning for the waiter.

As I relished the most exquisite cup of coffee and dessert, my eyes teared, knowing I may never see my friend again, at least on this earth. Sol, smiling, watched me enjoying my dessert while casually changing the subject. He had an idea for his one-hundredth birthday. It would take the place of what Sol considered a mundane funeral. He wanted his friends to remember him having fun and give them one more laugh. There was a long pause as Sol lowered his head and looked down. For the first time, he seemed to be without words. Holding back the tears, I gathered my courage and told him I would miss him every day, thanked him for all he taught me, and if God willing, I would tell his story someday. Our tear-filled eyes connected, and more words were not necessary. Sol rested his elbow on the table, his hand on his forehead, covering his eyes.

Then glancing again at me, he held his hand tightly over his mouth. Nodding his head in breathless silence, he slowly picked up his spoon, then took a big scoop of my dessert. Shocked, I looked at him in puzzled amazement, as it was a strange response, and besides, I did not think Sol ate desserts. "What's the matter? You don't want to share?" Sol said to me. We both burst out laughing, then I cried. Only Sol Saks could say a profound goodbye and make you laugh. We ended our lunch, and I drove him home. I watched him walk through the squeaking gate and listened as the latch connected, closing the gate one more time. I slowly backed out from the driveway and paused as he turned to look and wave goodbye. Tears ran down my face; time seemed to stop for a brief, uncomfortable moment as I waved goodbye; with an indescribable emotion.

In the following days, arrangements came together for his 100th birthday celebration, culminating in his biggest party. Sol was thrilled to see all his friends gathered as he dreamed. Served were cocktails and food with a side of thought-provoking stories. Stimulating conversation, jokes, and contagious laughter filled the house, the yard, and the air surrounding Sol. Profound gratefulness at the joy upon each face filled him like never before.

Sol's favorite birthday gift was to see lingering smiles of satisfaction, feel the love radiating from each person, and hear stories about times spent together; it was a perfect party lasting into the night.

At the party's close, Sol stood at the doorway as each friend parted with grateful tear-filled hugs. He lingered with bittersweet gratitude until the last car drove away, then reluctantly closed the door. Resting, for a moment, his forehead against the closed door, he noticed a tingling sensation in the pit of his stomach; Sol sensed that a new beginning lay ahead.

A short four months and three days later, the splendor miraculously offered him came to pass. Perhaps the angel returned, taking his hand once more and, this time, releasing all that constraints, escorted him to the destination shown to him alone. The following day, a rare rainbow appeared in the sky across the Valley, and I wondered if, somewhere close by, Sol and Anne had united again. It seemed the perfect splendor across Sherman Oaks, reaching across with joy to all his friends and family saying, "This chapter is over, and another great one is beginning."

Then, ten years later, almost to the day, I finished his story, which I sincerely hope you have enjoyed.

Never, the end. xo

SOL SAKS

I Would Enjoy Hearing from You!

Thank you, dear reader, for joining me on this honored journey. It is such a privilege to be given the task of writing about another's life. It's been my prayer from start to finish that I have done justice to the commentaries, stories, and time spent taking notes.

I would appreciate your reviews on Amazon and hope to travel again with you soon.

To contact me, write to:

Email: addictivebooks@yahoo.com

Or you can reach or follow me at:

- **Authors Page:** https://www.facebook.com/lloydhaynesroom222/
- **Facebook:** https://www.facebook.com/carolynhaynes5050
- **The Lloyd Haynes Blog:** https://thelloydhaynesstory.wordpress.com
- **Twitter:** https://twitter.com/carolyngrace505
- **Instagram:** https://www.instagram.com/carolyn_haynes_author/
- **LinkedIn:** www.linkedin.com/in/carolyn-haynes-14752a100
- **Goodreads:** https://www.goodreads.com/author/show/1068835.Carolyn_Haynes
- **YouTube:** https://youtu.be/zmPlcIctKJM

About the Author

CAROLYN HAYNES-AUTHOR OF ADDICTIVE BOOKS, wrote two masterfully crafted memoirs: The Lloyd Haynes Story, A Remarkable Journey to Stardom, reviewed by the Tribune as "Superbly Written" and Bewitched, Secrets from Comedy Genius Sol Saks, noted by LA Times as "First-Class."

She's a member of the Screen Actors Guild, American Federation of Television & Radio Artists, Author's Guild, and a widespread writing and poetry community. In addition, she attended the American Film Institute, CBS Workshops, and the Pasadena Playhouse and received an invitation to the Royal Academy of Dramatic Art in London, England.

For many years, Carolyn assisted Saks with books, plays, theater, television productions, and university classes on writing. As wife to Samuel Lloyd Haynes, she also helped with his screenplays, short stories, and photography.

"We anticipate more adventures with this author of addictive, engaging books."